Caradoc King is chairman of the literary agency, A P Watt Ltd. He represents a wide range of adult and children's authors, among them Philip Pullman, whom he met on his first day at Oxford. This is his first book.

Praise for *Problem Child:*

'*Problem Child* is immensely readable and moving. I have to confess that the author is an old friend, but there are depths and shadows and mysteries in the lives of even our closest friends, and Caradoc King has illuminated his own difficult and complicated childhood in a way that I found both moving and revelatory. It took courage to tell this story, and an unusual degree of emotional intelligence too. Those qualities would have counted for little, though, if the story had been poorly told, but at every point it's clear and compelling. It's a most impressive book'
Philip Pullman

'fascinating memoir which balances devastating honesty, warmth and irony . . . a strong and courageous piece of writing and it tells an extraordinary story'
Helen Dunmore

'devoured *Problem Child*, drawn in immediately by its addictive combination of little-boy-lost, aberrant motherhood and period detail – peculiarly English Spartan lost age. It is a tale fluently told – one would expect nothing less from a man with King's background and training – but what will raise it above the competition is its compelling honesty and intense evocations of place. King makes his boyhood at once as full of arcane social detail as any costume drama and as painful as fresh wounds, its trauma unsalved by nostalgia'
Patrick Gale

'Reading Caradoc's memoir, you can't help fizzing with rage and sorrow on his behalf. It is not so much the moments of cruelty that catch your throat as the long shadow they left on a bewildered child. Caradoc grew up desperate for affection, falling hopelessly in love with other boys at boarding school and attaching himself like a limpet to any happy family that happened to invite him home for half-term. It is testimony to his strength of character that he grew up able

to write about these appalling times without a hint of rancour. If anything, he is grateful to the rackety crew of schoolteachers and other people's mothers who gave him brief glimpses of what it felt like to be loved. *Problem Child* is an exhilarating read . . . one that has taken a lifetime to write'
Kathryn Hughes, *Mail on Sunday* 4 stars

'Far from being a"misery memoir", the book is infused with a sense of yearning for a lost past. Beautifully written, it captures superbly the pleasure and pain of childhood'
Ian Critchley, *Sunday Times*

'A compelling and courageous piece of writing that tells the extraordinary story of [Caradoc King's] own childhood and adolescence ... Despite its painful subject matter, the book is shot through with King's warm, ironic sense of humour and an optimism that makes it in some ways quite exhilarating'
Lisa O'Kelly, *Observer*

'For a teenage boy to lose his mother is a tragedy. To lose two, as Caradoc King did, is barely comprehensible, and to survive, not just to tell the tale but to tell it with lucid generosity, is truly remarkable . . . This book tells a shocking story of the damage inflicted by respectable, well-meaning middle-class parents on a child; but it also testifies to that child's resilience and enduring capacity to love . . . with its touches of the Brothers Grimm, [it then] enters Evelyn Waugh territory'
Anne Chisholm, *Evening Standard*

'The problem is less often the child than the parent. Caradoc King's misfortune was first to be abandoned by his birth mother and then adopted by a loveless woman who treated him cruelly as a "problem child" until he was again left to fend for himself at 16. That was the beginning of his new life as a student at Oxford and later as a successful literary agent. More than 30 years later King tracked down his natural mother soon before she died and re-established good relationships with all his siblings. The story ends happily, mostly because King presents himself as a happy adult who can recall his childhood with candour and compassion but without rancour'
The Times

Problem Child

A Memoir

CARADOC KING

**SIMON &
SCHUSTER**

London · New York · Sydney · Toronto · New Delhi

A CBS COMPANY

First published in Great Britain by Simon & Schuster UK Ltd, 2011
Paperback edition first published by Simon & Schuster, 2012
A CBS COMPANY

1 3 5 7 9 10 8 6 4 2

Simon & Schuster UK Ltd
1st Floor
222 Gray's Inn Road
London WC1X 8HB

www.simonandschuster.co.uk

Simon & Schuster Australia, Sydney
Simon & Schuster India, New Delhi

A CIP catalogue record for this book is available from the British Library

ISBN: 978-1-84983-350-9

Typeset by M Rules
Printed and bound by CPI Group (UK) Ltd, Croydon, CR0 4YY

To my children: Charlie, Flora and India.

Contents

Prologue

I am in Southwold, an old-fashioned seaside town on the Suffolk coast. I first stayed here as a five-year-old with my paternal grandparents who owned a house called the Old Mill on the common. For a couple of years I visited until my grandfather died and Little Granny moved to a smaller house. Although I had four sisters, my visits to Southwold were always on my own, a bit scary for a small boy staying with a strict elderly couple, but the visits are still happily remembered – solitary tricycle rides across the common from the town to the water tower, ice cream on the pier, climbing the old bear pole on the golf course watched anxiously by Granny below, prodding the famous whale washed up and dying slowly on the beach.

The visit I clearly remember was in spring 1953, when I was six. It was just after the Great Flood, which on the last night of January overwhelmed the east coast, drowning two hundred people and leaving a swathe of dead livestock and smashed houses, among them Strood House, my family home on the

Essex marshes. That night was the most exciting of my life, and as a temporary refugee in Southwold I remember walking with Little Granny in our wellington boots along the mud-silted road to the harbour gazing in wonder at the roofs of the seaside houses decapitated by the wind, with attic and bedroom contents spilled across the gardens.

I didn't return to Southwold until 1988, with my then wife and our two children. We stayed a night at the Swan Hotel for an eightieth birthday lunch for my Aunt Mavis, my father's oldest sister. My father didn't come to the lunch because he hadn't had any contact with Mavis (or me) for twenty-five years. But it was a happy family reunion. Manfred, Mavis's partner of thirty years and regarded in the family as a bit of a bounder, to everyone's surprise proposed marriage to her during his after-lunch speech; and, for the first time for half my life, I re-met my sister Priscilla, as delightful and affectionate as I had remembered, a meeting which started the process of reclaiming my childhood.

Since that birthday visit I have come back every year to Southwold, staying at the Swan, now with my partner Ingrid and our daughter India. But this time I'm on my own, renting a holiday cottage for a fortnight to start this book.

The book has been marinating for several years and two things have prompted me to write it. The first is coincidence. A new client of mine, a novelist living in Bloomsbury, mentioned my name to one of her neighbours, a painter called Patricia. The neighbour asked her to ask me whether I was the Caradoc King who lived at Peldon House in Essex in the mid-1950s. I said I was if she meant Strood House, Peldon, and, when we met, Patricia told me a surprising story.

When she was a schoolgirl, Patricia had been a friend of my oldest sister, Jane, and had stayed at Strood House a couple of times when I was a small boy. This was itself surprising because my mother, Jill, was a family recluse who disliked visitors, even her children's friends, and had once substituted teatime sandwich spread with hot chilli paste to scare away some particularly unwelcome child.

Then Patricia said that she remembered Jill telling her quietly before she introduced me'... and this is Caradoc, who's adopted but don't tell him because he doesn't know.'

Her words were a shock. I hadn't been told I was adopted until I was fifteen, a year before my parents threw me out of the family. I had thought that until then none of my siblings knew I was adopted, that this was my parents' closely held secret and that the explanation for my abrupt disappearance was that I was a problem child, adopted from a bad family, a cuckoo in the nest. How could my mother have told an eleven-year-old stranger a secret she had kept from me until I was in my teens?

It was of course naive to believe that my older sisters thought I was their natural brother, born mysteriously without pregnancy and already fifteen months old. Much later I was told that both Jane and Janet had always known but it was never mentioned. But this late discovery deeply upset my memory and perception of childhood.

The other catalysts of the story are family photographs, and one in particular.

When in middle age I met my natural mother, already an old woman crippled by a stroke, my half-sister gave me copies of a batch of family photographs. One of them was of me as a baby, in the garden of the family home.

Four years later, after a reunion with my adoptive siblings at a family funeral, my sister Priscilla gave me three King family photograph albums covering my childhood. Looking through the albums, I discovered that the same picture appeared in both my natural mother's collection and in my adopted mother's album – one a memento of an abandoned baby and the other welcoming that baby as a new member of the family. Why one mother gave up her year-old child for adoption and the other sixteen years later banished that adopted child is a puzzle this book tries to solve.

ONE

Small Problems

I

I start with my first memory. I am on my back in a pram in the front garden of Strood House. It is a bright, cold spring morning. My hands are in mittens. They are tied to each side of the pram so I cannot move them or roll onto my side. The mittens are not for warmth but to prevent me from sucking my thumb which, underneath the mittens, is smeared with 'bitter aloes', a disgusting thumb-sucking deterrent applied daily by my mother.

My family started ten years earlier on the 5th of May 1939 when Catherine Cecilia Beavan (hereinafter known in the family as Jill, her brother Sidney's nickname) and Eric John Ferguson King (hereinafter called Da) both from Enfield, Middlesex, got married in secret.

There was no particular reason for the secrecy because both of them came from neighbouring middle-class families, but Jill, according to her older sister Molly, had always been a contrary and difficult child and, after a fierce row with her father over his refusal to pay for her to go to the Royal College of Music, deliberately married Eric without asking her parents.

The Beavans were the older Enfield family. Jill's father, Thomas Beavan, had been brought up there and apprenticed by Weld & Son, a local family firm of solicitors. He married the senior partner's daughter Barbara and on his father-in-law's retirement inherited the partnership and changed its name to Weld & Beavan. Grandpa Beavan lived in a beautiful Queen Anne house called the Hermitage and had a chauffeur named Yates to drive him several times a week to the firm's central London office in Soho. The Beavans had three children: Sidney, educated like his father at Blundell's in Devon and then joining the family firm, and his younger sisters Molly and Jill, who were sent to non-academic but bracing boarding schools in Sussex to prepare them for marriage rather than professional careers.

Grandpa King was Yorkshire born and bred, married a farmer's daughter from the Scottish Lowlands, known to us as Little Granny because she was so small, and moved south. He became a director of the Far Eastern trading company Jardine Matheson and was prosperous enough to buy another grand Enfield house called Holmwood and a substantial holiday home, the Old Mill House, on the Southwold Common. There were four children in the family – Eric, his older brother Graham and two younger sisters, Mavis and Jessie. The boys went to the Leys School in Cambridge and the girls to Saint Felix, Southwold.

According to Molly, the Kings and the Beavans were acquaintances rather than friends though their children met regularly at grander Enfield parties. There was no just cause or impediment to the marriage of Jill and Eric and no doubt, if asked, both families would have given their blessing. But for whatever reason the marriage, rather than uniting the two families, caused deep and lasting estrangement. The rift between Jill and her father only healed (just about) after the death of her mother in 1953. Eric's siblings lost all contact with their brother after the marriage and

4

there was no contact between the cousins from opposite sides of the families until more than a decade later when my cousin Tim, Jessie's second son, and I were sent to the same Suffolk prep school.

Jill and Da, soon after their wedding.

Jill was the one who was blamed. The King family thought her a difficult and unfriendly woman who deliberately isolated Eric from the rest of them. Their dislike was at first restrained because she was Eric's wife but would later become open and vehement.

Despite this rift Jill and Eric were ideally suited and deeply in love. They didn't need wider family and social contacts. They were self-sufficient within their own family. As with most enduring couples their differences complemented each other, complying with allotted roles in the tacit conspiracy of their marriage. Eric was gentle and considerate, Jill could be angry and mean; Eric was weak and Jill dominating; Jill was shy, antisocial and fearful of outsiders; Eric was outgoing, friendly and protective. They were a single unit, combined to keep the world at bay.

The early years of their marriage were extremely happy. During the war they lived at Horse Cross, a simple cottage in rural Hertfordshire, and the albums are full of roly-poly half-naked children, pony rides and rural jollity. At demob time Eric was lucky to get a job as town dentist in the small town of Chagford in Devon; when I visited in the early 1990s, his name was still remembered. Here Caroline was born and I first entered the picture.

I don't know what the Kings knew about me when they adopted me. It should have been nothing, in accordance with the strict secrecy which applied to adoption at the time. But according to Janet it was a private adoption arranged by the Chagford doctor, who may have known more. Jill's story was that I was the illegitimate child in a broken marriage and that my father was a professional footballer.

Nor do I know why Jill and Da adopted me. They already had three girls, one still in nappies. By the date of my adoption, 13 May 1948, Jill was already pregnant with Priscilla, born in January 1949. One possible clue is that Jill, having been strongly advised to have no more babies after repeated miscarriages, particularly wanted a son. Priscilla told me recently that she was a twin to a small boy born stillborn, a loss that must have upset Jill deeply and possibly affected how she treated her adopted son.

There is also a mystery about how the Kings found me, apart from some vague geographical clues. My adoption certificate was issued in Poole, Dorset which is a hundred miles from Chagford where the Kings lived in early 1947. But the certificate also shows that I was adopted from a Barnardo's Home and, although it doesn't indicate which home and Barnardo's records don't go back that far, I am certain that it was from Farm Hill, Coggeshall, just twenty miles from Strood House, Peldon, Essex where the Kings moved in late 1947.

I recently visited Farm Hill. The place was immediately familiar – a collection of mock-Tudor buildings built in the 1930s set in a spacious garden, no longer a Barnardo's but an opulent family home, with two Mercedes parked in the drive. I knew at once I had been there several times, when still in nappies in a nursery with lots of other cots and then as a toddler playing on the lawn. The matron, a kind lady dressed in blue and white called Miss Simcox, knew my mother and, I found out later, offered to take me back for an occasional week to give Jill respite from her large family and clamouring new baby.

Strood House is next to the causeway over the marshes leading to Mersea Island. Built in the mid-eighteenth century by a local smuggler, it had an upstairs spyhole window in which to burn a candle if the Excise men were nearby. When we lived there the house was stuccoed Essex pink and behind the pleasing symmetrical facade there were five bedrooms, two attic rooms, a large ground-floor room at the back we called the nursery, a music room and living room at the front, separated by a hall, and

Strood House, c. 1950.

a galley kitchen. The only bathroom and separate lavatory, known as the potty room, were off the lobby by the back door, conveniently close to the nursery when it was bath-time but a miserably long dark walk from the bedrooms which meant we had to use chamber pots.

The house was sparsely furnished. Apart from matting on the landing and stairs the only carpet was in our parents' bedroom and the spare room. Other rooms had painted boards or lino and in the nursery there was a polished red concrete floor. The walls were whitewashed. The music room, so named because it housed Jill's Erard grand piano, was only used by the children on Sunday at teatime. In winter a driftwood fire was often lit and in front of the blaze was a threadbare hearthrug. The furniture in the other rooms was functional. In the living room were my mother's Heal's bureau and two upright armchairs with wooden arms in which Jill and Da sat listening to the wireless or reading after the children had gone to bed. A protective plastic cloth was kept over the mahogany living-room table. Except in the music room, where there was a standard lamp, the lighting was from overhead bulbs. Our beds were metal-framed school beds with hard horsehair mattresses.

My bedroom looked out onto marshland. Mersea Island, to the left, was linked to the mainland by the half-mile Strood causeway. Straight ahead was a marsh track marked by wooden poles leading to Ray Island, a small deserted stretch of grass, brambles and windswept trees, and a regular spot for our family picnics and sailors from West Mersea.

Behind the house were two fields surrounded by a sea wall and more marshland. At the end of our garden was the 'Cow's Field', in which we exercised the dogs, and played in two wrecked Second World War landing craft and a pair of concrete pillboxes on the sea wall. The Cow's Field and the wheatfield next to it were tenanted by a local farmer, Mr Alan Maskell, whose ramshackle farm buildings were in the far corner of the fields.

Our close neighbours were an elderly couple called the Hardings, who lived in the large house next door. Occasionally we children were invited over the garden wall for lemonade and to collect overthrown tennis balls but, apart from an invitation for all of us to watch the 1952 Coronation on their television set, I don't recall any social contact between the Hardings and our parents. Our other real neighbours were the Maskells, Alan and Judy, who lived in a bungalow across the road from the farm and were a much more friendly couple. They had no children and Alan would let us play in his straw barns, ride on his trailer, and sit on his lap to help steer the tractor.

One other person lived nearby, an eccentric man known as Old Jack Williams. He lived on his own in a Second World War pontoon, converted into a makeshift houseboat and moored amidst piles of rusting bikes, fishing gear and oil cans, on the edge of the marshes near Maskells farm. He sold freshly caught herring out of his bike basket around Peldon village and spent most of his earnings in the public bar of the Peldon Rose. Old Jack was very grumpy and when we walked past on the sea wall he would shout at us to clear off.

The Strood House garden was large and wonderful for children. There was a big scrappy lawn next to the house and a barn, home to Dimple and her kittens, born during the flood and named after Noah's children, Shem, Ham and Japheth. The barn also housed Da's workshop, my sisters' hamsters and guinea pigs and my two rabbits, both of whom died in the 1955 myxomatosis pandemic, and there was a loft store for animal food. On the other side of the house was the garage, and a bike shed with Elsan lavatory, a good place for sulky escapes from too much family life. The dogs, first Hamley and Bumble, and then Dyvodd and her children Madam and Eve, were Welsh collies trained to bark at strangers, and kept chained to their kennels by the garage.

Behind the house was a weeping willow, overhanging a ditch verdant with weeds, fertilised by a link to the family cesspit. Beside the ditch ran a grassy track where my sisters had their shops and dens, leading to the Wilderness which was used for bonfires, and the stile into the Cow's Field. A long wall and wooden door separated the lower garden from the upper garden, known as Martha's Vineyard and my parents' smallholding. It had a small orchard and vast vegetable beds, weeded by the children at weekends and regularly tilled by my father with his rotovator. The Nile, a small enclosed brown and reedy stream, bordered Martha's Vineyard with a wooden bridge across it to Howard's Piece, a small field for the ducks, hens and geese who helped to keep us self-sufficient.

10

Self-sufficiency, thrift and independence were essential to my parents and common in the early 1950s when rural family life was tough and simple. Televisions were scarce and in our family not permitted. We seldom owned a car. Newspapers weren't delivered; *Punch* and, for the older girls, the *Elizabethan* magazine, were sent by post. The cinema was half an hour's bus ride away and a very rare treat. Our most direct link to the outside world was a handsome mahogany wireless which promised on its elaborate tuning dial access to radio stations as far away as Berlin, Moscow and Hilversum, although the only English ones were the BBC Home Service for plays and discussions, the Third Programme for classical music and the Light Programme for entertainment, which my parents didn't approve of.

Domestic life was hard then for a mother of five children, a long daily routine of washing, cooking, cleaning, bathing and bedding, though with the benefits of home delivery. Jill hated going to the shop so the West Mersea baker delivered special large family-sized wholemeal loaves, the International Stores delivered weekly groceries and, after the end of meat rationing in 1954, Dewhurst the Butcher made occasional deliveries. Fresh herrings and mackerel appeared regularly, sometimes direct from Old Jack's bike basket or from a Mersea fishmonger in his rusty Ford van.

Despite the austerity of those years there were also liberating inventions. The Electrolux vacuum cleaner came first, then the Kenwood mixer. The Hotpoint washer and rotary iron arrived next, easing Jill's burden of the Monday and Thursday family wash, although the drying was still done in the garden, with double-pegged sheets billowing like galleon sails, except on rainy days when wet clothes were hung on pulleys in the living room. Then came a Belling electric cooker which Jill used only in high summer, preferring to cook and keep a kettle always boiling on

11

the coke-fired stove in the living room. Later a radiogram appeared, bought from money Jill inherited from her mother, and LPs of Tom Lehrer, *The Sorcerer's Apprentice*, Holst's *Planets* and Britten's new *Young Person's Guide to the Orchestra*.

Books were the family's lifeline, armchair links for Da and Jill to the outside world, and for the children escape routes from boredom to imaginary worlds of adventure and romance. The landing outside my parents' bedroom was wall to wall with books, shelves of colour-coded Penguins, orange for general fiction, green for mysteries, blue for Pelican general non-fiction and the specialist brown for archaeology and yellow for anthropology or perhaps the other way round. There were classic reference books – *Gray's Anatomy*, *Encyclopaedia Britannica* and Shell Guides to Britain – mainstays of post-war self-education. There were also *Punch* omnibuses handsomely bound in brown cloth, the first going back as far as 1927, inherited from Da's father, and expanding annually thereafter. In the nursery were shelves of children's classics, *Black Beauty* and *What Katy Did* and *What Katy Did Next*, and books our parents had enjoyed and passed down – those by Harrison Ainsworth, and *Little Lord Fauntleroy* by Frances Hodgson Burnett. Later I would discover my mother's book club choices from The Reprint Society – Daphne du Maurier, A. J. Cronin, Nicholas Monsarrat, Irwin Shaw – glorious middlebrow classics which helped me bridge the gap between childhood and adolescence. I read fluently by the age of five and in 1952 could master not only *The Tale of Sly Tod* and *The Velveteen Rabbit* but also *Royalty in Essex*, an illustrated history book given out to all Essex children to commemorate the Coronation. A love of reading was the most valuable thing my parents gave me.

My next distinct memory is about my tricycle and the first time I was severely punished. It is like a slow bad dream. I am sitting in a high chair confined by a notched bamboo cane inserted through the holes in each arm of the chair. The cane is called the dog stick, normally kept on the window ledge beside the back door. Its main purpose is to discipline the dogs but it is also used on us children. 'Fetch the dog stick' was a dreaded instruction, issued by Jill. She also normally administered the punishment; but this was an exceptional occasion and I am waiting for Da to come home from work and beat me. My crime involves the tricycle.

I loved my tricycle. It is old, with chipped blue paint and spoked wheels, which I have just taken over from Caroline who has gone on to her first bike, inherited from Jane and Janet. I also have a red two-wheeler trailer which hooks onto the back, a fourth birthday present from Jill and Da. Priscilla now has the small black trike and she follows me everywhere, standing up on her pedals to get enough speed over the grass tracks. I load sand and grass cuttings into the trailer and collect and deliver them to special places in the garden. Priscilla helps with the shovelling. It's an elaborate game we both love.

That morning we found the main gate half open, so I suggest to Priscilla that we go out onto the road because it is much smoother to ride on. Priscilla is too scared so I go on my own, pedalling furiously away from the house until I am halfway across the causeway where the high tide is lapping up from the Pyefleet channel onto the path by the road. I feel exhilarated by this sudden bid for freedom, but scared of the consequences. When a man in a passing car stops to ask if I'm all right and where do I live I nod and point back to Strood House. As soon as he has driven away I start pedalling furiously back, fearful of being found out.

Too late. I see Jill come through the gate. She shouts furiously and runs towards me. Now I am locked in the high chair, waiting for Da.

That afternoon was the longest and scariest of my life. Da didn't get home until bedtime so the waiting went on for ever and I became ever more fearful. After her initial outburst Jill became cold and silent. I too was locked into my own silent obstinacy, refusing to say sorry and admit I had done wrong. The other children passed through the nursery with doleful looks. I was allowed down once for a pee. I missed my tea.

Poor Da. Although Jill's official executioner, punishment was against his nature. When he finally came through the front door to be confronted by this bleak tableau I am sure he shrank from his responsibilities and longed just to have his solitary supper which Jill kept warm in the oven. But he had to use the dog stick and afterwards I sat painfully in the bath with a wide-eyed Priscilla until Jill, punishment now complete, forgave me at last and wrapped and towelled me with such unusual gentleness that I burst into tears and was carried to bed.

That tricycle confrontation started a pattern in my relationship with Jill. The shift from cold anger to tenderness. Her fury and my obstinate refusal to give in.

Parents treated their children differently then. Like Mr Banks in the *Mary Poppins* song, Jill and Da believed in 'discipline and order'. At Strood House life was very strict. We got up at six and went to bed very early – six o'clock when I was six and even in my teens no later than eight. We had to work hard – making beds, tidying rooms, cleaning out the hens, housework, gardening, washing up, sawing logs and polishing shoes. We had to behave ourselves. Answering back, cheek, lying, spite, laziness, tantrums were serious offences with punishments ranging from curfew, banishment to room, extra chores, stony silence, cancellation of pocket money, the dog stick and, perhaps worst of all, Jill's towering temper and withering tongue.

But the photograph albums show that life was also fun. We had a healthy, simple childhood, mostly spent outside, playing in the sand-pit, walking the dogs in the Cow's Field, crabbing, picking mushrooms and blackberries, collecting driftwood with Jill and Da at the weekend, helping at the farm. We swam a lot, either in the Pyefleet, or in the marsh creeks beyond the sea wall, which were filled and drained daily by the tide. There were bus trips to West Mersea for sandy sandwiches and a Wall's ice cream on the beach and bike rides to East Mersea with the young ones strapped into the basket-work seats on Jill and Da's carriers, where we fried sausages in billycans and played in the wartime gun fort. There were mud-larking walks to Ray Island, piggy-backed when I was very small, then hands held by older sisters, and finally stumping and squelching along with the rest of them.

Winter was exciting too, even though the east coast winds were freezing and too long in the garden meant chaps and chilblains and constant snotty noses. There seemed to be more snow and ice then and we would toboggan on trays down the sea walls, slide on the frozen pools in the Cow's Field, and have proper sledge rides along the Strood with the older children playing at being reindeers. Inside, in the nursery, there were cards and board games, my Triang lorries and crane, school and hospital games with Caroline's dolls and a secret cupboard under the stairs in which I once locked Priscilla before going upstairs for my afternoon rest.

This was the happy side of my childhood – but between Jill and me there was a serious problem.

Guy Fawkes Night, six weeks before my fifth birthday, led to the next confrontation. Da loved Guy Fawkes and helping him to build the bonfire was a big event. He chose two assistants, who that year were Caroline and myself, a special honour because the year before I had been scared by the fireworks and watched from inside the house with Priscilla. This year, with Jill's help, Caroline had stuffed and sewn the Guy Fawkes effigy and, while Da laid out his fireworks with bottles for the rockets and Catherine wheels nailed to the tree, she told me about the terrible Gunpowder Plot.

At six o'clock after tea we went out with lanterns into the garden. Da sprinkled paraffin over the piled wood and threw on a lighted paper spill which set the bonfire ablaze instantly. The night was cold and clear. Rockets shooting into a star-filled sky and then breaking open to make more stars and coloured balls of fire was the most beautiful thing I had ever seen. Later when the fire had died down we came out again and Da put potatoes wrapped in silver paper into the hot embers.

Everything was fine until the next day when I was caught trying to relight the bonfire with rolled-up paper and a box of matches. I had already been severely cautioned for playing with matches and once smacked on the hand with a ruler for audaciously lighting a candle on the landing. This time the punishment was much worse.

Both of them administered it. I was given a stern lecture by Jill and then led by Da into the nursery. Jill took my hand and lightly and quickly pressed it onto the scorching hot metal over the chimney of the stove. The pain was intense and I screamed. Jill rushed me to the kitchen to put my hand under running cold water. The other children watched looking shocked. The punishment was over. All was forgiven and forgotten, except for the blisters on the palm of my hand.

II

Even so, there are many good memories.

I am sitting on a bus and can see Strood House down the hill at the far end of the causeway. I am on my way home from Mersea where I now go three mornings a week to Mrs Harris's kindergarten. I can remember only a little about the place – that it was housed in the village hall, which it shared with the Women's Institute, and that Mrs Harris was a plump and kind lady. I don't remember any of the other children. The important thing is that I am travelling on my own because the conductor of the number 75 Colchester to Mersea bus which stops outside our house has agreed to keep an eye on me and make sure that I get off at the right place. I feel deep pride at this new independence.

I remember, too, Da's 1937 Bullnose Morris, his first motoring folly.

The Bullnose was an eight-seater convertible, the size of a small tank with a windscreen you could wind open for extra ventilation, long leather bench seats front and back and two 'dickie' seats in the boot. It was very handsome and we children spent happy hours cleaning and polishing it under Da's guidance. It had a deep growly engine and a journey with all of us on board, either enclosed by the black canvas hood and Plexiglas windows or with the roof down, was a thrilling experience.

Driving my sisters.

Da had bought the Bullnose on impulse from a local garage without telling Jill. The car was too big to park in the garage, so it took up a large space in the garden beside the house. That it often failed to start didn't matter to Da who adored tinkering with engines, nor to Jill who when she occasionally agreed to come for a ride would be secretly glad the car wouldn't go. When eventually the Bullnose needed some crucial but unavailable part Jill made Da pay the garage to tow it away for good.

A passion for cars was something Da and I shared – a special father–son link which made us both butts of Jill's displeasure. If my childhood was short of love, Da's marriage was short of things he loved but Jill disapproved of.

Another was sailing, which he had learned as a boy in Southwold. Although we lived surrounded by water and other people's sailing boats, the only sailing we did was in the Strood in an army surplus inflatable dinghy with a red sail, until the rubber perished and caused a terminal leak and it was thrown out. Perhaps if Da had stood up to Jill, bought a proper boat and taught me to sail my childhood would have ended differently. As it turned out he had to wait another forty years and separation from Jill before he resumed sailing in old age, too late to share with me.

The lack of a car was not only because of Jill's displeasure but also shortage of money. Apart from occasional windfalls when a parent died the only family income was from Da's job as a National Health dentist in Colchester. With five children to support and the drain of private education the Kings lived in proud and sometimes embarrassing poverty.

Another economy was on family holidays, though also for practical reasons. With a smallholding of livestock, the numerous family pets, and later a trio of goats, a fortnight's family holiday was rarely possible. We had just four in fifteen years which, remembering the rows and sulking which accompanied rainy fortnights in railway camping coaches, were probably quite enough.

The first one, in June 1952, was the best of them all with an exceptionally happy memory.

It is well past my normal bedtime and Da and I are standing at the end of a platform at King's Cross station looking up at the driver of an enormous green and gleaming railway engine which is going to pull our train. I am old enough to read the words on the nameplate – *Flying Scotsman* – and I am overwhelmed with excitement.

'Would you like to come up, young man?' asks the driver, and when I nod he gets down from his seat, reaches out of the door and pulls me up the steps. He sits me on his knee, tells me what the different levers do and then lets me pull the one for the engine's whistle, which blasts a cloud of steam around the station.

The journey which follows is magic. We are all in one compartment and I am given a top bunk, head to tail with Priscilla, which means I can peer out through the edge of the blind onto the moonlit scenery and the blur of lights when we race through a station. I manage to stay awake until Darlington where the train stops and a man goes up and down tapping the wheels. This is bliss, like Christmas night. Finally I must have fallen asleep because suddenly I am awake and a man in a white jacket hands up a cup of tea, something I'm never allowed at home, and tells us there is another hour to Edinburgh.

There are a few blurry black and white snaps of that chilly holiday on the shore of Loch Earn, grinning little Kings grouped in front of magnificent mountain scenery, swimming in the icy loch, the small rented caravan which had to sleep six of us. It rained quite a lot and we spent one day in the caravan playing board games behind misted windows. My clearest memory is leaving very early one morning for the station in the back of the farmer's van and the long train-ride home.

The caravan holiday must have been a nightmare with bickering kids and irritable parents crammed together in a small steamy space full of damp clothes and muddy shoes. No wonder Jill avoided family holidays. At least at home she could retire to her bedroom, take the dogs for a walk or shut herself in the music room to play the piano, and Da could spend hours tinkering in his workshop. I remember the babble of family meals and hating them, the argumentative Sunday family board games, the pressure of always being expected to join in, the non-stop noise of family life.

Kings united.

So what were my sisters like? I have only seen Janet and Caroline twice in the last forty years and Priscilla infrequently. Jane, who died young, was thoughtful, quiet and musical and after I left home she changed her name to Martha for religious reasons. Janet was vivacious, strong-willed and rebellious. Caroline was busy and bossy, and Priscilla was the sweet-natured baby of the family and my little sister. All of them, except Janet, wore their hair in pigtails which involved long sessions of Jill's fierce brushing and plaiting. Only Janet was allowed to keep her blonde hair in a pony-tail or loose and held back by a snood.

Jill scared me from the beginning. There was something deliberately severe about her, the double plaits pinned round her head, her plain unmade-up face, her tweedy unfeminine clothes, her proud aura of rural simplicity. Occasionally her warmth, wit and sharp intelligence would shine through, a balm of happiness, but this could be swiftly eclipsed by her sharp tongue, her quick Celtic temper, her troubled mix of strength and insecurity. She worked hard at motherhood – a slave to the kitchen, the washing, the garden and the housework. She was fulfilled by her children, but resentful of the self-martyrdom motherhood and family life involved.

She also played the piano beautifully. I remember being allowed once to listen alone to her playing the *Moonlight Sonata*, her face and mood softened by the music, and afterwards there was a rare moment of just the two of us when she told me about my unusual Christian name.

'Caradoc was a famous Welsh chieftain who fought against the Romans,' she explained. 'We named you after him because my family, the Beavans, are from Wales near where Caradoc lived. So you must try to be brave like him.'

I wish there had been more moments like that. I deeply wanted Jill's love and attention but there was a barrier between us, which I couldn't cross or understand. She didn't cuddle me as she did the girls. The physical contact I most remember was her fierce rubbing of my face with a spit-dampened handkerchief to remove the smuts. I must have been a disappointment from the start.

Da was Jill's opposite. His main interests were mechanical – car engines, trains, traction engines – and books. He was brilliant at making things and, like many men, probably happiest in his own workshop. He was bullied and enthralled by his wife, devoted to his children, gentle and courteous. He had glasses, a quiet voice and scholarly look, which made him a popular dentist. But he was a weak man, dependent on Jill's strength. I loved his bookishness, the crosses he put by programmes in the *Radio Times* he wanted to listen to, his workshop with its painted silhouettes of his tools to show where to hang them, his special voice for reading *The Jungle Books*, the two identical grey three-piece suits and black crêpe-soled Oxfords he always wore for work and his weekend brown corduroys and flappy khaki shorts. I loved him because he loved me, at least for as long as he could.

Later that summer Jill's brother Sidney visited with his wife Effie and their daughters Patricia, Barbara and Linda. They drove from Enfield towing their caravan, and stayed in a caravan site in West Mersea. It was the first time we cousins had met. It was also the first time that we could see how another family behaved and certainly the Beavans were very different from the Kings. Sidney was a genial pipe-smoker with the easy charm of a successful solicitor, now senior partner of Weld & Beavan, living (as I discovered the following year) in a comfortable house called Hennons on the outskirts of Enfield. He and Da knew each other from childhood and got along well. Jill and Sidney, both tough Beavans, had an affectionate sparring sibling relationship. Effie, called Aunty Bevvy, was the complete opposite of Jill – a little, cuddly, feminine woman who clearly adored her husband and the comfortable life they shared and to whom life at Strood House would have been a nightmare. The children, in the mould of their mother, seemed like little princesses compared with their wild country cousins.

That hot weekend the two families had a ball. It was afternoon high tide and Da inflated the rubber dinghy, filled it with small children and sailed up and down the Strood, the bigger children swimming alongside. The Beavan girls, at first shy in their flowery bathing dresses and prim about the muddy water, were soon splashing about happily and competed fiercely in the races which Da and Sidney organised afterwards in the garden.

The next day we set off early at low tide to Ray Island, mudlarking children pushing ahead led by Jane and Janet and the grown-ups behind – with a lot of squeamish giggling from Aunty Bevvy gallantly guided by Da. We swam from the beach when the tide was up and had a barbecue lunch with sausages on sticks and bacon and mushrooms in a billycan, washed down with fizzy orange Corona. When the tide had dropped we walked back to Strood House where Da and Sidney hosed us down in the garden and the two women prepared tea before the Beavan cousins, now sworn friends, drove home.

That autumn I was sent to proper school for the first time at Endsleigh in Lexden Road, Colchester, where Jane and Janet were already in the senior school.

It was a long journey for a five-year-old. Colchester was eight miles by bus from Strood House, then there was another bus ride to Lexden Road but Jane and Janet delivered me to Endsleigh every morning and collected me in the evening. This meant that I was always last to leave because the senior school finished an hour later than the pre-prep, so the headmaster's wife would give me orange juice and biscuits in her kitchen before I went home.

I started being a bad boy at Endsleigh early on, not because I was naturally naughty but because Endsleigh was a tough little school and it frightened me. One boy – Brian Baker – had a big influence on my behaviour. He ran a gang called 'Brian Baker's gang' and belonging to it was a crucial indicator of status in the school. Membership depended on Baker's whim, and initiation tests, which involved wrestling other candidates and the amount of cheek you dared to give the teacher. I achieved entry in my first term.

I am not sure what Brian Baker's gang actually did, probably chasing non-members through the shrubbery at the back of the school, but gang seniority was indicated by how you wore your school cap. All members wore them back to front. More senior members wore them back to front with the peaks turned up, very senior members inside out and back to front and Brian himself wore the full caboodle of upturned peak inside out and backwards.

Despite a bad end-of term-report, Jill and Da must for some reason have felt sorry for me because that year on my birthday in December I was given the best present a small boy could wish for.

That morning I was sitting in bed eating a biscuit, a regular Sunday treat, and waiting for Jill and Da to come in and start my day. The door opened very slowly, there was a pause, then a black and white dog bounded into the room, took one look at me and my biscuit and leapt onto the bed. Hamish had arrived – and got the biscuit.

How I wish he'd lasted! But Hamish was a King family member for only a month because in that short time he turned from a cute biscuit-eater to a frenzied chaser of Alan Maskell's cows. Da had bought him from a Peldon family but hadn't established why the farmer wanted to get rid of a handsome one-year-old black and white spaniel. Alan Maskell was too polite to complain but a dog-chaser was bad for his cattle and, after a phone call to the embarrassed previous owner, Jill and Da decided that Hamish would have a safer and more interesting time as a town dog and at the end of January he was dispatched to a family in Colchester – or so I was told.

Christmas was the most magical moment in the year and a lavish treat after Jill and Da's normal tight economy. It followed fixed traditions, starting with a family expedition on Christmas Eve morning to collect holly and ivy from the lane to Maskell's Farm and mistletoe from Peldon Woods. Then in the afternoon, with the King's College Cambridge carol service turned up loud on the radio, the young children licked coloured strips of sticky paper into paper chains, Jane and Janet pinned up the holly and ivy, Da erected the Christmas tree, and Jill cooked. We did the first stage of decoration all together, looping the paper and silver and golden tinsel chains from one corner of the nursery to the other and hanging paper lanterns and balls in a cluster in the centre and in the corners. After tea the older ones played Monopoly with Da and the little 'uns Ludo with Jill. Then came the distribution of Christmas stockings, a collection of khaki army surplus knee socks, size depending on seniority. Finally, after washing and cleaning teeth, we laid out carrot sticks, cake and a glassful of Drambuie by the music-room fireplace.

Waiting in bed for Father Christmas that year was the best time. The rest of the house is quiet. Priscilla and I whisper to each other about hoped-for stocking presents until she drifts off. Downstairs I hear murmuring adult voices. The lights from passing cars flicker round the room, the wind rustling the poplar trees and the hot water gurgling through the central heating pipes.

I am sure I didn't sleep at all, but at some point Father Christmas must have come because I am awake again, my feet nudging the heavy, well-stuffed woollen sausage lying on the end of my bed. What seems like hours passes in delicious suspense. No one is allowed to open their stockings until Jill and Da come to our rooms, switch on the lights and say 'Happy Christmas'. But the weight at the end of the bed is pleasure enough, toes massaging the different lumps to guess what's inside, almost better than opening up the dolls and pencil cases, the Dinky Toys, water pistols, books, gloves, mandarin oranges and nuts with which the stockings are filled.

Outside our bedrooms the house has been transformed into Christmas fairyland. Puffs of cotton-wool snow fall past the landing window. A giant candle-burns on the table, its reflection flickering onto the darkened glass. Fairy lights illuminate the stairs down into the hall. In the nursery stands the Christmas tree festooned with angels, chocolate money, glass balls and glittering tinsel. Around the tree are piles of more presents, big presents to be opened later in the morning.

Normally the day which started so early stayed magical until after lunch when the surfeit of goose and stuffing, chipolatas, roast potatoes, Corona, Christmas pudding with silver money, brandy butter and a general overdose of crackers and excitement began to take effect, and the children would be sent for compulsory rest time in our bedrooms.

But that year, 1952, it was different. For the first time Grandpa and Gamma would join us for Christmas. After the summer visit Uncle Sidney had finally brokered peace between Jill and her father, and my parents must have realised this might be the last chance for a family reunion. Careful plans had been made for Aunty Molly, who still lived at the Hermitage, to drive the elderly couple to Colchester on Christmas Eve for a two-night stay at the George, and for us all to meet for lunch and tea at the hotel on Christmas Day.

The day went well, all things considered. Gamma, pale and papery thin, could only walk with a stick, supported by Molly. 'You look like Queen Mary,' Da said gallantly, which clearly pleased her. After lunch she showed me her rings and I was struck by her claw-like hands and their prominent blue veins. Grandpa looked rather stiff in his dark double-breasted suit in marked contrast to Da's brown corduroys, but that was probably because he and Jill had been on distant terms since the row following her secret marriage. But the prattle of his granddaughters and a couple of glasses of red wine cheered him up and by the time we got to the Christmas pudding, to which Da had asked the waiter to add the specially polished silver coins, everyone was in fine form. Aunty Molly and Jill, never great friends, laughed over childhood memories at the Hermitage and Molly told us exciting stories about her travels in India.

After lunch presents were exchanged in the drawing room and coffee was served. I had already done well with a big Triang crane as my main present, but the Beavan present was even better – a battery-operated red car which could be steered with the help of a rubber plunger attached by tube to the exhaust pipe. Molly showed me how it worked and I had a great time steering the car around the other guests.

I had watched the door of the hotel lift opening and closing on a trip to the lavatory with Da before lunch and later, when everyone was busy with their presents, I drove my new car out of the drawing room and tried out the lift for myself. I reached the third floor by pressing the button marked three, but when the lift door closed all by itself with me standing out in the corridor, I lost my nerve and had to be escorted weeping downstairs and back to the drawing room by a chambermaid.

This misdemeanour provoked a sharp dressing down from Jill and almost led to me being banished from another treat, proposed by Grandpa over Christmas lunch. For a return visit the King children were invited go with Jill to Enfield by Empire's Best Coach on the 6th of January. There we would be met by Grandpa and Aunty Molly and driven up to London for a slap-up lunch at the Trocadero, Piccadilly, followed by a matinee performance of *Where the Rainbow Ends* at the Festival Hall.

But two days before I was suddenly sick all over the nursery floor, and confined to bed for Jill's usual twenty-four-hour semi-starvation cure with just hot Marmite to drink, dry toast and doses of a morphine-laced medicine we called 'Miss Kaolin Said'. The next day I felt much better, although hungry and weak, and Jill at the last minute agreed that I could go after giving me half a Kwell and telling me I was on a strict diet which would rule out the best of the lunch.

The coach journey was a headachy ordeal but thanks to Grandpa's special attention I enjoyed the day hugely. I sat between him and Molly in the front of the car while the rest of them sat in the back behind a glass partition. Grandpa also put me beside him at our table in the grand restaurant and personally supervised the ordering and preparation of the white fish and boiled potatoes which I was allowed to eat while my sisters tucked into roast chicken and chips. After lunch each child was given a present and the head waiter made a special point of giving me the largest box of all which contained a plastic model of a Spitfire. *Where the Rainbow Ends*, which for three years became an annual pilgrimage, was enchanting and everyone was in such a good mood afterwards that I was allowed a full Lyons Corner House tea with crumpets and chocolate cake before we started the long journey home.

In January 1953 I started my second term at Endsleigh School and dreaded it. Although now a junior member of Brian Baker's gang, the pressure to conform to the gang culture and earn promotion to second-grade cap wearer made me very anxious. But two weeks into the term something happened which was even better than my childhood dream that school would burn down. A devastating storm and flood, the worst since records began, savaged the Essex coast.

The flood was the most exciting event of my childhood. There had been warnings on the wireless that evening as we drank cocoa in our dressing gowns, and Da went out with his torch to lock up the chickens and ducks, a tragic error as it turned out because if he had left them loose the ducks might have survived, instead of being washed up, drowned and locked in the duck house several miles down the coast the following morning.

I fell asleep, snug against the sound of gales rattling the windows and battering the trees in the garden. Then, in the middle of the night, I woke and knew at once that something was different. The wind had dropped; there was eerie silence. I got out of bed and opened the curtain. In front of the house, in the moonlight, I could see water everywhere, flooding the road, lapping over the garden wall, puddling on the lawn and sidling towards the house. It was all very calm and beautiful.

The house was silent and there were no lights on so I put on my dressing gown, walked down the landing and quietly opened my parents'bedroom door. Da awoke immediately and switched on his bedside light.

'What's the matter, Caradoc? Is something wrong?'

'I think the flood has come,'I said, grinning.

Events moved very fast after that. Jill woke the other children and told them to get dressed. Water was already seeping under the front door at the bottom of the stairs and I watched Da prising up floorboards hoping he could stop the flood by letting it fill the cellar. But the water just kept on coming until it was knee deep on the ground floor. My parents were shouting at each other, panic in their voices. Da pulled on his waders and climbed over the lower half of the back door to rescue the dogs tethered in their kennels.

The rest of us went up to the attic. Through the dormer window we watched the water lapping over the sea wall into the Cow's Field and turning the ponds where we paddled into giant lakes, a blur of cows huddling in the corner of the field. Then in the moonlight we saw something terrible and wonderful. Cracks began to open in the sea wall; the water was breaking through. Another crack, and then another, and the sea wall gave way in a vast section of grass and mud, shunted forward by an overwhelming torrent of water. Fifty yards further along it broke through again and a second tidal wave swept across the field towards the house.

Jill told us sharply to come away from the window. Caroline had started to cry.'What about the cows ... and the hens ... and my guinea pigs?'But Jill was already running down the attic stairs to find Da who was still in the garden, and Jane told us all to sit down and that we would sing a song.

Once the worst had happened, everything quietened down. Water filled the ground floor and, peering over the banister, I saw our breakfast places laid on the plastic tablecloth floating like a magic carpet. I remember cuddling the cats, and sleeping on cushions in the attic. Then, in daylight, we came downstairs to see the devastated house and upstairs, from our bedroom window, the grey chaos of mud and jumble left in the garden and the fields beyond by the tide which drained back through the gaps in the sea wall before rising again a few hours later. The coastland of East Anglia was devastated and, until repairs could be made, the sea flooded and drained the countryside twice daily, covering it with mud.

Apart from the dogs and cats sheltering with us in the attic, all our livestock was drowned. The one remarkable survivor was Old Jack who, like Noah, had untied his houseboat and floated on the tide until he was washed up on dry land several miles away.

Two days later we children were evacuated. I went for a short trip to Southwold then joined Caroline and Priscilla at Hennons, Uncle Sidney's house in Enfield, for an exciting reunion with our cousins, with the added challenge of attending their convent day school as temporary refugees.

Aunty Bevvy was a kind and gentle mother and although Patricia, Barbara and Linda didn't have the high spirits of my elder sisters, it was a big relief to escape Jill's quick temper. It was also exciting to be with a family who owned a car, a Standard Vanguard with column gearshift and a push-button radio, and we went out for treats to the zoo and the cinema. The one disappointment was that we saw Grandpa only once on a teatime visit with Aunty Molly. The Hermitage was only just two miles away but Gamma was extremely ill so visits were impossible.

Leaving Hennons two months later to return to Strood House made me homesick for the first time. Life with the Beavans had given me a glimpse of a more loving and easy-going family and I missed them. I was also anxious about returning to Endsleigh for the summer term.

The school itself wasn't too bad. The weather was getting warmer so we were outside a lot and that term I started playing rounders, running and doing long jump which I enjoyed and was quite good at. My reputation as a flood survivor must have helped because by the middle of the term I was at last promoted to wearing my school cap inside out.

The problem was at home and most of all between me and Jill. Twice that summer she beat me with the dog stick, once for taking a square of dark chocolate from her special tin and the second time for lying.

The lying started at Endsleigh, a habit which stayed with me for several years and was a serious problem for Jill and Da. I am not quite sure what I lied about – probably, thanks to Brian Baker's gang culture, my achievements at school, but lying became one way of trying to get out of trouble and escape into fantasy. This led to a crisis in which for once Da took my side against Jill.

We had started training for Sports Day and I had to travel to school in sports gear. I can't remember the actual cause of the shouting, tearful row. Maybe boasting about my athletic skills, skipping homework, or fibbing about some broken crockery. But I clearly remember the shameful punishment.

Jill sent me to school with the words 'I AM A LIAR' embroidered in large red letters on the front of my sweatshirt. I managed to endure the stigma of the bus journey branded in this way, but when the form mistress arrived for the first lesson I had already faced fierce taunting by other kids in the playground, egged on by Brian Baker. Although another sweatshirt was swiftly found, the damage was done and I spent the rest of the day trying hard not to cry.

The result of this humiliation was dramatic. When Jane and Janet arrived to collect me I locked myself in the school toilet and shouted through the door that I hated Jill and I would never go home again.

Urgent phone calls were made to Jill and Da and it was decided that I should stay at school for the night with the headmaster and his friendly wife. Da would come to the school the following morning and talk things over. I remember having supper with the headmaster's family and listening to something funny on the wireless. That night I did something I had never done before or since. I shat in the bed.

Da arrived early the next morning for a serious talk with the headmaster and then took me home on the bus. I don't think he said much to me but he must have had firm words with Jill who gave me a little hug when we got back and said she was sorry. Both of us burst into tears. Then she told me that Gamma had died.

This crisis led to an important and swift decision about my future. I don't know how Jill and Da discovered Nowton Court. Maybe they just read about it in the Association of Preparatory School Headmasters' brochure. I don't remember either of them going to see the school and they must have decided very quickly because there was only eight weeks before the start of the new term. The news was told to me formally by Jill in the music room. It didn't take long but I remember what Jill said clearly. She spoke in her firm but gentle voice, which from then on she would try to use with me as much as possible.

'You have some problems, Caradoc, so we have decided to send you to a boarding school at the beginning of next term, which we think will be good for you and help you to grow up a bit. It's a small school with only about fifty boys in a big house in the countryside near Bury St Edmunds, thirty miles from Colchester, and is run by the Blackburnes, a family of two brothers and a sister.'

My response was a mumbled 'Thank you' and an immediate feeling of relief.

The next few weeks were hectic with preparations. I was the first of the family to go to boarding school and my sisters treated me like an Indian bride before the wedding. There were two trips to London with Jill to buy my uniform at the school outfitters Daniel Neal. The list was long and the clothes no doubt expensive, with two grey-flannel short-trouser Sunday suits, three dark-blue corduroy suits with zippered jackets for weekdays, grey Aertex shirts for summer, white shirts and grey shirts, black Oxfords and gym shoes, football gear, a navy-blue mackintosh and a bright-yellow school cap and tie.

One of our London trips included a detour to Enfield to visit the grieving Grandpa at the Hermitage, who clapped when I appeared for him in the garden wearing my grey flannel suit with bright-yellow cap. Before I left he gave me an envelope enclosing a five-pound note and a letter saying how fond he was of me and wishing me the best of luck on this big new adventure, which much later I discovered he had offered to pay for.

I still have an estate agent's photograph of the Hermitage drawing room with a photograph of me on Grandpa's writing desk, known as Lord Mayo because it had been made for the Indian Viceroy. Years later I would inherit the desk from Aunty Molly.

The last weeks before school passed in a happy blur of hot

weather, swimming and picnics, and also a long weekend cara-vanning in the New Forest with Uncle Sidney and family. I was now allowed to bike on the road and deemed tough enough to tackle the five-mile round trip to East Mersea beach. In the last week I rode to West Mersea with Da for a haircut at Mr Hart's the barber. Jane and Janet were delegated to help Jill with the major task of sewing the tapes with my embroidered name on every article of my school gear. Da bought a new trunk in Colchester which had to be packed for dispatch by British Road Services three days before term started. The big adventure was about to begin and I felt very excited.

Small problems.

TWO

Happy Days

III

On the first day of term Jill took me to Nowton Court. We went by bus from Colchester to Bury St Edmunds taking seats in the front where I could watch both the driver and the road ahead and we didn't talk much. Although the school had suggested that we take a taxi for the last two miles from Bury bus station to Nowton, Jill wanted to save the expense. So we got off at the Nowton turning and walked a mile and a half along a country lane to the school, Jill carrying the brown overnight suitcase with my washing things and two toy elephants. By the time we arrived at the lodge at the end of the drive Jill looked hot, hardly surprising as she was wearing a tweed coat and skirt although it was a warm afternoon in early September.

As the school grew closer my excitement shifted to anxiety. Nowton Court looked huge with a tower over the entrance and smaller turrets with high pointed roofs at each corner, like a fairy castle. At the end of the drive there was a gate into a large courtyard. We stood there watching parents unloading cars and boys in uniform greeting each other. I knew that Jill felt as anxious as I did. But then a tortoiseshell cat which had been basking against the courtyard wall got up and came towards us, tail upright, meowing loudly.

I knelt and held out my fingers to the cat who sniffed and rubbed her nose under my hand.

'She's welcoming us,' Jill said. 'We'd better go and introduce ourselves.' She smiled at me. 'Don't worry. It'll be fine.'

And it was fine, almost from the moment we entered the school.

Jill disappeared quickly. A man with a moustache, wearing a light-grey suit, had greeted us warmly in the hall and took her into another room. I was handed over to a smiling lady in a white uniform who said she was Matron, picked up the overnight case and led me upstairs to a room with eight beds which she said was the White dormitory for the new boys. Her bedroom was next door, she said, in case anyone became frightened in the night.

She went away and a younger woman in white helped me to unpack the suitcase and put my elephants side by side on the pillow. Then she took me to another room where there were other small boys and Matron, or 'Mato' as we were to call her, was serving tea. Two of the boys were crying and all of us were very quiet, although I felt quite brave and sat at the table, enjoying the sandwiches, biscuits and a glass of orange juice.

Mato tried to help us relax, telling each boy to say his name, his address, and the names of his pets. I sat in frozen shyness until Mato, passing the window, said brightly, 'Come and see who's out there.'

There was Jill, walking in the garden below with the man in the grey suit, who Mato said was Charles, which didn't mean much to any of us until the young Mato – 'my assistant, Miss Parkhurst, but you may call her Parkie' – explained that he was Charles Blackburne.

Jill and Charles were busy talking, Charles pointing out different flowers and encouraging Jill to sniff one of the roses. I wanted to call out through the open window or rap on the glass to attract her attention, but the presence of the other boys made me nervous and I thought Jill and Charles might not be pleased if I interrupted their conversation. So when Mato said behind me, 'Come on, everybody, let's listen to my favourite programme,' I turned quickly away from the window and sat down again at the table.

The favourite programme was exciting but a bit scary. It was called *Journey into Space* and was about a group of spacemen trapped in a spaceship hurtling out of control towards Mars, from what I could tell through the spooky music and the disjointed voices of Jet, Doc and Mitch, names I got to know well over the next few weeks listening to Mato's regular bedtime treat.

I was asleep before the programme ended and faintly aware of being picked up by Mato and carried to the dormitory. After helping me into my pyjamas, she kissed me goodnight and I heard her say 'Poor little mite' to Parkie as the two matrons stood by the door waiting for the last of the new boys to scuttle into bed.

I lay there feeling sad and tearful that Jill hadn't said goodbye, then drifted off to sleep.

I was fast asleep the next morning when Parkie woke us, clapping her hands and calling, 'Wakey, wakey, rise and shine.' At first I had no idea where I was and when I remembered I didn't want to get out of bed. Parkie explained that today I should wear my blue corduroy suit, which she had laid out on my bed, and when we were all dressed and had brushed our hair, she led us down to the dining room.

It was a big room with lots of tables. All the new boys from the White dormitory sat at the same table with Parkie at the head of it. Bigger boys handed round the food. This was much nicer than at home. Instead of lumpy porridge we had cornflakes, white bread instead of brown and bacon with fried bread. But the biggest treat of all were the cups of hot sweet tea; in the King family no child was allowed to drink tea until the age of thirteen.

After breakfast, while the dining room was cleared, Parkie took us to the Conservatory at the end of the dining room and introduced us all to the junior form teacher called Miss Pizzey, who was very young and pretty. Then a bell rang and we all went back to our tables in the dining room for prayers.

The teachers were already assembled, in a row of chairs on either side of the top table and, as soon as everyone was settled and all was very quiet, another door opened and in came the Blackburnes.

Charles led the way, today wearing a dark-grey suit with a red tie. His moustache made him look like a soldier and his searching glances at both boys and staff as he walked up to the top table made it clear who was in charge. His sister, Betty, was next – stumpy and fierce-looking, with short manly greying hair and wearing a tweed suit. Last came their brother, Neville, with a half-bald dome-like head, like the Mekon in *Dan Dare*, dressed in baggy corduroy trousers and jersey.

Most of what was said passed me by. First there were prayers and a Bible reading, a novelty for me as a child of parents who didn't believe in God. Then there were announcements – new and departed members of staff, teams and football matches, this term's house captains and seniors, who, Charles explained, would each be a guardian for a new boy during his first term to help him settle into the school and deal with special problems.

Next, the new head boy explained the house system by which the school was divided into three teams, Red, Blue and Green, who competed against each other at everything.

Then Charles got up with all the seniors and came down the room to our table.

'Last but not least, I want to introduce this term's new boys, whom I want you all to make very welcome, and introduce the new boys to their guardians. Stand up, boys, and tell us who you are.'

I was last and said my name as clearly as I could. A boy called Roly Thomas shook my hand. Then Charles put an arm round my shoulder and said loudly: 'Caradoc is the youngest boy ever to come to Nowton. He is only six and a half and I want you all to be very kind to him.'

The rest of that day was a blur of trying to do new things in the right place at the right time. Roly was there to help, taking me back to the junior form room after prayers, collecting me when the bell rang for break, showing me where to queue for milk, where to wash before lunchtime hand inspection, explaining the library's borrowing system, taking me to the dormitory for rest and then to the boot room before football trials, then to beevers (Nowton teatime and originally a term used by Suffolk farmers for a mid-morning snack), back to class, showing me the ping-pong room and the train club in the cellar, queuing with me for supper and escorting me to junior baths. By the time Parkie wished us sweet dreams and switched off the light I was dead tired and disorientated. But I felt that I had found my new home.

It took me several weeks to settle into Nowton life, to know my way around, start to make friends and to stop waking up each morning with a feeling of quiet dread. The first and most important thing I had to learn about the Blackburnes was to call them by their Christian names. I had been taught that all grown-ups, except Jill and Da, were to be respectfully addressed as Mr, Mrs or Miss; and even in the family relatives had titles like Aunty Molly and Uncle Sidney, Grandpa and Gamma, so to call this formidable trio by their Christian names was rather odd. But, as Roly told me over the next few weeks, this was just one of many odd things about the Blackburnes.

Later I found out about their background – that their father had been the Dean of Ely, that Charles had taught at Charterhouse, but had had to leave after falling in love with one of the senior boys; that Neville had had a glittering theatrical career at Cambridge, and had served as aide-de-camp to Louis Mountbatten, India's last viceroy; that Betty had become worn out playing housekeeper to an elderly and cantankerous father. And that the three of them had decided to open a prep school and in 1947 moved with twenty boys into Nowton Court, which they acquired on a fifty-year lease from the local Oakes family.

What I had to learn now, from school lore passed down by Roly, were the individual foibles of each Blackburne and how to deal with them.

Charles was the older brother and senior headmaster. He ran the boys, the teaching staff and all the school activities. He taught Latin and history, administered punishment and was a lay reader at the local church where he took morning service each Sunday. During the war he had been a major in the army and with his well-groomed moustache, stripy ties and commanding voice, still had a military bearing. But it was mostly appearance. He was, according to Roly, also very funny and theatrical, a brilliant teacher and storyteller. He adored the boys and, although he clearly had favourites, made a point of dealing with everyone fairly. What the boys most liked about him was that he treated them as grown-ups. He could be terrifying but was also the best person to share a serious problem with.

Neville Blackburne looked very brainy and could appear grumpy with a bald head the shape of a pumpkin, eyes that were round and protuberant like a bullfrog's and pale skin, which flushed when he was angry. He had little contact with the boys. According to rumour (much exaggerated), generally he didn't like them, had a dangerous temper and didn't know his own strength. He had caned one boy so savagely that his parents had reported him to the police and in a fit of rage had punched another boy unconscious. He was also far too clever to do any teaching and spent all his time in the library writing biographies of dead people (although I can remember only one was actually published – about Mary, Lady Wortley Montagu). His only school responsibilities were to supervise the Nowton Court grounds and gardens and make costumes for the school plays.

Betty was the most down to earth and approachable Blackburne. She played a crucial role in school life, in charge of all Nowton Court's domestic arrangements and the boys' health, and was a general mediator between the boys and a tough and primarily male regime. Her manner was bossy and her voice gruff, partly from heavy smoking and also because, being short and dumpy, she had to stand up for herself with two tall and dominating older brothers. To the boys she was a mother figure, strict about food faddiness, constipation and badly written letters home, but with a warm heart and protective instincts. Betty was the lynchpin of Nowton Court life, confidante of the boys and staff who ran into difficulties with Charles or Neville, counsellor to troubled parents, and adored by and devoted to her brothers.

The Blackburnes lived in the Small House, a large pink cottage with its own garden, halfway down the drive, but during term Charles slept in the school, on the top floor close to the two senior dormitories. He supervised baths, turned off the lights and woke the boys by standing outside his bedroom ringing a hand bell. He was moody, said Roly, and the best way to understand his mood was to check the colour of his two corduroy jackets.

The beige one meant he was in a bad mood and the dark green a good mood and his mood affected both boys and staff and could send the whole school into light or dark. Neville was easier to fathom when it came to moods: he was always supposed to be in a bad one.

The rest of the male staff in the school were almost entirely military or naval, demobbed wartime officers who, like the Blackburnes, had drifted into prep-school life with nothing better to do.

Brigadier Collett-White was the senior army officer and taught French. According to his son who was in my year, the Brig had done something very secret in the war and, because he was also tall and beaky, had possibly once been a decoy for General de Gaulle. He was most famous at Nowton for his ferocious 'Brig clip', a hard flat hand flick over the back of the head which could make even big boys cry. There were two equal-ranking naval officers, Commander Miles Child, gentle and friendly, who told great bedtime stories about life at sea, and Commander Prendergast, louder and more bossy. The two commanders taught a miscellany of subjects – history, geography, maths and science – but only up to the fifth form because neither of them had much knowledge and certainly no qualifications to teach the subjects. Slightly below the commanders was Major Kitto who, according to rumour, had been with the Desert Rats and loved reading Kipling aloud.

Apart from our junior form teacher Miss Pizzey and Parkie, the women on the staff seemed much older than Jill. Miss Gaunt, who taught maths, was white-haired with a quavery voice and carried a stick. Mrs Belfrage taught Latin, had a figure like a barrel and a terrible temper and was nicknamed Breathless because of her bad halitosis. The most formidable of them all was the art teacher Beryl 'Sadie' Sedgwick, red-haired, theatrical and the owner of two yappy Pekinese who went everywhere with her.

Sadie had been a stage designer and had met Neville in theatre and was a Blackburne family 'chum', which put her in a special category among the teaching staff.

Further down the Nowton ladder were the domestic staff, led by Mrs Fenner, the school cook, reporting directly to Betty and supported by a gaggle of local girls who served food, washed up and kept the place clean. Mrs Fenner's husband was the school gardener and the couple had a flat in the Stable block where, under the benevolent eye of Commander Child who also had a room there, they kept watch on fifth-form boys in the Stable dormitories.

On a par with Mr Fenner was Sergeant Sharrock, the school groundsman, who occupied the Lodge at the bottom of the drive with his wife and family. Sharrock, as he was called by the Blackburnes, was an archetypal company sergeant, loyal to and respected by both the commissioned officers and the ranks. Both he and Mr Fenner reported to Neville and their roles were clearly marked. Mr Fenner was in charge of the school flowerbeds and the Small House garden and Sharrock was responsible for everything else, particularly the playing fields. From his HQ, known simply as Sharrock's Shed, he ran a platoon of heavy garden artillery, a Ransomes' cultivator for the vegetable garden, three Atco lawnmowers of different sizes and a massive Massey Ferguson roller for the cricket pitches. In my last year, I was put in charge of the giant sit-upon Atco, a non-sporting school honour on a par with playing for the first XI.

The other important members of the Nowton Court family were the school cats. At any time there were around eight of them, led by the flirty tortoiseshell Mrs Toast and a formidable black cat called Baron. The Blackburnes adored their cats and framed pencil sketches of them, drawn by Sadie Sedgwick, hung on the dining-room walls.

During my first year Miss Pizzey was the central person in my life because she taught us for several hours each day. It was easy to adore her because she was young and beautiful, with a soft voice, gentle manner, and a deft understanding of the new boys in her class. To me, she was the perfect woman, an idealised alternative to Jill and my three bossy older sisters.

The junior form was in the Conservatory, a glass-ceilinged annexe to the dining room with a red and black chequer-tiled floor, and white metal poles, once used for climbing plants and now for athletic boys. There were lots of radiators to keep us warm in winter and French windows with direct access to the garden in summer. Life was snug there with the daily round of 'the three Rs' – reading, writing and arithmetic – all taught by Miss Pizzey. Most days there was also an extra afternoon class after beevers (our mid-afternoon snack) – Bible stories taught by Betty, singing classes with Mr Mackinnon the music teacher, who had fish-like eyes behind ultra-thick glasses, or history lessons taught by Charles, who in general school encounters could be terrifying but in the Conservatory with the new boys was gentle and funny, telling quirky stories about Alfred burning his cakes, the poor princes in the Tower and London burning like rotten sticks in the Great Fire, and teaching us silly rhyming songs to remember the kings and queens.

I was also slowly getting to know my fellow new boys, whose names I remember in roll-call order. Blackie, Cameron, Dickson, Duval, Folkard, Higson, O'Hagan, Ullstein and Vaughan-Jones would be my closest friends in the school, and three of them would remain so for a long time after I left.

There was no Brian Baker in the junior form. Charles was astute about picking both boys and parents who would 'fit in' at Nowton and the school was much too disciplined to allow disruptive behaviour. As the youngest, Miss Pizzey treated me as the class pet and helped me with any problems, and particularly with my first moment of trouble, which happened soon after the beginning of term.

'So where did you all go on your holidays last summer?' she asked one day in a geography class, overlooking how fiercely competitive even seven-year-olds can be.

There was a clamour of answers – from family homes in Devon and the Lake District to more exotic locations like the South of France and Positano. I was silent until Miss Pizzey turned to me.

'And what about you, Caradoc? Where did you go?'

'The Taj Mahal,' I said without hesitation, remembering Aunty Molly's stories about her Indian travels. There was a hubbub of surprise and laughter. Suddenly everyone was looking at me and I knew they didn't believe me. I blushed and Miss Pizzey's help was swift.

'Did you, Caradoc? How wonderful! I've always wanted to go there. Lucky you! Can you tell us the story about the Taj Mahal?'

I shook my head. 'I can't remember.'

'Never mind,' she said briskly. 'I can. It was built by Emperor Shah Jahan in memory of his wife Mumtaz Mahal whose death at the birth of their thirteenth child in 1653 so broke the heart of the emperor that his hair turned grey overnight. It is certainly the most fabulous monument built for love and one of the Seven Wonders of the World.'

Someone interrupted. 'But do you think he actually went there?'

'Of course he did, if he said so. Didn't you, Caradoc?'

I nodded. It was all I could do.

They were all laughing. Miss Pizzey clapped her hands.

'Now, now, it's not for us to judge whether Caradoc is telling the truth or not. Everyone sometimes tells a story which is not absolutely true.'

I still feel amazed that I said it. Why could I have not simply been honest and said that I had gone on a caravan trip to the New Forest with my Uncle Sidney? And why somewhere so fantastic which would have been completely out of reach for a small boy in the early 1950s unless he had parents who lived in India? But the need to embellish and glamorise my life was planted early on.

Another embarrassment was my tuck allowance.

The Nowton tuck shop was in a cubbyhole off the stone back stairs. Every Sunday and Wednesday, after lunch and before rest, boys would line up while Betty dispensed sweets to each boy according to the tuck allowance contributed by his parents. The general rate was between one shilling and sixpence and two shillings and sixpence. For this money you could buy a feast. Mars bars were the most expensive at sixpence, but there was a delicious range of Palms Toffee bars, Crunchies and Bounties at fourpence and, further down the range, Fruit Gums and Polos at threepence per tube, and Refreshers at tuppence. Even cheaper were Trebor chews and Sherbet Lemons at a penny each in old money.

The prospect was mouth-watering, since at home we were only allowed one boiled sweet a day, and on my first visit to the tuck shop I followed the lead of the boy ahead of me and ordered several expensive chocolate treats until Betty interrupted me.

'I'm sorry, dear, but you will have to cut back. You see your weekly allowance is only fourpence.'

She spoke quietly but the word was already passing down the line – 'Poor Caradoc, he gets only fourpence.' I dreaded walking back down the stairs, past all the sympathetic grinning faces. Then Betty saved the day.

'But this time Caradoc wins the youngest new boy of the year Chocolate Award,' she said, her gruff voice loud enough to be heard down the line of boys, and she added first a Mars bar and then a Crunchie to my very small pile of two Sherbet Lemons and a Trebor chew.

There was another embarrassing moment that term although I feel disloyal and ashamed to admit it. It was the half-term exeat weekend: Da had written to say he would be coming on Saturday to take me out for tea and deliver my bike. That was fine and I had been looking forward to the visit – not realising he would turn up in Alan Maskell's rusty old Ford van.

Da, in his familiar brown corduroy suit, was unaware of the impression he made, and of the boys sniggering at the old van parked beside their own parents' gleaming Fords, Humbers and Jaguars. My bike was an embarrassment too – a tiny old-fashioned beginner's bike repainted in black by Caroline who had owned it before me. Boys watched us curiously as Da lifted the bike out of the back of the van and we wheeled it down to the Stable bike shed and parked it alongside the BSAs, Raleighs and Dawes with Sturmey-Archer or derailleur gears, the gleaming equivalents of the parents' cars.

The tea trip made up for it – not the slap-up ham, egg and chips high teas at the Angel Hotel in Bury after the Odeon matinee that richer boys bragged about – but scones, sandwiches and sponge cake at an old Tea Shoppe in the neighbouring village of Sicklesmere after a drive to Lavenham church to look at the brass rubbings, one of Da's hobbies. Over tea he asked me gently about life at Nowton and gave me family news about my sisters and life and death among the Strood House livestock. Dimple had just given birth to another batch of kittens, a fox had got into the henhouse, Hamley had caught a seagull. I felt ashamed of my earlier embarrassment, but also relieved when he dropped me back at school, gave me a hug and a ten-shilling note and disappeared noisily up the drive.

That grotty little bike transformed Nowton life for me. The

school was surrounded by lawns and flower gardens and set in beautiful parkland, with a lake and an island reached by a rickety bridge, two large woods – the Stable Wood and the Summer House Wood – the ruins of an old chapel and miles of paths and driveways. On a recent walk though the grounds (now sold off to Bury borough council as a public park) I was overwhelmed by the variety and beauty of the trees – massive cedars, firs, oaks and yew trees, most of them well over a century old and planted by some visionary landscaper when the house was built. For a boy from the featureless Essex mudflats, the Nowton grounds offered a feast of nature and a magical playground. Boys were allowed to cycle wherever they wanted and could play games and have adventures well out of sight from staff – cops and robbers, den-building, bike races, or just companionable rides to quiet corners away from everyone else. I remember the deep pleasure of wobbling along the Nowton paths on my diminutive bike cheered on by bigger boys speeding past, and parking my bike on its stand at a far corner of the lake and watching the ducks and moorhens. At home I was restricted to journeys along the Strood under the bossy supervision of older sisters. Biking at Nowton in that first term felt as liberating as, years later, passing my driving test.

Outdoor life was the essence of Nowton. There was football on either Wednesday or Saturday afternoon, which for a timid and very small six-year-old wasn't much fun, particularly as the weather got colder. I liked my football gear – navy shorts and a smart blue team shirt with white collar, and dauntingly large football boots needing regular applications of waterproofing dubbin and their studs hammered back on by Mr Fenner on an iron foot last in the boot room. But the matches were muddy no-man's-land encounters, a blur of shouting bigger boys, and a sodden leather ball erupting with stinging velocity out of fog.

I was never much good at games, which didn't matter because

the Blackburnes were not very interested in football even though Charles enjoyed driving the first XI to matches at rival prep schools in his 'Battleship', a large American estate car acquired through a parent from one of the nearby US air-force bases.

The Blackburnes were more passionate about gardening than football and estate work took up the other half-day afternoon. It involved three labour gangs, each allocated an estate task for the afternoon – sawing logs, clearing undergrowth, bonfires, and in the summer some weeding and mowing in the garden of the Small House. The smaller boys were supervised by seniors, who reported directly to Sergeant Sharrock, but the whole operation was master-minded by Neville, who went around the different gangs issuing languidly imperious orders along the lines of 'Oh you stupid boy, not the buddleia' or 'Please be careful with that axe, Henry. He's not Mary Queen of Scots.' It was slave labour but instilled in me a deep-rooted love for the beauty of Nowton and the smell of bonfires.

The biggest Nowton outdoor adventure was the game of Merchantmen played annually on Tip's Day, so called to com-memorate a dog. Under the yew trees beside the lake was a small but beautifully carved gravestone with the words:

In loving memory of Tip
A faithful friend to all at Nowton Court,
who died aged 16 years
on 30th October 1914

It was typical of the Blackburnes, not dog lovers, that they adopted this obscure 'faithful friend' as the Nowton mascot and made Tip's Day an annual half-holiday.

Merchantmen was played over the whole Nowton grounds and involved all the school. The actual merchantmen were three 'convoys' of junior boys from the Red, Blue and Green teams who had to race against each other around a circuit of 'ports' situated in different parts of the school grounds. Each round completed without being tagged earned ten points. The older boys played Royal Navy ships according to speed and seniority – one battleship, two submarines, three cruisers and three destroyers – and had to protect their team's merchant fleet from being sunk or tagged by enemy ships as they raced between the ports. Points were graded according to the importance of the sunken ship and the team which earned most points won the game.

The most destructive weapon was the mine, one per team. A mine had to walk and carry a croquet mallet and was usually played by slow, fat boys with sadistic streaks. When the mine struck the ground with the mallet and shouted 'I explode' any ship within ten yards was sunk.

After that first game I was singled out as a fast runner and given swift promotion to 'lone merchantman'. This meant I could separate from the convoy and score as many points as possible running the circuit on my own. Running, and running away, would be my only sporting childhood achievement.

My first term ended on a high note at the annual Carol Service. At prayers a week before Charles solemnly announced that I was to sing solo the first two verses of 'Unto us a boy is born, king of choirs supernal'. There was laughter at Charles's little joke and I felt immediately terrified.

Sunday Matins at Nowton Church was always a dramatic event. Dressed up in his lay-reader's cassock, Charles's magnetic and theatrical personality excelled. As the oldest son of the Dean of Ely, he took Christianity seriously, but in the pulpit he couldn't resist an opportunity of playing the entertainer.

His sermons were mostly retold Bible stories, camped-up and

with a modern twist. The Hittites were 'the horrible Hittites', St Peter was 'an awful silly-puss', Mary Magdalene was 'a bit of a minx' and the Pharaoh who slew the innocents and brought down the plagues was an Old Testament Adolf Hitler.

The sermons were spiced up with Charles's pulpit salvoes against the boys who annoyed him. 'Cato, if you must pick your nose, kindly use your handkerchief' or 'Minchin, if what Bolam has just told you is so extraordinarily funny, why don't you come up here and tell us all the joke.' 'Wake up, Dickson, or are you just saying a private prayer?'

The Carol Service was magical and frightening. Snow started falling as we walked from the school to the church, a straggling crocodile of boys with scarves and yellow caps led through the winter dusk by torch-waving seniors. The church was transformed with holly, ivy, lilies and candlelight – a Neville and Sadie co-production – and as soon as the service started with Charles's favourite *Veni, Veni, Emmanuel* my excitement swelled. Then my turn came. I felt sudden panic, standing alone on the altar steps in the silent church with everyone looking at me. My voice wavered in the first verse but grew in strength and soared into the second verse. When I finished there was silence then a murmur of '*Oh*'s from the older parishioners. Charles, standing up to read the lesson, made a little bow towards me and a clapping gesture with his hands. I felt at that moment intense happiness.

The end of term also had a bit of magic. It was the Nowton tradition for the 'car boys' to be collected by their parents directly after lunch on the last day and for the 'train boys' to spend an extra night at the school before leaving by taxi for Bury railway station the next morning. For the rest of their extra day the train boys had special treats. The afternoon was a glorious free time to ride bikes or play hide-and-seek round the almost empty school. Beevers was followed by a special discount trip to the tuck shop where Betty sold off sweets at half-price. Supper was egg and chips with ice cream and before bed there was either a film on the ancient cine projector or an exclusive television evening with the Blackburnes' antique television projecting an enlarged picture onto a white wall.

Of course I wasn't really a 'train boy'. The Morris Oxford taxi which collected four of us the next morning dropped me off first on Angel Hill in Bury St Edmunds for the bus ride to Colchester before taking the rest of the boys to Bury station for onward journeys to distant exotic places like London, Hertford and Bishop's Stortford. It was on that ride to Colchester I felt something which would grow stronger over the years. I wanted to stay at Nowton much more than I wanted to go home.

It wasn't surprising. One term at Nowton had changed my life. I was fired with excitement. I felt happy. People liked me and I fitted in. Life at Nowton could be scary but never boring. I had fallen under the spell of the Blackburnes. They were an extraordinary trio – charming, witty, formidable, cultured, non-conformist, camp, each different and, in their own particular way, brilliant as well as terrifying. Even after one term, as the youngest boy in the school, their magnetism had taken hold. I loved Nowton Court – and life at Strood House, with quarrelsome sisters and an angry, intimidating mother, already seemed a strange world to which I didn't really quite belong.

It was also different at home. I was treated with more respect. The beatings and punishments tailed off, as if Jill and Da realised that my 'problems' were now the responsibility of the Blackburnes, to whom I might talk about how I was treated at home. I had a separate life away from Strood House now, and that feeling of separateness became essential for survival in a family from which I would become gradually estranged.

IV

I have always been prone to mood swings, especially as a child. My first term at Nowton had been a huge adventure and, as the youngest boy, I was treated like the school pet. I had taken to this new world like a fledgling discovering flight. But in the second term the novelty and excitement disappeared. Nowton was cold and the weather drab. My mood sank.

There was soon a good reason for feeling low – a flu epidemic. It started with a few boys being isolated in the sick room, but within a week the sick room had overflowed into the Blue dormitory. When I caught the bug the White dormitory was converted into an isolation ward and the healthy boys moved out.

I had never felt so ill before. The symptoms were fever, shivering, and a terrible sore throat. I must have been one of the worst cases because I was checked by the school doctor, Dr Mole, on each of his twice-daily visits and, although too feverish to take in much, was aware of Parkie giving me Disprin dissolved in orange juice and urging me to pee in a bottle.

The worst was over after three days and, though still too weak to do more than doze, I felt content lying in bed with a group of other ill boys, pampered by Mato and Parkie, and their emergency staff of two giggling girls from the kitchen upgraded to white uniforms, whose main job was to keep our beakers topped up with Robinson's Barley Water.

I got to know the two boys in beds on each side of me. Lane was a bit older, from the Blue dormitory, and a cocky little boy whose cheek made the matrons laugh. Ian Nixon on the other side was a doctor's son from Kelvedon, in my class and dormitory but with whom until now I hadn't exchanged a word, because of his shyness. Now, bedridden, the two of us swiftly bonded with school and family chit-chat. We swapped names of siblings, pets, holidays, and the make of family car – and this time there was no need to lie because Nixon had heard about Da's visit in an old Ford van. After a couple of days our friendship had blossomed enough for Nixon to tell me his family nickname – Nini, and although he swore me not to tell anyone else it was the name I always called him.

Nini was my first best friend at Nowton. The closeness didn't last because as my confidence grew I turned to more popular and outgoing boys, but when I decided to run away from the school at a low point a couple of years later it was Nini Nixon I persuaded to come with me.

I didn't get close to Lane during the flu epidemic but he was passionate about cricket and persuaded Mato to let us listen to the commentary on the wireless of a Test match taking place somewhere hot and a long way away. For the first time I heard the names of legendary players – Bedser, Bailey, Hutton, Tyson, Sutcliffe and Compton – which became a childhood litany as familiar as the rail stations between Colchester and Liverpool Street. Lane also taught me to play fantasy test match, scoring runs by rolling dice.

One sick-room treat was the open coal fire which Betty

allowed during the flu epidemic. The White dorm had once been one of Nowton Court's principal bedrooms and the fireplace was the original with marble mantelpiece and glazed tile surround. My bed faced it so that during the day I could watch the fire then fall asleep with its pink glow flickering on the ceiling – a memory which in winter still makes me yearn for firelight in a dark room.

Like the Great Flood the flu epidemic was an exciting relief which lifted my spirits. Afterwards life settled back into a dull Easter-term routine of classes, muddy football, and huddling round radiators. By the second half of the term, I had changed from youngest and most innocent new boy into one of the cheekiest members of the junior form. I was soon in serious trouble.

A mild Nowton punishment was to be sent out of the classroom to stand in the dining room, where you ran the risk of being spotted by one of the passing Blackburnes. This had happened a couple of times already.

I was now back in the White dorm and a regular in after-lights-out pillow-fights. One night a boy who had gone to the lavatory came back saying urgently, 'Sadie's coming, Sadie's coming!' We raced for our beds, but I tripped and when a moment later the door opened the light was turned on and Sadie said loudly '... and Sadie's here!' I was lying on the floor in the middle of the room clutching a pillow.

There was a predictable penalty. Sadie ordered me into my dressing gown and led me down to Charles's study. I waited outside in the hall while she told him what I had been up to. After Sadie had gone, Charles summoned me to enter.

I would get to know that study well from many anxious visits – its electric red and green enter/engaged sign outside, the red-leathered partners' desk, Charles's wing armchair and the sofa facing it, the scary cat's head with glass eyes on the mantelpiece, red Collins Crime Club novels on the bookshelf, the smoky reek of his Player's cigarettes and, in the corner, the notched bamboo cane, a size thicker than the Strood House dog stick. That night Charles spoke gravely about my bad behaviour, then the stick was in his hands and I was told to take off my dressing gown and bend over the chair.

As a veteran of several beatings at home I was prepared for the pain. I heard the first loud thwack, but I felt nothing. I waited for the next one, but then Charles said, 'Turn round, Caradoc' and I realised that instead of beating me he had diverted the blow to the arm of the chair.

That first mock punishment was typical Charles. He ran the school as a benign despot, sharing out terror and affection in equal measure. His mood swings, marked by the green or beige corduroy jackets, were extreme; when Charles was in a bad mood the whole school, including the teachers, quaked. He had a sharp wit and natural authority, derived from a mix of insight, cleverness, and simple charisma. His teaching was an intellectual challenge as well as brilliant entertainment. The few Nowton boys I still know remember him with awe and deep affection.

The rest of term settled into a wintery routine of lessons and indoor recreation. Canasta was the Conservatory craze that term. Other indoor activities took place in the cellar, a warren of musty rooms that housed the train club, ping-pong room, and the stamp and chess clubs. I loved the train club with its massive layout of miniature electric trains, the stations, bridges, houses and flickering lights, four boys at a time controlling different terminals and trains racing round overlapping routes, leading to occasional massive crashes and derailments. I also became a nifty ping-pong player, coached by a demon player called Bolam, a more senior member of the Blue team, mastering a flashy range of chops, spins and smashes, with which, despite my small size, I began to beat much older boys.

There was brainier relaxation in the library. It was an elegant sky-lit room whose walls had been stylishly wallpapered by Neville with a collage of old book jackets and whose shelves were stocked with rattling boys' adventure stories by G. A. Henty, master of the pop historical, and author of more than fifty books with stirring titles like *Richard the Lionheart* and *With Clive in India*; also Arthur Ransome of *Swallows and Amazons*, John Buchan, Sax Rohmer and Edgar Wallace and the best-selling children's historian H. E. Marshall whose *Our Island Story* of how Alfred burnt the cakes and Harold lost an eye at the Battle of Hastings never quite matched Charles's enthralling history classes. The Nowton library with its polished parquet floor, leather armchairs and compulsory silence was my first hunting ground for a good story, a quest that for thirty-five years has earned me my living.

Food was also a Nowton treat. Betty's diet was much more varied and enticing than the cheese, cabbage and milk puddings of Strood House and meals appeared every two or three hours. Breakfast was followed by elevenses of fresh fruit. Lunch was a red-blooded affair of beef on Sunday, roast mutton with onion sauce on Thursday, fish pie on Friday and during the rest of the week a hearty range of stews, and steak and kidney pudding. After the main course was a large pudding – apple turnover with suet crust, jam tart, chocolate and treacle sponge. There were two puddings I hated – marmalade sponge and rice pudding – but on Sunday there was Betty's special –'jelly whip', a simple but delicious blend of jelly and sweet condensed milk which everyone loved and stirred my adult taste for exotic desserts like crème brûlée, zabaglione and syllabub.

Beevers, named after a Suffolk farmers' snack, was at four o'clock, with jam, chocolate spread, or Marmite on half slices of white bread and on Wednesday a scooped handful of potato crisps. High tea was at six with a dish of baked beans, sardines or, my favourite, cheese and potato pie, and at seven-thirty biscuits were served out of the kitchen hatch to boys queuing in the adjacent corridor.

As well as controlling our diet, Betty was also in overall charge of health and general well-being. Mato reported directly to her and was available to dish out Dettol and plaster for cuts and Junior Aspro for headaches. There were daily doses of cod liver oil and handouts of Horlicks tablets to help restore vitamin deficiencies picked up during wartime rationing. The state of our bowels and personal hygiene was also a major concern. Outside the dormitory lavatories there were lists on which boys daily ticked off success-ful performance of number twos and each Sunday morning before Church there was Betty's embarrassing underpant skid-mark check when we handed in our used laundry.

The first thing Jill said when I arrived home for the Easter holi-days was: 'You've put on weight!' But my well-being owed less to Nowton's hearty nourishment and preventive health care than the happiness I felt after only two terms at the school.

Judging from the photo album, only one thing memorable hap-pened that Easter holiday: a family production of *The Princess and the Pea* in the Attic Theatre, an attic room with two levels of floor Da had made into a theatre with a curtain between the auditorium and the raised stage. The production starred my sisters and was directed by Janet, who also played the Real Princess. The two small male roles were shared by me and my one home friend, Paul Spendlove.

I am not sure how the friendship started or was approved by Jill, who didn't welcome my schoolfriends coming to stay. Paul might have been at Endsleigh with me, or maybe the family were Da's patients, but he became a regular visitor and a year later I was allowed to go on holiday with the Spendloves, which would have serious consequences. Paul was a tubby gentle boy my sisters liked to tease. His parents, Michael and Sylvia, were vegetarians and ran a health food shop (exceptional in the early fifties) on East Hill in Colchester, next door to the run-down Empire cinema where Michael was the manager, although we were only allowed to go there once, for a rare family trip to see *The Inn of the Sixth Happiness*, a historical drama about Gladys Aylward, a missionary in China.

I have never liked Easter very much, a festive non-event with deceptively bright cold spring weather, and in our family even the chocolate feasting was strictly regulated. We were given a couple of Easter eggs each, the main one from Jill and Da, and another bought on behalf of Grandpa and Aunty Molly. There were usually extra treats from the Maskells or the Hardings next door, so we each compiled a good-sized chocolate hoard. But Jill – possibly at Da's tooth-caring instigation – insisted that we hand it all over to her. Each child was given a chocolate ration of four ounces per day, two in the morning and two in the afternoon, weighed out on Jill's kitchen scales.

It must have been this strict rationing that made me squirrel-like about chocolate. I hoarded mine in a tin nailed to a beam in the bike-shed roof and I would feast there secretly until Priscilla discovered my secret. It was chocolate temptation which led to my early stealing – of Bendicks Bittermints, from Jill's personal tin, an addiction I still have, though now I can pay for it.

Another King family tradition was the Easter first swim of the year and I shiver to imagine how cold the water must have been in early April. But this was a family dare which the girls in their Jansen regulation swimsuits loved or pretended to, screaming with delight as they plunged into the Strood or Pyefleet channels, watched from the bank by Jill and Da.

By the end of the Easter holidays I was eagerly looking forward to going back to school. Nowton was at its best in summer.

Recreation between tea and supper was now a blissful time for biking, building dens and tree-climbing until the bedtime bell was tolled at seven-thirty. On Sundays and half-holidays there was fishing in the lake, Sergeant Sharrock's outdoor judo classes and croquet for senior boys on a special lawn behind the pavilion. For juniors there were regular evening Dinky Toy rallies along mini-dust tracks round the trunk of the giant cedar on the south lawn.

That term there was a new temporary member of staff, one of the trainee teachers Charles employed each summer to help with games and outdoor activities. Mr Reed was waiting to 'go up' to university and because he had been in the first XI at his public school was put in charge of teaching the junior boys cricket. He didn't have much success with me. Although I enjoyed lazing in the outfield watching the sky and birds and hoping the ball would keep away, I showed little aptitude for batting and my bowling looked, said Mr Reed, like a monkey's with a bad shoulder.

Mr Reed was also in charge of training junior forms for Sports Day, particularly exciting that year because on the 6th of May Roger Bannister, once at school with Mr Reed, ran the first four-minute mile. Surprisingly I turned out to be one of Mr Reed's stars. The qualifying heats for the races had been held the week before and my 220 yards had been good enough, thanks to Mr Reed's determined training, to make me the only Blue team member of the six junior finalists.

Sports Day, in mid-June, was the high spot of the Nowton calendar. Doting parents arrived in the early afternoon to watch the finals then joined the Blackburnes and members of staff for afternoon tea in a marquee on the back lawn, followed by the presentation of prizes, and Charles's annual speech. Later, after parents and boys had enjoyed their own picnic suppers, there

64

was an outdoor performance in the rose garden of the annual Shakespeare play.

That year it was *Romeo and Juliet* and I had been given the non-speaking role of Juliet's pageboy. Charles and Neville, ex-Cambridge theatricals, applied professional dedication to their Nowton productions. Charles directed and would sometimes tackle a significant walk-on role, such as his definitive black-coated Mercade in *Love's Labour's Lost* a couple of years later. Neville was responsible for sets and costumes, helped by Sadie who for each production would first sketch the new costumes and then spend a fortnight shut away with Neville in the Sewing Room making them.

Charles, assisted by a harassed junior member of staff (that year Miss Pizzey),would start rehearsals at the beginning of the summer term after arbitrary selection of favourite boys to play the male parts and auditions for the women's parts at Moreton Hall, a neighbouring girl's school. Rehearsals were both terrifying and hilarious, particularly for the girls who Charles treated with charming rudeness and withering remarks like 'For God's sake stop plucking your knickers, dear, and pay attention!'but he managed to secure from the cast superb performances which deeply impressed the parents.

With both sporting and acting roles to contend with my first Sports Day was alarming, though I was more worried about how Jill and Da would behave than my own performance. Da had already embarrassed me by turning up in the old Maskell van but I was even more fearful about Jill, who could appear very rude to strangers.

Everything turned out fine. Jill and Da had gone to the expense of renting an elderly but respectable Austin Cambridge from a local Mersea garage. Both were dressed in their best – Da in a cream linen jacket and Jill in a flowery summer dress like other mothers.

I didn't win the long-jump final but got bronze, which for the youngest boy in the school wasn't bad.

The day's big event was my debut performance as Juliet's pageboy in the school play. This was only a minor walk-on part but, thanks to Charles's master touch, added at the dress rehearsal, it stole the show. After Juliet had taken poison and collapsed on a stone garden table, the Capulet family tomb, I appeared in the glare of the spotlights. Wiping a stage tear from my eye, with a penknife I cut a red rose from the flowerbed and laid it gently on her stomach. A gasp of delight from the mothers was followed by a loud burst of applause. I stood bedazzled in the lights, grinning. A great moment.

A real-life love story also started that term. Two seniors had seen Mr Reed and Miss Pizzey sitting by the lake holding hands. The news was swiftly circulated. Miss Pizzey and Mr Reed were in love. No further sightings were reported because the lovebirds were too careful, but excited rumour spread throughout the school. The junior boys were on the look-out. Every encounter between them was closely observed – soft conversations, exchanged smiles, hints of blush, were eagerly watched and listened to. The junior form was humming with romance.

We loved Miss Pizzey and admired young and handsome Mr Reed and were longing to know whether it was true but too bashful to ask. Finally, as the youngest boy in the school, I was given the challenge to find out and, to make the question more discreet, the seniors briefed me to ask it in Latin. At last I found the right moment – by the lake on a Sunday afternoon when Mr Reed was on duty and Miss Pizzey was watching the fishing.

I got the words a bit muddled but clear enough to be understood.

'Excuse me, sir, *amat* Miss Pizzey? And, do you *amat* Mr Reid, Miss Pizzey?'

I don't remember the answer, just that the two of them and the boys around laughed, that this was a sunny moment of happiness by the lake and that soon after that someone hooked a fish. Nor do I know whether Mr Reid did *amat* Miss Pizzey. It was almost the end of term and by the following September, the beginning of our second year, we had moved up from Miss Pizzey's cosy Conservatory form and into the larger school with different teachers for different subjects.

According to the school photographs, Miss Pizzey stayed at Nowton for a while. I doubt if she became Mrs Reed – life is rarely that simple – but I'm sure she married and hope that the love she showed my junior form was later given to children of her own.

Nowton Court School, summer 1956. In middle of seated row, from left:
Commander Predergast, Sadie, Charles (in dark glasses), Betty, Neville, Commander Child,
Miss Pizzey (second from left)

V

My memory of that first year at Nowton Court is exceptionally sharp, reflecting the acute importance of what was
happening to me. My daughter India's teacher, when asked how
well India was doing after a term and a half at prep school, told
me it was as if a light bulb had suddenly been turned on inside
her. It was like that for me at Nowton.

Leaving Miss Pizzey's junior form was a big step forward. The
third form was in a ground-floor corner room in the private part
of the house and uncomfortably close to Charles's study and the
drawing room. Next to the drawing room was the Blackburnes'
library where Betty and Neville spent most of the day sitting at
adjacent desks, Betty doing her catering lists and general school
administration and Neville, shielded by a large bookcase from
Betty's gruff phone calls to the school suppliers and anxious parents, writing his current biography. The library led into the dining
room and it was from there that the Blackburnes made their formidable appearance at prayers and lunch, joined on Sunday by
seniors for a small sherry beforehand.

Visits to the drawing room were restricted to Thursday evenings when the Blackburnes invited older boys in dressing gowns to listen to high opera on their radiogram while needle-pointing or rug-making. My own handicraft, when old enough, was sewing military badges onto an old blanket. Listening to a complete opera with recitative could be a turgid experience for small boys, but it planted in me a love of Italian arias and a strong aversion to Wagner.

In charge of the third form was Mrs Sketchley, a heavily tweeded French teacher. We had now moved on from one all-subject teacher and had specialists to teach different subjects. The thin, beaky Miss Gaunt taught us maths and algebra, Commander Child geography, Betty scripture, Major Kitto English and Charles history. 'Specialist' is not quite the right word because although Miss Gaunt was a trained maths teacher, Mrs Sketchley was French and married to an Englishman; and Betty, as the daughter of the Dean of Ely, had been brought up on the Bible; the military and naval contingent were complete amateurs who obligingly filled in whatever gaps Charles had in his staff. Major Kitto's knowledge of English was an army version fortified by regular muggings of Ronald Ridout's *English Today*, and Commander Child's knowledge of geography, outside wartime experience commanding a cruiser in the Mediterranean, was restricted to the world's capitals, their populations and main exports, which could have been learned in my Letts Schoolboy's Diary.

Charles's history lessons were high spots of the week because every encounter with him provoked a mixture of excitement and dread. He was a brilliant teacher, gossipy, irreverent, and funny. His historical approach was 'broad sweep' and during the year we swept at high speed from the Roman Conquest through the Dark Ages, the Normans, Tudors and Stuarts, Hanoverians and the Victorians up to the Great Queen's death, a witty *1066 and All That* burlesque of our island story.

Another important step forward in my second year was a new Hercules, which arrived by carrier in early March, a late Christmas present from Grandpa. This was my first new bike after my sisters' hand-me-downs and, although without gears, put me on an equal level with the other bikers in the school.

Biking was essential to my progress in the school; the boys I biked with – Gus Ullstein, Nick Duval and Paddy O'Hagan – became close friends. There is also a revealing entry in my diary – 'Joined Chris White's den'. The den was a palisade of logs and branches in the Stable Wood and, as Chris White was already a senior and the following year became head boy, membership of his den put me on the fast track of Nowton society and meant that I was becoming popular.

There were two key indicators of close friendship. The first was to be on a boy's 'cake list', one of a dozen boys who were handed a slice of birthday cake at teatime by the birthday boy; I was already on several. Even more special was to be invited out by a boy on one of the twice-termly Saturday exeats or 'going out' days.

My first 'going out' day was with a boy called Higson. His father had a farm near Thaxted, a pretty Essex town, and 'going out' meant a drive along twisty roads to the Higson home, a round trip of seventy miles. On the trip there I felt just a little queasy, but the return journey after a large tea was a disaster. Halfway back I very suddenly and violently threw up a ghastly mix of cream cake and sandwiches all over the upholstery of the family's new lime-green Jowett Javelin. The invitation wasn't repeated and my friendship with Higson came to an end.

Car sickness was a problem throughout my childhood and I nursed the shameful belief that Yates had given up his job as Grandpa's chauffeur to work on the buses because I had once been sick all over his trousers sitting in the front of the Triumph.

'Going out' trips with other boys were more successful and I 'went out' with Nick Duval, whose father was the vicar of Great Barton on the other side of Bury and with Nick's best friend, Paddy O'Hagan, whose parents lived at Rattlesden, another nearby village, where his father was headmaster of the village school. Both Mrs Duval and Mrs O'Hagan were kindly women and must have had a soft spot for me because I remember these trips with great pleasure and affection, and Nick and Paddy became good friends.

Another family I got to know well was Gus Ullstein's. Gus's father, a member of the distinguished German publishing firm Ullstein Verlag, had moved to England and taken up farming when the firm was sold to the Springer publishing group in the early 1950s. The family home was at Great Barnadiston Hall, near Haverhill, and I spent several happy days there mucking around on the farm. Gus had a lovely warm-hearted mother, and his younger brother, Bart, also at Nowton, took up publishing like his father, so our paths have crossed regularly since then.

Nick, Paddy and Gus were my best friends at Nowton and, if I hadn't left the school two years before them, we would have probably stayed in closer touch. Although I remember exactly what they looked like and the sound of their voices I don't think there was anything very distinctive about us – just averagely bright, cheeky, and likeable eight-year-olds. Gus was small for his age, a bit bossy and with a slight German accent. Nick appeared shy and timid, but with close friends had a wicked sense of humour. Paddy was the most extrovert and acted as Nick's protector. I must have been the naughtiest because after my second year I remember frequent trips to

Charles's study and nervously walking the diagonal patterns of the hall carpet waiting for the red engaged sign to turn green. Whatever I did I don't remember – probably lateness, cheek to staff and talking during silence – but these misdemeanours were to be eclipsed by one act of very serious misbehaviour.

There were about sixty boys in the school, all of them I think English apart from the Ullsteins and Cons, the son of the Commanding Officer of USAF Mildenhall. Nowton was a small, close-knit, happy school where all the boys were carefully selected by Charles as sons of 'suitable parents'. The boys were the Blackburnes' family and I was much happier there than at home – so the fact that I ran away from Nowton in the summer of my second year is surprising.

There are two revealing pictures in the family album taken during the Easter holiday of that year. The first is of us all setting

off by bicycle for a picnic on East Mersea beach which Jill has captioned 'The Kings setting off to enjoy themselves' and the second shows us arriving at East Mersea and presumably getting ready to collect wood for the picnic fire. This one Jill captioned 'The Kings enjoying themselves'. These pictures disturb me because they convey vividly that strange mix of misery and enjoyment which was the essence of my childhood. Jill looks frankly terrifying in her dark glasses and the rest of us look pretty tense as if there had just been some big family row, perhaps caused by the effervescent Janet who is the only one in the picture smiling. None of us look as if we are enjoying ourselves at all, although Priscilla told me later that we were told not to smile in photographs because it might seem like showing off.

But my memories of those beach picnics are happy. When we went to West Mersea beach we always took sandwiches because fires weren't allowed but East Mersea Beach was a wilderness of tangled woods, a pillbox and a rusted gun emplacement, a strip of beach and lots of mud where we could climb trees, build dens and race around playing wild games of hide and seek. Best of all were the fry-up picnic lunches of eggs, bacon, sausage and baked beans cooked on sticks over the open fire or fried in Da's army billycans. We would also swim once the tide had risen above knee height over the vast mudflats of the foreshore.

The reason for my running away was a bout of acute homesickness triggered by a late return to the school for the summer term because of convalescence from chickenpox. Paul Spendlove had had it too and had also been in quarantine. When Michael and Sylvia Spendlove suggested I should join them on a late April holiday in the Lake District Jill surprisingly agreed. It was the only holiday I spent away from the family throughout my childhood and I loved it.

We travelled in the Spendloves' health-food-store Ford delivery van which, away from Nowton's car snobbery, I didn't find in the least embarrassing. Nor did I feel carsick, although this may have been because of a daily dose of Kwells. Paul and I sat on cushions in the back of the van and we meandered slowly northwards taking in the sights of Cambridge, Peterborough, Bakewell and Carlisle. We camped each night well away from the main road, cooking on a campfire and sleeping in a large tent. The vegetarian nut rissoles were a bit difficult to stomach, but Sylvia was a loving and inventive cook and I soon settled happily into a diet of grilled carrots and parsnips marinated in oil and herbs and grated cheese on potatoes baked slowly overnight in the embers.

We spent a week in the Lake District camping in a field next to Lake Windermere and enjoyed warm days trekking over the fells and boating. The Spendloves were easy to be with, nut-brown healthy and cheerful, with that special closeness of an adored single-child family. It was a wonderful and happy out-of-time adventure and I felt miserable returning to Nowton two weeks after the start of term.

The weather was hot and I spent sleepless nights in the White dormitory playing with a yo-yo, the craze that term, feeling lonely and cut off from the other boys – a sense of isolation and of being different which can still haunt my adult dreams. I didn't particularly want to be at home, but the desire to run away from school became irresistibly strong.

I must have kept my misery well concealed because neither the staff nor any of my close friends realised. But Ian Nixon, my friend from the flu epidemic, was also homesick and, quick to spot another boy's unhappiness, started joining my late-night yo-yo sessions.

How the joint escape plan started I'm not sure, though I was certainly the instigator and Nini Nixon the willing accomplice. We talked about it for several nights until finally making a decision. We would run away one Wednesday afternoon when the rest of the school was playing games or on estate work and our disappearance was unlikely to be noticed for several hours.

The execution of the plan was simple. At three o'clock, after an afternoon clearing undergrowth, we slipped away from our estate groups and met at the gate into Nowton Road near the ruined archway. All went according to plan and in twenty minutes we had walked through the village along the route Jill and I had taken on my first day at Nowton and were standing on the Bury St Edmunds to Sudbury road hitching a lift.

Today, it would seem incredible that two eight-year-olds could hitchhike for thirty miles without someone raising the alarm. But in the mid-fifties, before the age of television and paedophiles, there was much less anxiety and suspicion. People accepted much more on trust and my expertise as a liar, which Jill had exposed, was also very useful.

'Where are you two off to then?' said the man, unwinding his window.

'We missed the bus because we were kept in detention,' I said.

'Naughty boys then, are you?' the man said in a jolly voice.

'Not really,' I said. 'We just had to re-sit a maths test.'

Nini sniggered. I felt stunned by my glib falsehood.

The man laughed.

'Bloody maths. One of my worst subjects too. Hop in then.'

Fortunately his car was old and noisy so much further conversation was difficult. He told us he was going home to Bures, more than halfway to Colchester, and that his job was selling fertiliser. It wasn't until we reached Bures that things got complicated.

'So where do you live then?' he asked. 'I'll run you to the door.'

I had to think quickly before he asked for our address.

'Thank you very much. Next on the left please.'

The speed of my reply must have made him a bit suspicious, because when he had turned into the next street he looked at me closely.

'Which house then?'

'That one,' I said, pointing to a bungalow set back from the road.

The man stopped. We got out and thanked him but instead of driving away he sat watching us with his engine running.

There was nothing else to do but walk up to the front door and ring the bell.

The young woman who opened the door looked surprised.

'Excuse me. Could we have a glass of water, please?' I asked before she had a chance to speak, then I turned to the man in the car and waved.

The trick worked. He waved back then drove away.

Similar lies and two more lifts got us to Colchester and here the problems started.

My knowledge of the town was limited to Endsleigh School in Lexden Road, Da's surgery on North Hill and the area round St Botolph's Priory which was close to where the Spendloves lived. So I cheerfully said St Botolph's to the van-driver, who had picked us up on the bypass.

It was starting to get dark and also to drizzle. Fear took over the excitement. Although we had vaguely planned to go from Colchester to our separate homes we hadn't thought just how – hitching on alone or asking our parents to come and pick us up. Nini was now in a major funk. He realised we had come the wrong way for Kelvedon where he lived, which was eleven miles up the A12 towards London in the opposite direction to Mersea Island. I tried to put on a brave face and reassure him, but my own fear was probably worse. I knew that there would now be a major panic back at Nowton and I would be the one held responsible. I also started feeling very scared about Jill and Da's response.

We were saved by a large policeman who found us sheltering under a tree in a park behind St Botolph's.

He seemed to know at once who we were. The word about two runaways on their way to Colchester must have been phoned through to the local police.

He escorted us to the nearby police station and we waited nervously while phone calls were made. Nini's father would drive over straight away to pick him up, but as Da had only just got home I was to be put on the number 75 bus to West Mersea in charge of the conductor and met when it stopped outside Strood House.

As soon as I arrived home I was in deep disgrace. Jill and Da looked furious and said nothing to me at all. Priscilla and Caroline, both at home, were not allowed to speak to me. I was sent straight up to my room without supper and told that Jill would take me back to Nowton in the morning.

The silence lasted all through our Chambers bus ride and our second walk from the Nowton turning back to school. I was all ready to say how sorry I was and explain how unhappy I'd been, but Jill seemed too angry to speak.

Once again I was put in charge of Mato and Jill left without saying goodbye. I was finally called down to Charles's study as the lunch bell went. Boys coming out of class gathered in the hall to see what would happen to me.

The punishment was inevitable. After a stern lecture on the seriousness of what I had done and a faltering explanation on my part, Charles said that sadly he had no choice but to beat me.

It was eight strokes and the hardest beating I had ever had. I cried when Charles put his arms around me afterwards and told me that next time I felt unhappy at Nowton I should come and talk to him about it first. But as soon as it was over I felt better immediately. It was Wednesday and I remember walking late into a hushed dining room and sitting down painfully to warm shepherd's pie. At tuck afterwards everyone crowded round me to hear all about it and at cricket that afternoon, according to my diary, I scored twelve runs.

Nini returned to the school a week later, without punishment because his parents complained that it had all been my fault. My own cathartic beating by Charles seemed to erase my disgrace. The rest of the term was busy with rehearsals for *The Merry Wives of Windsor* in which I played a silent page to Mistress Ford. I was clearly back in the Blackburnes' favour and had become a bit of a hero in the school. I never felt homesick at Nowton again.

Jill's frozen response to my running away upset me badly. Why didn't she understand the deep unhappiness which made me do it – that I wasn't actually running away from school but running back to home for help? It was the first time that she used silence to control and punish me. Later I got used to it. It was her way of keeping me at a distance, of not having to deal with me. But it laid the pattern of my own behaviour towards her, cheeky defiance when I was in high spirits and silent withdrawal when depressed.

The next big event of my childhood was my brother Quentin's birth in February 1956.

The discovery that she was pregnant must have excited and scared Jill. She was already over forty and had had four children, the eldest then thirteen and the youngest seven. Childbirth hadn't been easy for her. All of them had been caesarean births and she had had one stillborn child, and, according to Priscilla, two miscarriages after losing her twin son. Although later her blessing, Quentin's birth was to have a serious effect on Jill's state of mind and the balance of King family life.

From the family album, however, the summer of 1955 seems a busy, happy one. There wasn't a family holiday because of Jill's pregnancy, but there are pictures of us swimming gleefully in the tide-filled creeks close to the house, a hobby-horse gymkhana in the garden, Caroline proudly in possession of the Shop, a plywood store Da had built in the garden for her birthday.

There are also visitors – Uncle Sidney again with his brood, a glamorous friend of Aunty Molly from India called Derida with her daughter Susan, and a bowler-hatted Major Fowles from the Colchester Garrison, who moved into Strood Cottage with his wife, Judy, and was the main donor of my collection of military badges.

The best moment of that summer was the opening of the Willow Cabin, a holiday retreat for us children, made out of a refurbished shed next to the garage. Its name came from the 1949 novel by the popular novelist Pamela Frankau, a favourite of Jill's.

All children in large families need a place of escape and the Willow Cabin was a perfect refuge. It had just two rooms – a living room and bedroom – but the pleasure was in the small-scale reproduction of Jill's kitchen and living room – the sink in the corner, the miniature coal-fired cooking stove, the dresser with shelved plates, food jars and mugs on hooks. There were only two beds in the bedroom so just two children could occupy the Willow Cabin at one time which in itself was a treat. The front door was in sight of Jill and Da's bedroom window, but the Willow Cabin symbolised freedom and temporary escape from their control.

The time for the new baby grew closer. When we returned for the Christmas holidays after the autumn term Jill was a different woman. The discreet bump which had shown cutely through her black Jansen swimsuit in the summer was now a very large lump which she carried with a mixture of pride, anxiety and quick irritation with the rest of us. That Christmas we all became aware of the dangers which might arise from the unknown baby's birth. Da and the big girls took over the cooking so that Jill could rest and I remember all of us gathered in our parents' bedroom, Caroline asking Jill whether the baby would be taken out of the same caesarean furrow which stretched across her abdomen, and Jill suddenly feeling sick so that Da had to hurry us all out of the room.

There was also a lot of sisterly debate about whether it would be a boy or a girl, with the older sisters all vehemently declaring in favour of a little boy, probably picking up on Jill's undeclared but evidently strong wish for one. Only Priscilla said she would be very happy to have a new little sister because one brother, especially a slightly older one who was her hero, was quite enough. As for me, now nine years old, I really wanted a brother. My three older sisters seemed bossy and quarrelsome, and although I adored Priscilla as she adored me, the thought of a cute little boy who would model himself on me was very appealing.

The baby was due in mid-February and when we went back to school for the Easter term we all had a suspicion that there might be complications. Rather than have the baby in a local hospital, Jill was booked into St Thomas's Hospital in London where Da's brother-in-law Dickie worked as a consultant surgeon and she could get specialist attention. At the end of January Jill moved to St Thomas's.

I got the news on the 24th of February, via a phone call from Da to Betty, that Jill had given birth the day before to a boy called Quentin: mother and baby were fine. But it was not until the 8th of April that Jill and Quentin came home, by which time I was back at Strood House for the Easter holidays.

The return home of mother and son was a special occasion, especially for me. Da had chosen me to go with him to bring them back home; but his careful plan had unfortunate consequences.

The previous autumn Da had bought a yellow Rolls Royce, a 1922 Silver Ghost coupé. The purchase had been impulsive and without Jill's approval. Da had seen the car locally and fallen in love with it. But a mechanically unreliable two-door gas-guzzler, with a single bench seat and two dickie seats in the boot, was totally impractical for a family of five.

For several months Da kept the car out of sight in one of Alan Maskell's barns, disappearing occasionally to tinker with the engine, and provoking Jill's withering reference to 'Da's Mistress'. But as soon as Jill left for hospital Da brought Primrose, as we called it, back to Strood House, and parked it in the yard outside the nursery, where he could tinker with it over the weekends while Jill was away. When we returned home for the Easter holidays there it was – a gleaming vision of polished yellow coachwork, mirror-like black mudguards and huge nickel headlights. Da was confident that he had now tinkered the engine into excellent running order.

In the photo album is a photograph of the car and his handwritten note of the price, £25, the registration number of G 373, and technical information about the chassis number, and front-axle steering. He felt very proud of it and decided that, for a special surprise, he would drive Primrose to London, accompanied by me, to collect his wife and newborn son.

We set off early on a warm spring morning. I remember clearly the hushed purr of the engine as we cruised along the empty B1026 towards Maldon and looking out from the high seat on the greening hedges, sunny fields and villages we passed. Da was happier than I had ever seen him and I felt the

Primrose, a.k.a. Da's mistress.

same, as his co-pilot on this expedition to bring home my new brother.

All was well until the far side of the turning to Tollesbury, just seven miles from home. Then, with soft splutters like a dying animal, the Rolls began to lose power and the engine tailed away until we were gliding rather than driving and Da had to brake the car to a standstill.

For a moment we sat in silence then, with just a muttered 'dammit', Da climbed down and opened the bonnet. He fiddled around for a few minutes, then climbed back and tried to restart the car.

'What's the matter?' I asked unhelpfully.

'No idea,' he said finally, after listening to the futile whirring of the starter motor. 'Probably a blocked fuel pipe. We're stuck, totally stuck.'

This was a major crisis. We had arranged to pick up Jill and Quentin at one o'clock. It was now twenty to ten, plenty of time for the fifty-mile drive to London but little time to make alternative travel arrangements. First, said Da, trying to be calm and organised, we had to move the Rolls, which had inconveniently stopped on a bend, off the road. It was much too heavy for the two of us to push even with the help of a passing motorist and there was no gateway near enough in which to park. The chance of a passing AA motorbike patrolman on the B1026 was minimal and anyway Da wasn't a member. We could try to get a breakdown truck from a local garage but we were out in the country with the nearest telephone box probably in Tollesbury two miles away.

Our best bet was to find a friendly farmer with a tractor. So, leaving me on the verge fifty yards back from the car holding his handkerchief to alert other drivers of the obstruction, Da set off across a field towards a farmhouse half a mile away. By remarkable luck the farmer's wife was one of his patients and within a quarter of an hour he was back, riding on a tractor driven by the helpful farmer and with a taxi booked to pick us up in twenty minutes. A tow rope was swiftly attached to the back axle of the Rolls and the two men cheerfully engaged in the tricky process of towing the Rolls backwards to the farm driveway with me walking behind the entourage like an undertaker's mute, waving the handkerchief.

The rest wasn't so easy. The local garage's only rental car, a Wolseley, was laid up with valve problems. Da graciously declined the farmer's offer of his own car, knowing that Jill would not be happy with a muddy beaten-up Land Rover to bring home her baby boy. Time was running out and the only option was to go by train from Colchester, even though it was twelve miles away.

In the taxi Da explained that he couldn't take me with him.

'I'm sorry, Caradoc, but there'll be too much to handle if I bring them back by train.'

I was disappointed.

'I could help with the suitcases.'

He thought for a moment, then patted my knee.

'I think you're a bit young for that. But thank you.'

I could guess he was really worrying about Jill's response to his lateness and that rather than being driven home in a hire car as promised, she and her baby would have to face the ordeal of train and bus journeys. Jill when cross could be very cross indeed.

It turned out fine. I was dropped at the bus station and put in charge of the number 75 bus conductor once again who promised to drop me at Strood House. Da raced off to North End Station and eventually, hours later when we were having our baths, the taxi arrived with father, mother and new baby. Jill looked exhausted, but was so pleased to see us children and touched by the 'welcome home Quentin' picture we had drawn on the nursery blackboard wall that she burst into tears as we all crowded round the carrycot to inspect our new brother and passed him round like a parcel.

The album shows how much Jill adored having a new baby. There are pages of Quentin photos, in his pram, lying on the lawn, held by aunts, grandparents, surrounded by children beaming at the camera. I am prominently included, a clear display of her strong wish to hold me within her family.

Strangely I have no memory of Quentin during the seven years I knew him, of what he looked and sounded like, of the games which, according to the photo albums, we played together, of him as my brother. My sisters I remember clearly, but they were closer to me in age and I knew them much longer; their personalities had been fully formed. Quentin, like most infants, was less defined and memorable, and not having seen him for over forty years, apart from sketchy details from the sisters, I have no idea what he is like as an adult.

Quentin's birth at first brought joy and closeness to the family, and that summer we had one of our most successful family holidays, staying in a railway camping coach in Llanberis Station in Snowdonia. The coach was a standard carriage, converted into sitting room, kitchen and sleeping compartments and parked in a siding off the main track. Few trains stopped at the station, but there are pictures of me sitting in the driver's cab of one of them and in another holding up a thin florin (two-shilling piece) flattened after being left on the track. Quentin, now six months old, was clearly the apple of the family eye. There are other pictures of us all at the summit of Snowdon after a long slog up the mountain with Quentin in Da's backpack, coming down on the Snowdon mountain railway, and Jill lying happily on her carriage bunk with Quentin clambering on top of her.

The photo albums also introduce two new members of the family – the goats Rosamund and Celia – who became our essential source of all dairy products when Quentin was diagnosed with an acute allergy to cows' milk. The goats lived in a tin shack built by Da next to the Willow Cabin and needed milking in the early morning and evening and to be led out to pasture in the Cow's Field or to the edge of the marshes at the front of the house. Responsibility for this was added to our rota of daily chores of feeding hens, ducks, geese and guinea pigs, and mucking them all out at weekends.

I remember milking the goats under hurricane lamps on icy winter mornings, the steaming fresh milk hissing into the tin bucket. Unfortunately I loathed the taste of goats' milk even more than cows' milk. Although willing to join in the weekly milk-skimming and butter-churning activities, I found the mugs of milk we had to drink for breakfast a revolting ordeal only alleviated when, aged thirteen and in accordance with Jill's strict regulations about family diet, I was allowed to drink tea.

Another newcomer into the King family, who doesn't appear in the albums until a year later, was Father Michael, a Catholic priest at Westminster Cathedral. The origins of his friendship with my parents are mysterious, particularly in view of their staunch agnosticism. It seems that they met during the war, possibly in Thurso, Scotland, where Da was stationed in the medical corps and Michael was an army chaplain, and then lost touch. But in 1956, the year of Quentin's birth, the friendship was rekindled, during Jill's three-month stay in London. St Thomas's Hospital is just a fifteen-minute bike ride from the cathedral and Michael must have been a regular visitor to the maternity ward, soothing an anxious middle-aged mother who had medical complications and was separated from her family.

Jill's official conversion to Catholicism happened the following year. Much later Janet told me that Jill had made a vow through Father Michael that if Quentin was born a healthy child she would convert. Her conversion was to have a very disturbing effect on the family and particularly on me.

VI

According to Charles's current affairs bulletins, 1957 was a year of big change. In January Anthony Eden, exhausted after the Suez Crisis, resigned as Prime Minister to be replaced by Harold Macmillan. The days of Empire were over and the wind of change was blowing through the colonies. Ghana became the first African state to be granted independence that year, followed by Malaya and Singapore. Warsaw Pact countries met to plot with Khrushchev in Belgrade while Macmillan and Eisenhower had a summit in Bermuda. The cold war was warming up and, with East Anglia fortified by USAF bomber stations, England would clearly be piggy in the middle.

At Nowton the naval presence remained strong. Commander Child was commanding officer of the Stable dormitory block for mid-school boys and Commander Prendergast was my new form master.

The Stables was a handsome two-winged building round a large courtyard. It now housed the bike room, the carpentry room and a couple of staff garages, and upstairs there were two connected dormitories for fourth and fifth formers, Commander Child's bed-sitting room and a flat belonging to Mr and Mrs Fenner. Sleeping there was a big step towards independence after Mato's snug domain of the Blue and White dormitories. Miles Child was a balding genial bachelor. Discipline was not his strongest point so there was plenty of bad behaviour after lights out – pillow fights, blanket chariot races, reading by torchlight, and the new craze of lying in bed listening to crystal sets, the primitive but brilliant tiny radio transmitters which required no batteries or electric power, just a long single-wire aerial and a pair of headphones.

The best thing about the Stables was bath night which happened only once a week because there were only two baths and they involved using each other's water. Commander Child supervised them and would tell gripping stories of Sole Bay, Trafalgar, and Jutland.

I was very fond of Miles Child. It turned out he only had a year to live and it may have been precarious health which weakened his discipline and made him such a kindly man. He seemed stranded at Nowton, like most of the ex-officers in the school, washed up after the war years with no training or much appetite for civvy street, idling time in the genial shabbiness of a boy's prep school. He told us that he had been engaged to a girl before the war who had died of tuberculosis and claimed there had been plenty of girlfriends since then, but none were ever seen.

Commander Prendergast, whose career at Nowton would also end unhappily, was a tougher and bluffer character. Strong on discipline, he treated us like miscreant midshipmen. But at his chosen subject of maths he was pretty hopeless. Commander P, as he was generally known, had a wife, whom Charles was fond of so she was allowed to stay with him in the school. It was also rumoured that he liked a tot of gin at lunchtime, which was why he was more genial in the afternoon.

The fourth and fifth formers were generally the naughtiest boys in the school and I was one of the worst. I cannot remember any crimes as bad as my great escape – probably no more than cheek to grumpy Miss Gaunt, skiving football or biking out of bounds – but I became a regular visitor to Charles's study and familiar with the painful thwack of his knobbled cane on my trousered bottom and the squirming homily which would follow. Despite that I was a popular boy with staff, a 'cheeky little monkey', according to the Brig, and liked by Charles and Neville because I was good-looking and clever.

Nick Duval had become my best friend and on 'going out' days I often went with him to Great Barton Rectory, playing football in the garden, and watching Elvis, Adam Faith and Lonnie Donegan on the new TV pop show *Six-Five Special* before being driven by Mrs Duval at high speed in her Morris Oxford to get back to Nowton before seven o'clock with Nick and I singing: 'The Six-Five Special's coming down the line, the Six-Five Special is right on time.'

My cousin Tim Battle had now entered the school a class below me. Although the one-year age difference prevented us from becoming close friends, his delightful parents Dickie, a plastic surgeon at St Thomas's, and Jessie, Da's youngest sister, made a point of taking me with them whenever they drove down in their Ford Zephyr convertible to take Tim out and treated us both to slap-up lunches at the Angel Hotel.

One wet afternoon we went to the cinema for a matinee of *The One That Got Away* with Hardy Krüger playing Captain von Werra, the only German to escape from a British POW camp, somewhere in East Anglia, and get back to the Motherland across the North Sea. It was a gripping adventure story and began my childhood passion for illicit escape to the flickering light of a darkened auditorium.

My own 'going out' days were more cerebral and spartan, always with Da because Jill was too busy caring for Baby Quentin. Once he caused a stir arriving in Primrose but his normal arrangement was to bring his bike on the train from Colchester to Bury St Edmunds, get off at Sicklesmere station and ride the last couple of miles to the school. I would then join him for a bike ride on my Hercules. If the weather wasn't good we would have afternoon tea at Bury's second hotel, the Suffolk, and wander round the Abbey, go on a guided tour round Greene King's brewery or visit the town museum with its book about the fabled 'Red Barn Murder' of Maria Marten, bound in the skin of her murderer William Corder.

On fine days we would go further afield to Lavenham or Melford to look at Suffolk's beautiful wool churches or to a traction engine rally, Da's favourite pastime. Once we took our bikes on a tiny branch-line train to visit the memorial stone near Woolpit where St Sebastian had been tied to an oak tree and died in a fusillade of arrows.

I loved these trips. It was good to have Da to myself, and I have fond memories of riding along the Suffolk lanes to the tick of his Sturmey-Archer gears, the wind filling out my blue corduroy zipper jacket, and stopping at village shops to buy apples and Bournville chocolate. Da was always more relaxed and affectionate away from Jill and, although I wasn't at all interested in brass rubbings, I felt very close to him when it was just the two of us.

Everyday life at Nowton continued its familiar rhythm of classes, meals, rest, games and free time, with occasional highlights of Charles in a bad mood, the first XI beating Old Buckenham Hall 7–2 (a diary entry) or spontaneous treats like ice cream at beevers, a visit to Mildenhall USAF air base for open day or watching *Rawhide* on the Blackburnes' special wall-projecting television.

My middle year at Nowton was happy and untroubled until, at the end of Easter term, I nearly lost an eye.

It happened on the Sunday afternoon before the end of term. We were in the Stable Woods playing a wild game of Roundheads and Cavaliers with Chris White's den the Puritan stronghold. Some of us were armed with sticks and I would prefer to think that my eye was skewered under fierce attack by a Cavalier. In fact it happened as I was running through the undergrowth and caught my eye on a low-hanging branch.

It took a little time to realise that it was a serious wound. Blood was seeping through my closed eyelid but I felt just numbness and was determined to carry on with the game. Eventually a senior passing on his bike took a look and said I should go immediately to Mato.

Sunday afternoon was Mato's siesta time, and she was absolutely not to be disturbed. When at last she appeared, in response to our discreet but continual knocking, she was not in the best of moods.

'So, what have you done, King?'

'I ran into a tree, Mato, and got a branch in my eye.'

'Silly boy! Let's have a look.'

Her remedy, after finding her glasses to examine my half-closed eye, was to rinse it out with Optrex solution and send me on my way with instructions to come and see her again at normal evening surgery at five o'clock. Half an hour later my head was throbbing and the bleeding hadn't stopped.

This time Mato, having phoned Betty at the Small House, decided on more drastic action – to call out the school doctor.

Dr Mole, a plump and genial man with a boy in the school,

agreed to pop over to take a look, even though he had guests. He arrived in twenty minutes, took a look at me and agreed with Mato that an eye-wash was just the job.

'But eyes are tricky things,' he added, frowning. 'I think perhaps we should take Caradoc into the West Suffolk for a check-up.'

By the time we got to the hospital in Dr Mole's Humber I was in considerable pain. Within three-quarters of an hour Casualty had summoned the eye surgeon, Mr Storey, from Sunday relaxation and an hour later I was undergoing an emergency operation, involving four stitches straight into my eyeball. This was a pioneering operation in the mid-fifties and it saved my sight in that eye.

My main memory of the operation – and of my month's stay in the West Suffolk – was of everyone's kindness. The doctors and nurses calmed me with promises that the operation wouldn't hurt a bit and when the anaesthetist winked over his mask and said, 'Now try counting to ten and I'll bet you a chocolate cigar you'll be asleep before you get there,' I had the drowsy feeling that I was off on a magical mystery tour and that when I woke up my left eye would be able to see again.

It wasn't as simple as that. Although I don't remember acute pain afterwards it was a long time before I was able to use the eye. It was bandaged for a month, then covered by an eye-patch for another month, after which I had to wear dark glasses for several weeks.

My month's stay in hospital was a happy period of suspended time. For access to specialist equipment, I was put on adult general surgical rather than a children's ward. It was half empty and my bed was in a special curtained corner by the window. The young ward Sister and the half-dozen other patients treated me like the ward mascot and pyjamaed men would sit on the end of my bed telling me about their families and giving me packets of sweets, books and crayons brought in by their visiting wives.

I enjoyed the hospital routine, which was similar to boarding school – the morning wake-up call at seven o'clock, the regular meals, the ward rounds by the surgeons with their young housemen, and Sister's night-time switch-off of the ward lights. Even though I wasn't allowed to read for several weeks, I was happy drawing, playing card games, and chatting. I particularly liked the big sponge radio, placed under the pillow so as not to disturb other patients, and the daily episodes of *Nicholas Nickleby*, the most thrilling story I had ever heard. Nickleby's shout of ' "Stop!" with a voice that made the rafters ring', as the monstrous Mr Squeers thrashed the snivelling Smike, was for years my most memorable moment in literature, probably identifying with the unloved child and his heroic saviour.

I also fell in love for the first time. Nurse Carmen was a trainee nurse who took a shine to me because she had a brother of exactly my age. I have cherished memories of her sitting on my bed at night when the lights were low, telling me about the problems with her boyfriend and his parents and how privileged I felt that a grown-up – even though only eighteen – was treating me like an adult and sharing her secrets.

My stay in the West Suffolk General wasn't entirely happy. Nor was I a very good small boy. One patient called Jim with a bad cough and a crook knee took a shine to me and would hobble over to my bed to tell me stories about his wartime experiences – particularly the bad shoot-up in Normandy which had buggered his leg and for which he had very nearly got a medal.

Jim was a keen smoker and a regular visitor to the lounge at the end of the ward for a Woodbine. He was also a tippler, keeping his booze in a Thermos flask refilled by his only visitor, the brother he lived with. One evening in a state of mild inebriation he absent-mindedly offered me a fag, which I took and put swiftly into my bedside locker.

After a couple of days I decided to try it out and, having borrowed a box of matches from a winking Jim, locked myself in one of the lavatory cubicles, the only place I could have any privacy but also where smoking was strictly forbidden. I chose the worst possible time.

The one frightening person in the hospital was Matron, appropriately named Miss Savage. My only contact with her was on her ward visits, either with one of the surgeons when she was gracious and charming, or on her scheduled weekly inspections with Sister and the nurses when she was usually bossy and bad-tempered. Because of my youthful presence on an adult ward I was one of her 'special cases', so she would make a point of coming to my bed and ask a few kindly questions about how was I feeling, was I eating my food, did I have enough books to read and so on.

It was very bad luck that on the day of my first cigarette Matron paid a surprise visit to the ward, accompanied by two grand ladies who, Carmen said, were 'hospital visitors'. Mr Storey's pioneering operation to save my sight had stirred their interest and the hospital visitors were keen to see for themselves. When they reached my empty bed they asked where I was.

It was Carmen who saved me, at least from the wrath of Matron Savage. When she knocked on the door calling out my name, I was having some tentative puffs, but the whiff of smoke was enough to give me away. When I didn't answer she rattled on the cubicle door.

'Caradoc, please come out because Matron's here and on the warpath.'

Immediately I dropped the burning cigarette into the lavatory bowl, flushed it away, and opened the door.

It was a narrow escape. My breath, said Carmen, reeked of cigarette smoke and in a flash she had me brushing my teeth with minty toothpaste, before hurrying me back to the ward. But the smell must have lingered because although Matron and the two visitors didn't seem to notice, as soon as the visitors had left the ward Sister was in pursuit.

She came straight back to my bed, followed by an anxious Carmen.

'Caradoc, how come you smell so strongly of cigarette smoke?'

My lie was instant.

'I was in the lounge, sister. It was a bit smoky in there.'

Sister gave me a hard stare, then turned on Carmen.

'Is this true, Nurse?'

Carmen hesitated. 'I'm not sure, Sister.'

I felt terrible. I didn't want Carmen to tell a lie, and Carmen clearly couldn't.

'Caradoc was in the toilet when I found him.'

Sister frowned disbelievingly.

'Smoking?'

Carmen, now pink with embarrassment, just nodded.

Sister was extremely cross and insisted on finding out how I'd got the cigarette. Carmen genuinely didn't know and when I mutely refused to tell she clapped her hands and asked the whole ward if anyone knew.

Jim didn't have much choice but to own up. He was the one person on the ward who smoked like a chimney and had already joked to the other patients about how I had cadged one of his fags.

Jim bore the brunt of Sister's anger. The nursing staff already knew that he was smuggling drink into the ward through his brother and Sister gave him a very public dressing down for his irresponsible behaviour, warning him that if there were any more breaches of the rules, he would be sent home from the hospital on crutches.

Jim was so upset by this prospect he almost burst into tears. He had been on the ward a long time with recurring flare-ups of his war wound. For him the hospital was a haven from the troubles of his daily life – he was fed and taken care of by the nice nurses and had a captive audience for his implausible stories. Also he had clearly grown very fond of me. Hospital was far better than home.

I had the same problem when, after a month, it was getting near time for me to leave. Jill and Da had driven over once to Bury, bringing an Easter egg and a big hand-painted get well card from my sisters. I was allowed a telephone call every Sunday in Sister's office, but the phone calls tended to be one-sided and awkward. Da's stories (Jill didn't like the phone) of newborn guinea pigs, the goats' misdemeanours, and high tides flooding the Strood made me feel the opposite of homesick. I loved my pampered time in hospital, away from school and family.

My departure date was very close to the end of the Easter holidays and, as I still needed regular hospital check-ups, it was agreed that I would convalesce at school rather than go back to Strood House. It was Betty who came to collect me, and after poignant farewells to the nurses and my fellow inmates, and receiving a lovely fake-gold biro from Carmen which I treasured for years, we drove to Nowton in her Rover.

The four days I spent at Nowton as the only boy in the school was a special time. Mato was there – I am not sure if she had a real home to go to – and it was decided that I should sleep and convalesce in the San next door to her room. I had my meals in the San as well – tasty snacks sent up by Mrs Fenner – but during the last four days of the holiday I spent a lot of time with the Blackburnes.

Neville was busy with a major replanting of the Small House garden and appointed me his gardener's boy to help cut out new beds and dig holes for the plants. Betty had me help her in the kitchen unpacking the loads of cereal, crisps, biscuits, jams and beans necessary to feed sixty boys and staff in the term ahead.

Charles spent the mornings in his study preparing school programmes for the summer term but after lunch would take me with him on outings in the Battleship – one day to Moreton Hall to discuss likely girls for the new Shakespeare production, another to discuss cricket fixtures with the headmaster of Old Buckenham Hall, our rival school, while I played with his family in the garden. One afternoon we went with Neville into Bury for visits to the stationers and wine merchant and then to an appointment with their bank manager during which I sat outside the manager's office reading the *Eagle*.

Usually I had supper in the San and spent the evening reading, playing draughts with the fiercely competitive Mato, or listening to her radio. But on the last evening before the beginning of the term, as a treat, I was invited to supper in the Small House with Charles, Neville and Betty. To me it seemed a very grand affair with three courses of soup, chicken and cheese or ice cream, served by their housekeeper Mrs Chambers, with red wine poured from a decanter, which I was allowed to sip. I was too nervous to join in the conversation much but most of it was school gossip and plans for the summer. Charles, a natural actor, made us giggle with indiscreet imitations of a new boy's mother and the pompous public school headmaster he had been talking to on the phone about that year's Common Entrance candidates. Afterwards we watched a cowboy film on television and then Charles walked me back through the dusk to the school.

Those four days marked the beginning of my close relationship with the Blackburnes which would last until my late teens.

Even though I had spent almost the whole Easter holiday in hospital and was still convalescing in the San with only morning classes, that summer term was a special one, enhanced by new sunglasses and heroic status as a survivor of semi-blindness.

The happiest event of the term – and maybe of my entire childhood – was a surprise journey with Grandpa and Aunty Molly. Now a frail widower in his early eighties, Grandpa had never been to Nowton, and was honoured by an invitation from Charles to have lunch with Molly and me on the top table. In the afternoon, after a short tour of the school and a visit to the pavilion to watch the first XI open the batting against a rival school, we drove to Bury in Grandpa's gleaming dark-grey Triumph Roadster, with Molly driving, Grandpa beside her, and me in the back behind the chauffeur's partition window. We visited the Abbey, then a second-hand bookshop where Grandpa found a missing volume from his Kipling collection, and had a large tea at the Angel. At half past five we set off in the car again, I assumed to get back to school in time for seven o'clock, but instead of taking the Nowton turn we carried on towards Sudbury on the Colchester road.

Gradually I realised we weren't going back to school. Grandpa and Molly sat silent in the front and I had no wish to spoil the surprise. I thought we might be going instead to Strood House but when we took a turning towards Braintree, then another to Chelmsford I guessed we were heading towards London or maybe Enfield.

They kept up the mystery until the following morning when we were having breakfast in a restaurant on the A30 near Bagshot. When we had reached the Hermitage it was dark and late and I had fallen asleep in the back of the car. I was given milk and a ham sandwich in the dining room and told that we would be getting up very early because we had a long journey ahead of us. The next morning, when the first buses were rumbling to life in the Forty Hill terminal opposite the house, I was woken by Aunty Molly with a cup of lapsang, Grandpa's early morning tea which I always shared with him when staying at the Hermitage, and told to get dressed quickly in my school uniform and a clean white shirt from my overnight case which had appeared mysteriously from the boot.

'We're going to Devon,' said Grandpa with a smile over our coffee – an incredible treat – after breakfast of bacon and eggs. 'We're going to visit Blundell's in Tiverton, my old public school where Uncle Sidney went and I very much hope you will too.'

It was a long day's drive; in those days there were few dual carriageways. We didn't talk much because, even with the chauffeur's screen wound down, it was a long way between the fat leather back seat I had to myself and the front. Aunty Molly drove aggressively with much use of the horn, a habit she had picked up driving ambulances early in the war. I sat mesmerised by the passing countryside, half-listening to the conversation in front about places we were passing and the general gossip of Enfield, family and friends.

Lunch was a picnic in a field beside Stonehenge, prepared by Mrs Jones, the Hermitage cook, with a Thermos of coffee for the grown-ups and a bottle of ginger beer for me. Afterwards we wandered through the circle of giant stones wondering how they had got there and what they were for, Grandpa explaining that Stonehenge was one of the wonders of the world, a miracle of transport and construction before there were cranes and possibly before the invention of the wheel.

A lazy, hot afternoon followed, as we purred through the rolling Somerset countryside, with the smell of mown hay drifting through the open windows. We stopped for a tea of scones and whipped cream in the back garden of a roadside cafe then, when the lush green countryside had given way to moorland, we reached our destination.

I had never stayed in a hotel before and the Dulverton Station Hotel seemed incredibly grand. I had a room to myself looking out towards the moors with a four-poster bed and stag-hunting pictures on the walls. A porter brought up my overnight case and explained that if I put my shoes outside the door before I went to bed, I would find them polished in the morning. He also took away my grey flannel suit, which had been packed so that the housekeeper could press it for me. I was too tired and stuffed with teatime scones to eat more than some brown soup at dinner, but I watched in awe as the tail-coated waiter elaborately drew the cork from a bottle of red wine chosen by Grandpa, sniffed it, then poured a little in a glass for Grandpa to taste. There weren't many people in the dining room but they all seemed very smartly dressed. Grandpa too had changed into a dark suit and Aunty Molly was wearing a red dress. Hotel life seemed to me like staying in a palace.

Early the next morning was the best moment of the trip. I woke up to the sound of a chuffing steam engine and quickly put on my flannel suit, white shirt, yellow tie and highly polished black shoes and hurried through the quiet hotel out into the still sunshine of the station. Milk churns were being loaded onto a train. The guard gave me a smart salute and a lady in a white coat who was opening up a little cafe on the platform offered me a cup of tea. I said no thank you and stood on the platform watching the fireman connect the stubby black engine to the carriages; then a few early passengers climbed on board, and I watched the clock because Aunty Molly had said breakfast would be at eight.

The rest of that day and the journey home I don't remember so well. I think it was a slightly sad day because no one remembered Grandpa as well as he remembered the school. We went first to School House, which both Grandpa and Uncle Sidney had belonged to, and for which my name had been registered soon after my adoption. The housemaster gave us a warm welcome and delegated a house prefect to show us round. There were a couple of old masters, who had taught Sidney and were glad to see us, but the young headmaster, when we ran into him outside the chapel, clearly didn't recall the name Beavan although he pretended to. After a hearty shake of my hand and wishes of good luck at Common Entrance, he hurried off to meet the Lord Lieutenant of the County who was giving out the prizes.

We sat in a marquee listening to speeches just like at Nowton, and had lunch afterwards of chicken and strawberries and cream, then watched a cricket match and Grandpa proudly introduced me to some other old men. Then we got back into the car and soon after we left Tiverton I fell asleep.

It was good to get back to my friends and tell them about my adventure. I was proud that Grandpa wanted me to go on to his old school. My eye was better. I was rehearsing to play Dull in that year's production of *Love's Labour's Lost* and the end of term was close. But I didn't know that within a year Grandpa would be dead, I would have to leave Nowton and that I would never go to Blundell's.

That summer Father Michael appears twice in the family album, once serious and priest-like in his surplice and next in holiday mode, wearing a short-sleeved shirt with an open neck. We are having tea in the garden and everyone is smiling. This was the first of his regular summer stays at Strood House and marked his new position as an honorary member of the King family. It was a turning point. Jill's passionate conversion and decision that in future her children should be brought up Catholic was, as Janet said later, 'the start of the rot'.

VII

They told me on the last day of the Christmas holidays that I would be leaving Nowton at the end of the year. It was because they could no longer afford to keep three children at boarding school, Da said; as the youngest I would have to make the sacrifice and go back to day school. But I didn't believe them. It seemed much more to do with Jill's determination to move me to a Catholic school. She was now 'under instruction', with weekly visits to a priest in Colchester, and also in correspondence with a priest friend of Father Michael at a church in Ely Place in London, where in May she would be baptised.

The news clouded my last two terms at Nowton. I was in my second term of the fifth form, a confident member of the middle school, Common Entrance still three years ahead. We were the big boys of the Stable dorms, allowed a late bedtime by the benign Commander Child and special evening bun privileges by Mrs Fenner. Class was tougher because the fifth-form master was the fearsome Brigadier Collett-White, though the Brig's bark was worse than his bite and concealed a warm heart. I was a friend of his delicate youngest son and occasionally invited to tea at their Sicklesmere house and, unless he was in a very bad mood, the Brig treated me with gruff affection. I was also in the third football XI, enjoying weekend trips in the Battleship to away games and large cooked visitors' teas if we were playing at home. Life was good.

The reason I had to be told so soon was that in April I was to take the eleven-plus exam, which I needed to get a place at St Joseph's College, Iposwich, the Catholic grammar school where Jill had decided to send me.

Nowton, like all prep schools, prepared its boys for Common Entrance, the qualifying exam for entrance to Public School. CE is a traditional exam with papers on eight subjects including algebra, Latin, French, geography, history and scripture. The eleven-plus is in some ways simpler because it calls more for quick wits and basic intelligence, but tough for children brought up on narrative history and classic textbooks like Kennedy's *Latin Primer*, Herbert Collins's *French Courses* and Ronald Ridout's *English Grammar*.

The first sign that I had been singled out for special future schooling was the eleven-plus practice papers I had to do a couple of afternoons a week on my own in Mr Mackinnon's turret music room. The other boys were curious to know why I had to practise for the eleven-plus. It was clearly a social stigma.

Two other bad things happened that Easter term. The first was a tragedy that shocked the nation – the death of most of the Manchester United football team in the Munich air crash. On a snowy February afternoon an Airspeed Ambassador taking off from Munich hit slush at the end of the runway and, unable to lift clear of the airport's border fence, crashed into an empty house. Twenty-three out of forty-three passengers, including eight of the team, died instantly.

The first announcement was on the six o'clock news, reported to us by Commander Child at bath-time. My only interest in football was token support for the local team Colchester United, then floundering in the depths of the third division. But Manchester United were a national legend. Commander Child's announcement stunned us all and as soon as lights were out the Stable dorms started humming with crystal-set static as we all tuned in.

That night the Home Service schedule was replaced by a solemn bulletin direct from Munich airport. There was good news, that Jackie Blanchflower had survived, and the manager Matt Busby was in intensive care but conscious, but the BBC report, against background shouting, crane engines and rescue workers speaking broken English, was a litany of bodies identified, spectators describing the grisly events and officials speculating on what had happened.

Our parents' lives had been blunted by wartime tragedy but, for us children, death and national disaster were a new experience, and so was live action reportage on the radio. By the next morning, after Charles's grave summary at morning prayers of overnight events, the school was in a state of shocked excitement. That evening, instead of prep, Charles set up his television projector in the dining room. The fifth and sixth formers were allowed to watch the grim news and then, to cheer us up, to stay up for *Sergeant Bilko*.

A couple of weeks later a more personal tragedy hit the school. It was generally known that Commander Child had a health problem, a peptic ulcer which kept him on a milky diet. But his death was totally sudden and unconnected with his ulcer. He had seemed fine the night before at bedtime and had told us about *The Dam Busters*, the film he had seen in Bury that afternoon. But the next morning he didn't wake us as usual. A

105

dormitory senior had to get us out of bed and then knocked on the commander's door. There was no answer so he asked Mr Fenner to take a look.

Poor Commander Child had died in his sleep, peacefully, Mr Fenner told us, a smile on his face. The cause of death was a heart attack, Charles told us sadly at prayers, a merciful way to go. He wouldn't have felt a thing.

Commander Child's death upset me deeply – the sudden loss of a kind and gentle man, a substitute father. It seemed unbelievable that one day he could be there and the next be gone absolutely and for ever.

The whole school was in shock for a couple of weeks and the death was a constant topic of conversation. A memorial service was held at Nowton Church and attended by several parents. The Brig and Neville read sermons; Sadie, who had been at Nowton with Commander Child since the beginning and was rumoured to have had a crush on him, paid tribute to his kindness and modesty. Charles preached a stirring sermon about death being just a threshold to immortal life.

His fellow naval officer and wartime comrade Commander Prendergast didn't speak at the service, but seemed to feel the death most deeply, with a marked increase in his afternoon tipsiness as the term progressed. Things came to a head one Saturday teatime when he was brought back to the school in a large Wolseley police car in a notably drunken state, to the great entertainment of the boys who witnessed his arrival. Clearly it was a sacking offence but Charles, with characteristic loyalty to the men under him, merely informed the school next morning that Commander Prendergast had been taken ill and would be going away for convalescence.

There were two other major events that term. The first was the eleven-plus exam; the other was my second crush.

I almost failed the exam, not surprising given the social stigma of taking it and my strong but unrealistic wish to stay at Nowton. But it was also an exceptionally hard paper that year with one notoriously difficult question – to decipher the mathematical sum:

$$
\begin{array}{r}
\text{CROSS} + \\
\underline{\text{ROADS}} \\
\text{DANGER}
\end{array}
$$

The only two clues provided were that $R = 6$ and $S = 3$. Very few got the right answer and even an Oxford mathematics don took five minutes to solve it when challenged by a newspaper because of all the fuss.

My first result, posted to my parents, was failure. Jill and Da were horrified. I was secretly pleased, assuming that my parents would not be able to tolerate the shame of me going to a secondary modern school and that instead I would have to stay on at Nowton and take the Common Entrance. But the middle classes are good at complaining. Da sent a carefully worded letter to the Essex County Education Service explaining my problems, supported by a testimonial from Charles. I was summoned to attend an interview in Chelmsford where, at last, I excelled myself.

This time the crucial question was what books I had been reading. My answer – *Oliver Twist* by Charles Dickens – was clearly exactly what the nice lady examiner wanted to hear. I am not sure whether it was true or influenced by parental prompting – adults of course are allowed to lie when strictly necessary – but the result was another letter to Jill and Da saying that after review my eleven-plus result had been corrected to a pass; I was now entitled to free grammar school education.

The crush was even more confusing than the eleven-plus. Why did I fall for a darkly good-looking sixth former nicknamed

Badger? It had nothing to do with Badger himself, who was blind to my passion and barely noticed me. It may have been triggered by another fifth former called Oliver who seemed to have first caught Badger's eye. But mostly I think it was just hunger for love fixing randomly upon a suitable object of adoration.

At first there was nothing I could do about it. Then, in the last week of term, I made a simple decision – declare myself.

In the boot room there was the cap rack, rows of neatly shelved compartments where we kept the rolled yellow school caps we wore for Sunday church. I can't remember what the letter actually said – but on Saturday evening, with deep anxiety, I folded it inside Badger's cap.

The next morning we walked to church as usual. I presumed Badger must have read the note and maybe shared it with some friends. The suspense was both agonising and exhilarating. In church we sang the Easter hymn 'There Is a Green Hill Far Away' and I exultantly trebled the high notes, proud and happy to have declared my love though fearful of the consequences. As for Badger, he didn't seem to have noticed, or maybe I just couldn't bear to look at him to find out.

After the Easter holiday love finally blossomed. Summer was always an intense time at Nowton, the heat and long light evenings, the outdoor freedom and the sheer beauty of the place fostering a hot-house excitement. For me that summer, my last and free now of exams, stirred recklessness.

I don't know who made the second move but somehow it was clear from the beginning of term that Badger, having had the holidays to think about my letter, was keen to find out more. As he was captain of cricket I had a rare opportunity to get close to him. For a special last-term privilege, Sergeant Sharrock had appointed me his deputy in charge of the large Atco mowing machine with attached roller seat so I could give Badger rides to the cricket field, an established Nowton tradition. But wooing wasn't really necessary. Badger, a sporty farmer's son, was short on words and I think just took my adoration for granted.

It started with a tongue-tied walk in the woods one evening after cricket. We reached the Summer House and to bridge the silence I took his hand and we sat on the bench by the door. Badger looked at me, frowning slightly, puzzled. Then he smiled.

'Did you mean all that? In the letter.'

I nodded.

Slowly he ran his fingers up my bare arm and upwards onto my cheek. Then he leaned forward and very gently kissed me.

That was about as far as it went – kissing in the woods. It never led to sex or even thoughts of it, surprising in a school with two discreetly gay headmasters where there was certainly sexual awareness if not actual misbehaviour among the sixth formers in the open bathrooms. My first love affair was passionate, exhilarating – and innocent.

It was also soon triangular. Badger's crush on Oliver was probably as strong as mine for him and he saw no reason why he shouldn't have two boyfriends to keep the balance. Happily it worked out without jealousy. Oliver and I had no romantic yearnings for each other. We were happy, possibly relieved, that we could share a passion for the handsome captain of cricket and proud to be seen in public as his favourite boys – until Badger's uninhibited habit of walking along with arms round both of us attracted attention, and finally got us in trouble.

Charles issued a public summons at prayers for the three of us to come to his study; we went expecting the worst. But Charles's response was remarkably tolerant – and to modern parents more aware of the sexual corruption of minors it might have been worrying.

'You silly things,' he said kindly, as we stood quaking in front of him.'I have no objection to special friendships between boys, as long as things are strictly above the belt. But you really can't go round in public with your arms round each other. It can be upsetting for others who might get jealous – and you can also easily make yourselves figures of fun.'

He paused, looking sternly at Badger.

'And James [his real name]. You are a very senior boy in this school and it's up to you to set a good example and not lead younger boys into trouble. Is that clear?'

'Yes, Charles,' Badger said meekly.

Charles flipped his hand to dismiss us.

'Just try to be good, dears.'

His words had the desired effect. By the middle of term grand passion had dwindled to tender affection. Badger was in the throes of Common Entrance and cricket, and Charles's reminder of the importance of his position in the school must have struck home. He was very careful to keep his hands off us in public places and after a while reluctant to be seen with us at all. Oliver must have got bored with playing second fiddle because he soon drifted off for Sports Day training and to muck around with other friends.

I also had something else to occupy me – the school play. That year it was *Twelfth Night* and, for the first time, I was given a very minor speaking role, as Curio, lord to the lovesick Duke Orsino. With love in the air, Shakespeare's bittersweet tangle of unrequited passion, sexual identity and human folly must have had a potent effect. By the end of term my romantic yearnings had veered sharply in a different direction.

I should have fallen for the handsome Sebastian or his twin Viola, both played in this production by boys. A shift from a beefcake cricketer to the romantic male lead would have been a natural step in the camp atmosphere of a Blackburne production. But this time it was the beautiful Olivia who stole my heart although, like Orsino's, my passion was sadly unrequited. Her real name was Penelope, a dark-haired and vivacious beauty from Moreton Hall girls'school who had even enchanted Charles, despite his preference for boys playing the female leads.

Penelope was dark, pale and incredibly beautiful. I loved to watch her moving easily across the stage, saying her lines with grace and intelligence (Charles's praise) and effortlessly charming everyone. As with Badger I longed to see and be near her.

Several of the cast were clearly enamoured and as an eleven-year-old fifth former I knew I didn't stand a chance. I was happy to adore from a distance. But she must at least have understood my feelings because at the after-show party, as the girls were fluttering around saying goodbye before being driven back to Moreton Hall, she made a point of coming over to me.

'It was lovely meeting you, Caradoc. I hope we'll be in a play together next year.'

'I wish we could. But I'm leaving Nowton at the end of this term.'

'What a pity. Where are you going?'

'St Joseph's College, Ipswich.'

Penelope frowned. She had clearly never heard of St Joseph's. 'Well, good luck.'

She was about to leave. Suddenly I blurted it out.

'You're very beautiful.'

Her face lit up.

'Do you think so?'

I nodded. She laughed.

'And you're lovely too.' She leaned forward and quickly kissed me on the cheek.'I hope we meet again.'

I got the same message – about meeting again – from my friends a fortnight later at the end of term. Leaving prep school is always tough, the switch from being a big cheese in a small world to starting as a new boy at some large, intimidating public school. There was, nevertheless, a challenge and glory in leaving childhood behind, one's name on the school's honours board, and going forward to battle on the playing fields of Repton, Cranleigh, Gresham's, Charterhouse or Felsted. But I was losing my good friends – Duval, O'Hagan, Ullstein, Vaughan-Jones and Cousin Tim – and, just when life was getting good, disappearing to a school no one had heard of. Next year they would be sixth formers with grown-up chats over sherry on Sunday, trips to the Theatre Royal in Bury and the respect of the rest of the school. They would be treated as grown-ups, which the Blackburnes were very good at, before having to start again as juniors.

At the time I handled it bravely. Leaving Nowton at eleven wasn't as tough as being dumped there at the age of six. My survival instinct was already second nature. Nostalgia, which transformed Nowton into golden memories, was well into the future. But now, looking back, I know that missing out on those two years was an acute loss, and triggered a sharp decline in my relationship with Jill and Da.

Charles and Neville were the last to say goodbye to me. The train boys had already left when we shook hands formally before I got into the taxi to take me to Bury bus station. They seemed almost as sad as I was.

'Come back soon, dear boy,' said Charles, patting me lightly on the cheek. 'We are all very fond of you, remember, and there's always a home for you here if things get tough.'

They were prescient words.

Jill and Da must have felt guilty about forcing me to change schools because that summer holiday I was given a special treat. A fortnight at a Forest School Camp, whose aim remains, according to its website, 'to encourage children to work and play together close to nature', was one of the happiest episodes of my childhood. It helped me overcome shyness and fit in quickly with children I didn't know, a good preparation for St Joseph's. It also provided a new romantic adventure.

The camp was by the sea in Norfolk. There were around sixty children between eleven and fourteen and we slept in tents of four according to age and sex. The days were full with swimming, games and nature expeditions. At night we had barbecues, put on shows and sang songs round the campfire. The staff were young volunteers and as the FSC policy was 'to encourage children to take responsibility for both small and not so small decisions' discipline was very liberal and everything but the sleeping arrangements was communal and happy-go-lucky. The weather was hot and after a couple days of anxiety settling in I had the time of my life.

My main buddy for the holiday was a boy called Dick who had just ended his first year at grammar school and led me on various daredevil adventures, from raiding a local farmer's orchard for unripe apples to taking out a fisherman's boat one evening for a clumsy and hilarious row round Brancaster Staithe harbour. Dick also introduced me to my first vice and symbol to Jill of my rapid moral decline – smoking. After my experience in the hospital lavatory I was already fascinated by the process and had long admired Charles's elegant habit of tapping his untipped cigarette on the packet to firm up the tobacco before twirling the tip between his lips to avoid the paper sticking. Now Dick and I tried it out, first with dried leaves rolled in newspaper – and with eye-watering results. One day walking back from the beach we found an open packet of Senior Service dropped in the road and lit up behind the nearest tree. Soon we were puffing away like a couple of jolly tars, blowing out clouds of fragrant smoke but without much noticeable effect. Then an older boy came by and started laughing.

'What's the matter?' asked Dick crossly.

'You're not supposed to blow on the fag but suck on it, to draw the smoke inside. Like this.'

The boy took a drag on the cigarette, expertly curling the smoke out over his lip and inhaling it through his nose, then handed it back. Dick and I were deeply impressed, but certainly didn't show it. As soon as the boy had gone we got down to serious business, sucking down the smoke like old ganja masters, and polishing off two cigarettes each until we both felt very strange. Shakily we got up and started walking back to camp until after a few yards Dick was suddenly and violently sick all over his plimsolls.

But the most thrilling moments of the holiday were with the girls and I still feel a bit proud that at the age of eleven I kissed a girl's naked bottom. I am not sure how it happened. I think there had been a wild game of French and English with much racing to and fro between rival forts trying to snatch the opponent's flag, during which I was taken hostage and imprisoned in a girl's tent, guarded by two feisty eleven-year-olds, one of them a buxom blonde called Anna. How one thing led to another so that soon most of our clothes were off I can't imagine. But Anna certainly mooned me, I gave her behind a smacker and we all fell about, squealing with laughter.

Laura Long was different. She was a dark, intense girl who shared Anna's tent but was not quite one of the gang. However, she must have decided that I was her kind of guy and that she was going to beat off all competition, because for the last few days of the holiday we were inseparable.

It was with Laura that I had my first night of chaste passion. On our last evening there was a farewell campfire sing-song and because it was so hot we were allowed to sleep outside in sleeping bags. The moon was large, the sky clear and full of stars. Laura and I lay down side by side, snuggled together through our sleeping bags, not saying much, listening to the owls, feeling incredibly close. Then in the morning after we had all packed up she came round to my tent with a copy of *The Last of the Mohicans*, said goodbye with a kiss on the cheek – and we never saw each other again. I still have the book with her inscription inside the cover: 'To Caradoc, with love from Laura Long, July 1958'.

There was another consolation treat that summer – a weekend at the Hermitage with Grandpa, now a shrunken and frail old man and very disappointed that I was leaving Nowton and would not be going on to Blundell's. Aunty Molly later told me that he had immediately offered to pay my fees, but had been rebuffed by Jill, who was determined that I should have a Catholic education, news which distressed Grandpa, a staunch Anglican, even more.

The highlight of my stay was a trip to London for lunch on Saturday at a restaurant called the Ivy. We were chauffeured up in the Triumph by Aunty Molly, who went off to do some shopping.

I put on my Nowton uniform for the last time and Grandpa wore one of his dark double-breasted suits, now a size too large, which he wore most days even long after retirement. The restaurant was terribly posh, with red velvet seats, stained-glass windows and an atmosphere of hushed opulence. The head waiter, who looked almost as old as Grandpa, greeted him as an honoured friend and solemnly shook my hand. We settled at our table and I chose roast chicken from the enormous menu. Grandpa explained that the Ivy was in walking distance of the old Weld & Beavan office in Golden Square and that he had lunched there regularly with his most important clients. It was also a favourite haunt of theatre stars.

Today was a lucky day. After glancing round the room and telling me not to look, he said in a quavering voice that two famous actors were having lunch at separate tables – Sir John Gielgud and Dame Peggy Ashcroft.

'Who knows, Caradoc,' he said, 'perhaps it will be your turn one day. I hear you like acting.'

He was wrong about my theatrical career, but half right: years later as a literary agent I too would go to the Ivy to entertain important clients.

That was the last time I saw him. Grandpa died after a short illness at the end of the summer, just before I started at St Joseph's. Jill told us after returning from an urgent visit to Enfield, alas too late to see her father before he died. His death, like that of Gamma's, coincided with my imminent departure to a new school.

I missed Grandpa deeply even though we met infrequently and I understood that, as a frail old man, he was soon going to die. He was for me my natural grandfather and that was how he always treated me. Maybe this was partly prompted by a sense of duty towards an adopted member of his family but I was, until two years before he died, his one grandson and I know that he loved me.

Jill too was seriously upset by his death, though she didn't admit it. Her relationship with her father had been distant since the quarrel twenty years earlier but, as Aunty Molly told me much later, his loss was painful. Despite her reactions against them, Grandpa and Gamma, and the secure, loving, affluent middle-class respectability of family life at the Hermitage were the bedrock of her life. Her effective repudiation of her own happy childhood was, according to Molly, typical of her wilful and contrary personality. Grandpa's death, and the end of his natural decency and good sense, caused an emotional upheaval which she would try and resolve with a divine but more troublesome father figure – God. Her conversion to the Catholic Church was the beginning of our bad times.

THREE

Holy Days

VIII

I went alone to St Joseph's on the first day of the autumn term, refusing Da's offer to accompany me, determined to handle this new challenge on my own. It was the longest and most difficult journey I had done by myself and I had to do it six days a week in term-time for the next two years.

Each morning I caught the 7.15 a.m. bus to Colchester from outside Strood House, transferred to the town bus for North Station and then caught the 8.10 train for the half-hour journey to Ipswich where I picked up a local bus to the school. If everything ran on time I arrived at St Joseph's by 9.00 for morning assembly. The return journey was the same in reverse so that on weekdays I would get home by 6.30, half an hour before Da. On Saturdays my four-hour journey time was as long as the time I spent at school.

There was one excitement about this daily trip – the trains. My trip on the *Flying Scotsman* and staying at the Dulverton Station Hotel were cherished memories. Steam trains were magic.

The 8.10 was a dumpy local with a chuffing tank engine and

four uncorridored carriages which stopped at the three stations en route – Ardleigh, Manningtree and Bentley. Sometimes, if it was running late, I would pick up a Great Yarmouth express pulled by large sleek Britannia Class engines with corridored carriages. In the evening if I wasn't delayed by detention, I would pick up the *Broads Express* which went non-stop to Colchester.

I don't remember St Joseph's as well as Nowton, and in the one school photograph that appeared in the album I can identify only two boys, one whom I adored and the other who got me into serious trouble, although the other faces still look familiar. The two years I spent there marked the beginning of a very difficult period, and my abrupt shift through puberty into adolescence. I started behaving badly. I also realised for the first time that my parents could get things wrong and began to resent them.

St Joseph's was a Catholic grammar school run by the De La Salle Brothers, a religious order founded in the late seventeenth century to educate poor French boys picked up from the streets. The school was at Birkfield, a handsome mansion on the outskirts of Ipswich surrounded by large grounds, and by 1958, when the De La Salles were in their heyday, smart modern buildings had been added to house classrooms, labs and gym. The education was strict, and regular up-and-over hand slaps with a leather spatula were used to enforce good behaviour, but despite the intimidating, Napoleonic head of juniors, Brother Solomon, it was generally a humane and civilised school, no tougher than Nowton but much less fun.

The teaching was strictly Roman Catholic and, as a new convert, I was given extra religious instruction to clear my head of the woolly Anglicanism taught at Nowton and to implant firmly the fundamentals of the Faith – devotion to the Virgin Mary, papal infallibility and Purgatory, a pre-heavenly period for the expiation of sins from which days could be discounted for extra prayers on earth.

My arrival coincided with a major change in the Church. On 7 October 1958 the saintly and ultra-conservative Pope Pius XII died. The school was thrown into a whirl of excitement about the choice of his successor. We watched the funeral on a giant screen in the school hall and then the election of the genial John XXIII, with a puff of white smoke from the Sistine Chapel. The papal funeral and coronation, choral high mass in St Peter's, the processions of gorgeously dressed cardinals, and the new Pope's balcony address in Latin planted the emotional fervour that would absorb me into the Catholic Church.

My conversion to the grammar-school curriculum was more difficult. Nowton education had been an easygoing mix of classical, literary, historical and basic maths taught by genial, relatively uneducated ex-servicemen. At St Joseph's the emphasis was on hard facts and information; the teachers were zealous young professionals who expected good results. I was reasonably good at English and history because I could write well but poor at maths and science. I was a clever child but with a disorganised, impractical mind, and inhibited by the science master, Mr Prescott, a martinet who decided swiftly that I was a lazy dunce. My problems with science led to increasing misbehaviour and a reputation as a troublemaker.

The biggest hurdles were the weekly testimonials, coloured bits of paper with marks for work and behaviour, handed out by form teachers on Saturday. The top mark was 200. Above 150 you got a 'gold' (yellow) testimonial, a 'pink' for above 100 and a 'blue' for below 100. Testimonials were signed by Brother Solomon and had to be returned on Monday, countersigned by a parent.

My performance was very average, generally a low pink, a rare gold for a good essay and as time wore on frequent blues. Each

Saturday, as soon as Da and I got home and before a late lunch kept hot in the oven, I would produce my testimonial, a weekly ritual probably as hard for Jill and Da as it was for me. Their response was restrained disappointment at the low pinks and blues and just muted pleasure on those rare Saturdays when I brought home gold and longed for a hug or at least a pat on the back. Da always deferred to Jill in dealing with the children and silence was her principal way of conveying displeasure. In my case she was very difficult to please.

Life had changed at Strood House. Jane and Janet were now both at different boarding schools and into adolescence. Caroline and Priscilla were at a day school in Colchester but soon off to Hengrave Hall, a convent boarding school. The centre of Jill's family universe was two-year-old Quentin whom she doted on; having me back home after five years away was not easy. I sense they didn't quite know what to make of me and after the idyllic and exciting times at Nowton I found it hard to balance living at home with the tough day-school routine.

Jill and I were both in a state of change. My voice was dropping. I was starting to get frequent erections at awkward moments, such as on the bus with my satchel rammed onto my lap, although it took me a long time to learn what to do with them. Jill was in the throes of her conversion, sweeping Caroline, Priscilla and me as swiftly as possible into the Catholic Church. By the end of that year we had all been baptised by Father Michael in Westminster Cathedral and taken our first communions.

Religious salvation perversely coincided with my moral decline. I don't know what started me stealing. It began in a small way, but the need to buy sweets, magazines and now cigarettes to keep up with my schoolmates meant that soon I was into a life of serious crime.

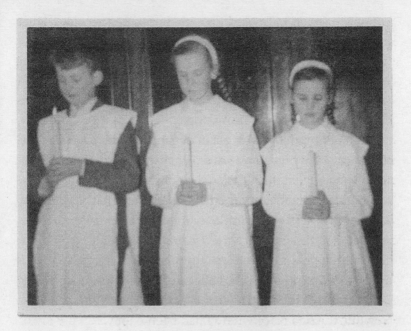

First communion.

Temptation was easily available in the form of the pile of silver change from Da's suit pocket which he left on a chest of drawers in his bedroom. A quick dip for a florin or half-crown when no one was looking and which Da wouldn't notice was easy enough. But escalating petty pilfering into taking pound notes from his wallet was a big step: in those days one pound was a lot of money. Da didn't carry much cash and being a precise man he would have known exactly how many pound notes there were. After my first raids on Da's wallet – usually on Sunday when the family were in the garden – he must have realised. But he never said.

Each raid was scary. The fear of being found out was the same as the fear of not being found out; only by being stopped could I stop myself. Even a strong hint – like concealing the wallet in a drawer – would have been enough. But there was only silence and the longer it continued the bolder I got.

Jill also kept her money in a wallet, in a cubbyhole behind the lid of her bureau in the living room. I must have watched her taking it out to know it was there and within a couple of months Jill's purse became my second target.

Stealing from Jill was an act of defiance. It was more dangerous because her bureau was downstairs in a public place and the act of opening first the lid, then the drawer, and finally the purse was burglary. Years later an analyst explained that my thieving was an unconscious plea for love, driven by a need for attention. I suspect it also expressed a need to live dangerously, to offset the blank unhappiness of feeling unwanted and to create in my life a secret, private place which made me different. It was an expression of the desolation I felt at having been removed from Nowton, the one place where I had been happy.

Why did Jill and Da stay silent and not try to stop my thieving? Until then my childhood had been governed by strict discipline and harsh punishment, with Nowton assuming the main responsibility when I went there. Now, at home again, Jill and Da probably didn't know how to cope. The beatings had stopped and corporal punishment was out of the question, not because I was a hulking adolescent who might fight back (I was small for my age) but because, in some way, I had grown outside their orbit of control. Nowton had turned me into a sophisticated grown-up child. St Joseph's seemed to be transforming me into a devious criminal. I was just *different* from Jill and Da's own children – a cuckoo in the family nest.

My domestic thieving soon became more serious, and early in my second year at St Joseph's I was almost expelled.

Jimmy Belton was a natural entrepreneur well known in our class for his dodgy behaviour – cheating and bribery, shoplifting from sweetshops, and telling extremely tall stories about his family's wealth and lifestyle. He was also a charmer, good at hoodwinking teachers and gulling susceptible boys like me.

We became friends because he was the only other 'train boy' in our class. His family lived in Manningtree, halfway between Colchester and Ipswich, and we usually travelled home together after school. His father was a director of Churchill's the cigarette makers, whose factory was in Ipswich, and Belton introduced me to the habit of smoking in the train lavatory or in the school woods which, when she smelled it once on my breath, triggered Jill's last attempt to get Da to give me a beating. He refused.

The De La Salle Brothers were good at extracting money from parents and the local community through fetes and sponsored sporting events to improve the school facilities. Raffles were one of their regular fund-raisers. Brother Solomon had a soft spot for Belton so he was given the privileged position of junior coordinator of the new music block raffle, a favourite cause for Brother Solomon, a gifted amateur pianist and conductor of the school orchestra. This involved the distribution of books of raffle tickets to junior boys who volunteered to sell them to parents, relatives and friends.

Belton's raffle-ticket scam was simple but brilliant. Taking into account that no one was very interested in the surplus number of raffle tickets supplied by the printers because of the minimal extra cost in over-printing, he adjusted the quantity of tickets officially in circulation so that there were a small number whose serial numbers were unrecorded. He then offered these tickets above the official quota to a few susceptible juniors as an 'extra incentive' from which they could pocket half the proceeds provided they paid him the other half. Each of these select salesmen was told that it was a very exclusive arrangement and so assumed that he was the only person involved.

Belton was my Artful Dodger. He taught me how to persuade passengers on the *Broads Express* to Ipswich to shell out half a crown for a book of five raffle tickets in support of a new music block for the town's premier Catholic day school. Like most cons it had little to do with logic and a lot to do with deceptive charm, and I swiftly picked up Belton's gift of the gab.

'Good evening,' I would say politely, sliding open the compartment door of the train. 'I wonder if I might interest you in buying some raffle tickets for a very good cause?'

Attention would flicker unevenly among the jaded businessmen absorbed in their newspapers and the women who were more easily beguiled by a pert schoolboy in short trousers. I would respond quickly to the person with the warmest smile to make my pitch about the value of music in education and the sumptuous prizes on offer, ranging from a Pifco fully automatic coffee percolator and an Ilford Instamatic camera to a week's holiday in a cottage in Connemara or a VIP ticket to the Eastern Counties Agricultural Show.

After initial nerves I turned out to be a natural. I quickly got used to the negative responses of irritable tutting and newspaper-blank indifference – and became an expert with the waverers who felt that it was better to give something to a good cause rather than publicly dismiss it. My boyish charm helped and after a few days I was notching up sales of a dozen tickets a journey, earning Belton and me one and sixpence each. As my weekly pocket money was only a shilling – based on one-penny increments for each year of my age – this was serious wealth and far less stressful than pilfering from Da's wallet.

The scam lasted only three weeks. It would have stopped anyway by the date of the raffle but it ended abruptly because of a complaint to the school. Stupidly I had ignored that there were many regular passengers on the train. Although one raffle-ticket sales pitch from a small boy in school uniform might seem a daring initiative worth rewarding, two or three identical pitches were intrusive and irritating. I don't know who made the complaint, but as the name of the school was printed on the ticket it was easy enough to do. The result was a solemn summons for the two of us from Brother Solomon at Monday morning assembly.

Belton was skilful at getting us out of this hole. We had to hand over some of the money to show it had come from legal sales, but because of his nifty surplus of unauthorised tickets we were able to keep a good chunk of it. Although suspicious, Brother Solomon finally decided that, as we had shown initiative in selling as many tickets as possible, he could only criticise us for 'overstepping the mark'. Tickets were to be sold only to family and friends – and not to members of the public. It made the school seem greedy.

I felt huge relief that Brother Solomon did not tell Jill and Da. Not only would they have been horrified to hear one of their children had been hawking raffle tickets to total strangers on a train, but also, knowing my tendency to steal, they would have been highly suspicious about where the money had gone, and finally confronted me.

And where had the money gone? I certainly didn't hoard it and there was only so much I could spend on sweets and cigarettes. Within a couple of years I would start spending money on clothes, such as pointed shoes and having a new pair of baggy long trousers secretly tapered to a more fashionable width. But at the time my only major expense was going to the cinema – the next of my compulsive secret vices.

I had two subterfuges to get to the cinema. The first was the basic schoolboy trick of being 'off games'. Every Wednesday afternoon there was compulsory sport – football in winter and cricket in summer – and I hated both. Any absence had to be supported by a letter from a parent confirming illness. By a stroke of luck the first one that Jill had given me when I was genuinely recovering from flu wasn't dated and I used it several times before it was crumpled up by the games teacher and thrown in the bin.

I was also good at feigning illness on the day – growing pale and silent and pushing away my lunch, a ploy which lasted until, without warning, Brother Solomon wrote to Jill and Da expressing concern about my regular ill-health. But until that crisis I was able to use the afternoon hiatus to take a short bus ride from school to the Ipswich Buttermarket and disappear for two hours into the cinema.

1958 and 1959 were great years for big films. *South Pacific* was my first and I was swept away by the sun, sand, and weepy music of the Rodgers and Hammerstein enchanted love story. Other favourites were *The 39 Steps* with Kenneth More, and the Colonel Bogey whistling epic of stiff-upper-lip survival *The Bridge on the River Kwai*. I also saw my first cinema western, the John Wayne classic *Rio Bravo*. I loved them all and cherished the brief escapes from school and Strood House into an imaginary world of heroism and adventure.

These were easy to get into because they all had a U rating, which meant they were suitable for a twelve-year-old in school uniform skiving off games. But the film I desperately wanted to see was *Ben-Hur*, the epic story of childhood friendship between the Jewish Judah Ben-Hur and his Roman friend Messala torn apart by ethnic hatred. The breathlessly exciting and violent chariot race between the two of them at the end earned it an A rating, suitable only for children accompanied by an adult.

When I asked the old lady in the box office for a two-shilling ticket she explained why she couldn't sell me one. Behind me in the queue was a fatherly looking man who, overhearing the exchange, offered to help out by accompanying me into the film, which the old lady happily agreed to.

Feeling it impolite to say no thank you, I found myself sitting beside a total stranger in the stalls of a half-empty cinema. He was friendly enough and laughed when I told him that I had got off football by pretending to be ill. After the trailers and before the main film started he bought me an ice cream and told me about his son Tommy who was about my age and nuts about football; in return I told him the names of all my sisters. Nothing happened until at a tense moment in the film I felt his hand squeeze my knee; when I didn't protest it stayed there. A while later I felt his fingers gently stroking my thigh. When they moved up slightly towards my flies, I stood up quickly, stuttering that I had to go to the lavatory, and swiftly made for the exit, too scared to go back and so missing the final chariot race.

I had another ploy to get to the cinema – missing Scouts. All my sisters were enthusiastic Brownies and Guides so Jill and Da decided that after my pampered life at Nowton, it would toughen me up to become a Scout. The 1st Colchester Scout Troop met at an old drill hall near the bus station at seven o'clock on Monday evening and my routine was to drop into Da's North Hill surgery on the way back from the station for a sandwich supper in his waiting room, change into my Scout uniform and then, when Da had closed up the surgery, walk with him towards the bus station. Close to the drill hall was the Empire cinema which picked up the smaller new film releases and, as attendance at Scouts was pretty casual and no one checked up on absentees, it was easy for me to wave goodbye to Da as he went off to catch his bus and then duck back into the Empire.

I had liked the Scouts at first. It was difficult not to get caught up in the saluting, knot tests, sing-songs, and hearty enthusiasm of the overgrown schoolboys who ruled the troop. At first I joined in happily and turned up dutifully every week. But things changed that summer when I went to my first Scout camp.

We drove to Holkham Park in Norfolk in great excitement in the back of an old army lorry. Then something went wrong. Sleeping in tents, with campfires and sing-songs like at the Forest Schools Camp the year before and the new challenges of digging latrine trenches, carving cup racks and lashing together basin stands added to the fun. The problem was sex – not the sexual interference of homosexual Scoutmasters, but the hormonal, sweaty, rancid fug of adolescent masturbating boys cooped up under canvas. Our patrol leader was the cock of the roost – literally because he greatly enjoyed showing us how large his penis was and wanking into a billycan. It made me hanker for the innocent fun of kissing Anna's naked bottom and lying under the stars with Laura Long.

So I lost my enthusiasm for scouting and started to slip into the cinema instead of going to the drill hall. The Empire was a seedier place than the Ipswich Odeon and didn't pick up the big Oscar spectaculars. Instead of a foyer there was just a poky box office in a badly lit corridor running in from the street and a small sloping auditorium with rows of creaky old seats, scarred upholstery and the stale reek of tobacco. The old man with thick glasses in the box office must have been a bit blind or simply didn't care because at the Empire I had no problem getting into A-rated films on my own nor, on one occasion, an X-rated chiller *Peeping Tom*, the story of a film cameraman obsessed with filming terrified prostitutes as he murdered them, which scared the life out of me. I also saw good family entertainment at the Empire, like *Whistle Down the Wind, Carry on Teacher* and *Gigi*. My favourites were the B-movie 'Alfred Hitchcock Presents Edgar Wallace' series, with their spooky prelude of the bald

130

'Master of Suspense' slowly turning to face the camera, wreathed in a cloud of pipe smoke and solemnly announcing the film of the week.

It was my end-of-term report that finally blew the gaffe. The comment that it was a 'shame that ill health made Caradoc miss so many sporting activities' coincided with a blistering attack from my science teacher, Mr Prescott, who had been targeting me since the beginning of the year and whose low markings had on several occasions landed me with blue testimonials.

Mr Prescott was a grumpy old lay teacher who mumbled inaudibly and couldn't keep discipline. Our class was divided into the swots, who loved science, and the troublemakers who were happy mucking around with glass tubes, magnets and Bunsen burners but made no effort to learn anything. I must have been one of the worst in his class and Mr Prescott had taken a strong dislike to me. I reacted accordingly and, as I did with Jill, lived up to his expectations of my bad behaviour.

A sudden putrid eruption of noxious liquid from a boiling flask, caused by the wrong mix of ingredients, was the final straw. It was explosively funny and, after a moment of shocked silence, the class was in uproar. Mr Prescott failed to see the joke. His face went white then purple with fury as he shouted for silence and summoned me to the front of the class. Ignoring my pleas of innocence, he said it was an act of deliberate vandalism, my behaviour was despicable, I was an inherent troublemaker, and one of the worst boys it had been his misfortune to teach. My punishment was the maximum available – a headmaster's report, which meant a visit to the very tall and awesome Brother Elwyn, normally too grand to be involved in everyday school discipline and called in only for very serious offences that might involve a public beating by Brother Solomon, an interview with the parents or ultimately expulsion.

The next morning after morning prayers I reported trembling to the headmaster. His response was appropriately fearsome. Brother Solomon would carry out the beating on the following day and Brother Elwyn would write to my parents to give the gravest warning that my behaviour in the school, including regular absences from games and possible fiddling of raffle tickets, was deeply unsatisfactory. Any more serious misbehaviour would result in immediate expulsion.

I spent that night at home so pale with anxiety that Jill decided I must have caught a bug and should stay at home the following day. But I knew that I had to face the music, which would no doubt result in the exposure of all my sins of smoking, stealing and skiving off to see unsuitable films, so the next morning I announced that I was feeling better and went off to school – and had a rare lucky break.

Brother Solomon, with the wisdom of his namesake, had decided to look into the matter further and questioned Mr Prescott and other boys in the class. His conclusion, explained to me solemnly when I reported for my beating, was that Mr Prescott's instructions about what to mix in the flask had been at best ambiguous and possibly plain wrong.

I was exonerated, said Brother Solomon. No beating. No official warning letter to my parents.

'But, Caradoc,' he added solemnly. 'I hope you have already had a chat with them about what has happened.'

I shook my head.

'Well, I think you should because you have some problems. Not only are there Mr Prescott's complaints about you, but we've also had that odd business of the raffle tickets, and your regular absences from games.'

All I could do was nod and suppress a sudden surge of panic. What would happen if Brother Solomon had a friendly chat with

Jill and Da? When he told them about my problems at school they would tell him about my stealing and then no doubt they would check with the Scoutmaster and discover everything about my life of lies and deception.

'Is everything all right at home?'Brother Solomon asked gently.

I nodded again.

'Glad to hear it.'

He got up from his chair and came round his desk.

'Well, tell your parents about what happened with Mr Prescott. I am sure it was a nasty shock and it's always best to share problems with them,'he said, gently squeezing my shoulder. 'Don't bottle things up, Caradoc.'

This crisis led to a surprising emotional upheaval.

I doubt if anyone really believed that I had a vocation, but by Easter of my second year at St Joseph's, just fifteen months after my baptism, I joined the chosen few whose names would be put forward as candidates for the De La Salle Junior Novitiate attached to St Peter's School, Southbourne.

My new religious fervour resulted from a mixture of ritual fever, guilt and loneliness. My first Christmas Midnight Mass had been a turning point. After the eight-mile bike ride with Jill and my sisters through a frosty star-filled night to our parish church in Colchester, I was entranced by the singing, the swirling incense, glittering vestments, the sense of exultation and belonging. Early in the New Year I volunteered as an altar boy and each Sunday, in red cassock and white alb, I processed down the aisle, and attended the priest, rinsing fingers, offering a towel, turning the pages of the missal, moving gravely around the altar bowing and genuflecting. Religion had got hold of me.

Jill's response was clearly one of relief, which she showed by new warmth and friendliness. The thieving cuckoo in the King family nest could be transferred to the nest of holy mother church. My departure to the De La Salle Junior Novitiate the following September would take me away from Strood House for long periods and once again shift the responsibility for my problems to someone else.

There was another reason for this change – an intense new friendship.

John Ashdown wasn't an older boy and school hero like Badger. He was a quiet, round-faced average member of my class and a month younger than me, who shared my dislike of games. The friendship wasn't physical and it may have been intensely one-sided, but during my second summer term we spent as much time as possible together, and when we weren't together I thought about him most of the time. I have tender memories of sprawling with him in the outfield watching cricket matches, not talking much, but feeling intensely happy.

This happiness sublimated religious devotion. By the end of that term I was quite certain that I should become a junior novice even though it would mean leaving St Joseph's and my new best friend. However, first I had to be approved by the De La Salle Brothers as a suitable candidate.

Brother Trevor was the De La Salle recruiting officer. Based at the Senior Novitiate at Dogmersfield, a small stately home in Hampshire, he scouted around the different De La Salle schools, following up leads on likely novices. He was friendly and enthusiastic and drove a green Vauxhall Velox with the dubious registration number of JOY 10. I first met him at the end of the Easter term when he spent a couple of days at St Joseph's and I volunteered for one of his seminars on the Brotherhood's worldwide mission. On his last day he offered me a lift back to Colchester and on the way took me out to tea. His technique was informal but effective. He mixed stories about jolly life at Dogmersfield with simple questions about my family, my work as an altar boy and how much praying I did. By the time he had got to the question, over chocolate cake, of whether I had ever thought of joining the Brotherhood I was under his spell.

The second stage of Brother Trevor's assessment was a visit to Strood House one Saturday afternoon. Jill showed him round the house and garden and was unusually enthusiastic, particularly when Brother Trevor said he knew Father Michael through a Catholic charity they were both involved with. After tea he chatted amiably to my sisters about their new convent school, Hengrave Hall, whose Reverend Mother he also seemed to know, and even crouched on the floor to help Quentin with his brick-building. After tea Brother Trevor, Jill and Da went into the music room for a quiet chat. I don't know what they discussed and whether Jill and Da told him about my stealing but after a while they all came out looking pleased. Brother Trevor gave me a cheerful pat on the back and said that although it was of course up to me and no one should try to influence my decision, he hoped very much that he would see me next term at St Peter's.

Jill seemed keen to discuss my plans and began to drop into my room at bedtime for little chats, mostly about religion – the joy of having faith, papal dogma, purgatory and the afterlife. It was slightly weird. Although she didn't actually say it, I knew she was trying to persuade me to join the novitiate. I liked the special attention and the sense that Jill was, for the first time, treating me like an adult rather than a delinquent child, but I felt disconcerted by her enthusiasm. I picked up echoes of Brother Trevor and Father Michael in what she was saying. I also knew that she wanted to send me away again.

Surprisingly it was Da, the staunch atheist, who most influenced my decision. In June the Religious Orders of Great Britain held a Vocations Exhibition in Manchester which Brother Trevor suggested I should visit to ensure that I was making the right choice in opting for the Brotherhood. I am not sure why Da was chosen to take me – perhaps because Jill would have found a day in my company difficult and Da shared my passion for train journeys.

It was a memorable day. We caught an early bus to Colchester, a train to London, then a tube ride from Liverpool Street to St Pancras to catch the 11.30 Manchester express, on which Da had reserved seats in the restaurant car for lunch as we sped northwards. I had never eaten in a restaurant car before and lunch was a serious business with a three-course fixed menu for 7/6d – asparagus soup, roast chicken and apple tart and ice cream – served by a waiter with white gloves who referred to me as 'the young gentleman'.

The exhibition was daunting. It took place in a vast hall full of separate stands for about fifty different religious orders. The 1960s would be the heyday of the Catholic Church and the competition for novices was strong. Monks, nuns and priests in a bewildering range of habits, wimples and soutanes manned their stands with eager smiles, enthusing about their order to apprehensive aspirants and their parents. We drifted between Franciscans, Dominicans, Benedictines and Carthusians, shaking hands and collecting pamphlets. Then at last we reached the De La Salle stand, the largest in the exhibition, reflecting its status as the largest Catholic teaching order in Britain, with almost four hundred brothers running forty different schools and communities. An effervescent Brother Trevor greeted us like old friends, gave us tea and biscuits, and introduced us to the other beaming Brothers. I felt we were coming home and this was a new family I wanted to belong to.

What clinched it was my conversation with Da on the train home. I was expecting a pork-pie supper bought at the station but Da, out of Jill's reach, decided that we both deserved an extra treat and booked us into the restaurant car again. Dinner was magic, the twilit countryside fading into dark, the light of our table lamp reflected in the window. The soup was the same as at lunch but on the dinner menu renamed 'crème d'asperge' followed by a grilled entrecôte steak, which I had never eaten before. I drank ginger beer but Da, who normally drank just an Adnams ale on Sunday, ordered a half-bottle of red wine.

It wasn't until the last course that he raised the question.

'So what do you think, Caradoc?'

I looked up from my ice cream.

'About what?'

'Going to the novitiate,' he said, slicing a piece of cheese onto a biscuit. 'Good plan?'

'I think so.'

'But what do you feel? Do you really want to ... devote your life to ...'

'God?' I said.

He nodded.

'Yes, I think so.'

'Good.'

He smiled and sipped his wine. I sensed his uncertainty.

'But what do *you* think?'

'How do you mean?'

'About whether I should go. You don't believe in God, do you?'

He frowned at the blunt question.

'No. But that's my loss. I am happy that you, Jill and the girls have found faith. Maybe I envy you a bit.'

'So you think I should go?'

He nodded.

'Absolutely. If that's how you feel it would be a shame not to.' He hesitated. 'Jill and I would be proud of you.'

Then he smiled across the table, and I smiled back, moved by his gentle voice and the kindness in his eyes. But I could tell he wasn't telling the truth.

The trip to the Vocations Exhibition was magical but deceptive. Da never believed in God and, maybe influenced by Father Michael's spiritual cuckoldry, thought organised religion was nonsense. But he had a religious wife whom he adored, which was why he happily connived at the subterfuge of my vocation. His lie to me at dinner on the train finally made up my mind. I sensed he was trying to protect me. He didn't believe in my vocation but he knew that Jill's wish had to be obeyed and to prevent total breakdown of his relationship with her, I had to go back to boarding school.

IX

My vocation didn't last long. I stayed at the Junior Novitiate, known as the Lodge, for just one year and a term before the rector, Brother Laurence Anthony, requested that Jill and Da remove me. There was no great shame in this polite expulsion because many were called but few were chosen, particularly among the thirteen- and fourteen-year-old aspirants. The Lodge was bursting at the seams, and in the year I joined there was the highest number ever, with seventy boys and half a dozen resident Brothers crammed into a family-sized Victorian villa.

There was also a question of money. So determined were the De La Salles to boost their numbers that the Lodge offered free education and boarding to all junior novices which, as the official history of St Peter's wryly records, led 'in a world far from perfect' to some abuse of this privilege by parents whose boys 'would be sent to the Lodge purely to obtain free private schooling'. So perhaps economy influenced Jill and Da's enthusiasm for my vocation. They were already paying boarding school fees for four other children and my abrupt departure from the Lodge certainly added to their financial problems.

I was a lonely, oddball novice and I don't remember the name of any boy at the Lodge, a self-contained boarding house next door to the main school. My one friend was a St Peter's boarder called Alan Marston, in the same year but several months younger than me, on whom I had a major crush. For me falling in love seemed easier than just making friends.

Life at the Lodge wasn't hard after the rigours of Strood House, but too full of religion. Each morning started at seven with mass in the school chapel. After breakfast and morning chores of washing up, bathroom and dormitory cleaning – to encourage humility and as an economy to offset the missing school fees – we would go to the main school for class. We wore exactly the same uniform as everyone else, but Lodge boys were supposed to be a bit different, more hard-working, better behaved, glowing with inner faith as they dutifully prepared for the religious life.

After lunch, which we had separately at the Lodge, there were prayers and Bible-reading and although we could mingle with the other St Peter's boys during break, as soon as afternoon school was over we were segregated again from the 'lay boys' and returned to the Lodge for homework and novice instruction in the Study Room. There was a final trip to the Lodge chapel for prayers and rosary before bedtime.

The Lodge food was quite good – particularly the fish and chips on Friday – and varied, with ice cream and Corona to mark special saint's days, birthdays and holy days of obligation. There were also television privileges, easily withdrawn, to watch favourites like *Hancock's Half Hour* and *Wagon Train* and occasionally the big treat of a Saturday-night feature film, preferably an old Hitchcock, of which the reverend brothers seemed very fond.

In one respect life was easier for Lodge boys than for the school boarders. At St Peter's Brother Ives, the deputy head, was in charge of discipline and applied it with old-fashioned military precision, which included exact dormitory layouts of symmetrically perfect beds and lockers so that the morning procedure of washing, dressing and bed-making could be achieved in six minutes flat. He also carried a cane in the inner pocket of his habit which he took pleasure in slowly exposing in front of scared boys before administering it or using it to whack the table to emphasise an angry reprimand. But the disciplining of Lodge boys was the responsibility of its more benign and quietly impressive rector. Lateness, disobedience or talking after lights out were the general limits of bad behaviour, usually dealt with by a serious chat.

As good little novices we were encouraged to discipline ourselves and keep free of guilt through prayer and regular confession. This more pious approach worked well for me at first. Although my stealing continued during the holidays, at the Lodge I tried hard to be a model of piety and good behaviour. Only in my second year, when I began to feel that I was play-acting the role of junior novice, did I get into the serious trouble, which led to my expulsion.

My first two terms at the Lodge were grim. Winter closed in quickly that year and I was entrapped by the harsh and muddy routine of compulsory twice-weekly games. Wednesday was football, at which I was useless, but as a boarder I had no opportunity to skive off to the cinema. Saturday afternoon was worse – either the traditional weekly cross-country run around Hengistbury Head or, if the weather was exceptionally bad, compulsory gym.

I am not sure which I hated most. The run was a three-mile race for boarders and Lodge boys along the promenade in front of the beach huts then up onto a dirt track across scrubland, up a grassy hill overlooking the sea known as the Head, round the top and then down through another track which wound back to the school playing fields. This was supervised by the new gym and sports teacher, Sydney Moore, ex-Parachute Regiment, winner of the Military Cross, plus two Brothers, one from the school and one from the Lodge, who kept staging posts en route to count the boys and time-keep. The general idea was to improve your personal time each week, a matter of pride and honour for Lodge boys, who had an extra spiritual target of combining fitness of body and soul. I was a good runner but had a flawed inner spirit, and each week would drive myself to frozen, muddy exhaustion trying to do better.

Gym could have been worse. Like most small boys I hated vaulting over the horse, a humiliating process usually ending with a clamber up the side or falling off the top. I was also useless at rope-climbing. But Mr Moore was a patient instructor. Despite a brisk military manner and passionate enthusiasm for physical fitness, he was a witty and good-natured man, sympathetic to weedy, nervous boys and keen to get the best out of us. My gritty performance on the weekly cross-country run had caught his eye and he gave me special attention so that by half-term I had mastered the horse-jumping and was also an accomplished pole climber which, he said, was the first step to climbing ropes. Mr Moore was also very good at encouraging personal motivation. 'It doesn't matter about being better than others, just better inside yourself' was one of his dictums, which I have observed throughout my generally unsporting life.

Then suddenly Mr Moore died during gym. He collapsed in front of a class of fifth formers and, as we were told at assembly the next morning, went out like a light. He was a heavy smoker but his sudden death without apparent cause seemed incomprehensible. The school was in shock.

Mr Moore's death upset me even more than Commander Child's at Nowton, although I had only known him a few weeks. He had been kind and his enthusiasm had drawn me out. Brother Laurence's talk to us all that night about God's wisdom, which we had to accept even though we couldn't always understand it, didn't make sense. Mr Moore's death by any reckoning was a cruel mistake.

The funeral at St Xavier's in Boscombe, a full requiem mass sung by the St Peter's choir and the special guest appearance of a professional soprano, was attended by the whole school. It was terribly sad, the flower-covered coffin on a bier in front of the altar, his widow and small children in the front row and two old wartime comrades paying tributes to his exceptional bravery and modesty. The Bishop of Portsmouth led the proceedings, assisted by Father Pierre the school chaplain, and gave a sermon about heavenly rewards which was as unconvincing as Brother Laurence's reassurances about God's wisdom.

Mr Moore's death and funeral planted my first serious doubts about having a vocation. Then, towards the end of the Easter term, thanks to Alan Marston and warmer weather, my gloom lifted.

Much older, I found that falling in love can often relate to depression. The sudden concentration of intense feeling, especially if heightened by the secrecy and excitement of an affair, is a reaction to loneliness and feelings of despair. My crush on Marston wasn't explicitly sexual, but it was certainly triggered by depression. I felt awkward and unwanted at home, at least by Jill, and at school trapped in a role-playing fantasy that I wanted to give my life to God.

Alan was a St Peter's boarder and we got to know each other through roller-skating. During the Easter holidays the school playground and the slope to it from the classroom block had been resurfaced and that summer term roller-skating was the craze. Luckily Aunty Molly had given me a pair of skates as a Christmas present and during the holidays I had been practising strenuously up and down the Strood causeway. When term started, with its long evening break times, roller-skating was the only thing I wanted to do, racing the slope, skating backwards, crossing skates, jumping, spinning and trying to impress Alan, like a male bird strutting his plumage.

He was just an ordinary boy with freckled skin and spiky hair; there was nothing very exceptional about him. But within a couple of weeks my crush on Alan gripped me like a fever. He was always on my mind and the amount of time I could spend with him each day was the measure of my happiness. I am sure he never felt the same about me but that was part of the attraction and challenge.

Although friendships between school and Lodge boys were generally discouraged, Brother Laurence must have been pleased that I had at last made a friend and had generally cheered up. To compensate for Jill and Da's firm decision that I should stay at the Lodge for the half-term weekend instead of going home, I was allowed an exeat to visit Alan's parents.

I have warm memories of the visit. Other boys' parents tended to be important in my friendships and the Marstons were no exception, a warm and friendly couple who owned a hotel in Lymington. As a special treat we were given lunch in the hotel dining room, served by a waiter and waitress in black uniforms who treated Alan like a young prince. In the afternoon Alan's father took us out on the Solent in the family motor cruiser which had two cabins and a shower.

144

Sadly this close friendship didn't last that summer term. My one-sided passion was one reason but near the end of term something happened, which would be the beginning of the end of my time at the Lodge.

The Charity Walk was a project started by Mr Moore – a sponsored road walk in support of a local charity for handicapped children. The target was to walk as many miles as possible on a circular route between Southbourne and Wimborne Minster. It was open to thirty St Peter's and Lodge boys, chosen for their sporting skills and toughness. Although I was generally unsporting, my performance at cross-country had earned me a place in the Lodge team. Alan, who played football for the school Colts, was also chosen for the Boarding House junior team.

The organisation of a thirty-five-mile road walk for teenage children was haphazard by modern standards, just a Brother with clipboard and camping chair waiting at intervals to log the mileage and two minibuses circling the route to collect exhausted boys. But the day of the Charity Walk was warm and dry. There was huge excitement as the thirty contenders, after a photo call with the *Bournemouth Echo*, set off down St Catherine's Road in plimsolls and gym clothes, with the school band playing and boys cheering.

Thanks to hours of roller-skating my leg muscles were strong. The first eight miles were along the seafront through Bournemouth with bystanders shouting encouragement as we passed. I was one of the leaders, soon ahead of the other four boys in the Lodge junior team. But two hours later, after Poole, the weather changed, the rain came down and I got a blister. By the time I passed the Broadstone staging point I was wet through.

The car was a convertible Zephyr like Uncle Dickie's, which

was the reason it caught my eye when it pulled up ahead of me. The driver, who reached across to unwind the passenger side window, was a smartly dressed man about Da's age.

'Want a lift?' he asked cheerfully.

Of course I didn't. Brother Laurence had made it absolutely clear that accepting a lift meant automatic disqualification from the run. So why did I say yes? Because I was wet and miserable and would have to trudge along the road or wait by the kerb for twenty minutes before the next school minibus. Maybe because the road was empty, no one could see me and adding some illegal extra miles undetected was a simple way to increase my sponsorship money.

I knew that I'd made a mistake. My sense of shame was immediate. So was the reminder of the man in the cinema, as the driver smoothly asked me questions about myself, checked where I was going to and made a joke about my squelchy gym shoes wetting the floor of his car.

We drove for about four miles towards Wimborne. The man chatted cheerfully, telling me he was a traveller for a toiletry firm and had two children of about my age. He laughed when I hunched down in the seat as we passed a line of walkers in the senior team trudging through the rain and another group huddling under a tree waiting for the minibus and said that he knew very well what small boys got up to.

He only got nasty when we had reached an empty stretch of road and I asked him suddenly to stop so I could get out.

'But I thought you said you were going to Southbourne?'

'Um, yes,' I said, feeling immediately anxious at the change of tone in his voice. 'But I shouldn't be taking a lift. I have to start walking again.'

'Ah, I get it. Never take lifts from a stranger, eh? Think you're going to get into trouble?'

'Not really.'

'Do you think I'm some kind of pervert then?'

'No, of course not.'

'Well, then.'

He looked at the road ahead and went on driving.

'Please stop,' I said again.

And then he did, sharply braking the car and pulling into the verge. I opened the door and said thank you very much and quickly clambered out. As I was about to shut the door he leaned across.

'Go carefully, young man, and good luck, because one of these days you might just get into real trouble.'

I had escaped, but it wasn't as simple as that. I was now five miles ahead of where I had walked to, but I couldn't claim that extra distance. If I did the group of senior boys that I'd passed in the car would quickly realise how odd it was that one moment I was behind them and an hour later I had mysteriously over-taken them without being seen. All I could do was hide off the road, wait for as long as it would have taken me to walk the five miles and for the other boys to pass me and then reappear to catch the next minibus.

For a short time I was a hero. When the individual distances were announced that evening, it turned out that I had walked much further than any of the junior walkers and everyone con-gratulated me. But the moment of glory didn't last long. One of the senior boarders I had passed in the Zephyr must have raised the question with Brother Ralph. How had I managed to be walking so close behind them? They had passed me several miles earlier clearly walking much faster than me. But I had ended my walk only a few minutes behind them – just about possible but somehow unlikely.

Brother Ralph must have mentioned this to Brother Laurence.

At supper he had tapped his glass and said how pleased he was with the Lodge's performance that day in the Charity Walk and made a special mention of me as the star performer. But later after prayers he called me in for 'a word' to repeat his praise, and add that there had been some surprise expressed by the St Peter's organisers about how well I had done given my age.

'Someone asked me whether it was possible you had accepted a lift, Caradoc?' he said with a quizzical smile, indicating that he couldn't quite believe that, but he expected me to answer.

I shook my head.

'No, I didn't. It would have been against the rules.'

He nodded slowly as if expecting me to add something. But I couldn't. I hated lying but now I had to stick to it.

'Good boy,' said Brother Laurence finally. 'And now to bed. It's been a long day and you must be exhausted. God bless ... and don't forget to say your prayers.'

To Alan, I couldn't lie. He was my best friend and had also been one of the walkers. The next morning after mass we had a roller-skating session, and he asked me bluntly.

'Is it true then? That you took a lift?'

I told him the truth, that it had been an accident, that I had had no intention of taking a lift, but once the man who stopped had asked me if I wanted one and I'd said yes, there was no way I could have got out of it. I also told him, because I couldn't bear the look of doubt on his face, that the man had been a bit weird and how I had told him to stop and let me out.

Alan listened solemnly. I didn't dare ask him, but finally he said it.

'OK. I won't tell anyone. But ...' He frowned, as if uncertain what else to say. Then, shaking his head and in a grown-up sad sort of way, he just said, 'I wish you hadn't.'

Those words I think dissolved our friendship. The term ended a week later and although Alan's parents were very friendly when they came to pick him up and suggested I might come to stay during the holiday no invitation followed.

It was hot that summer, but I felt under a cloud. Father Michael stayed at Strood House for a couple of weeks and I guessed from the silence when I interrupted him and Jill talking privately in the music room that my future was once more under discussion. It had to do with my end-of-term report from St Peter's. I was allowed to read the extracts on my school work and most of it seemed quite good; generally that I was a bright boy doing well but could work harder. What I wasn't shown was Brother Laurence's confidential end-of-year report about my spiritual welfare which came in a separate envelope and was the parents' responsibility to discuss with their novice child.

Jill and Da had given up having personal chats with me so it was left to Jill's resident spiritual advisor to have a quiet word, although I don't remember it going further than a walk along the sea wall with Michael asking how it was going, me saying fine, and him telling me that the spiritual life was hard work and needed time, patience and self-discipline.

I am sure that Brother Laurence's report was a warning that my future as a novice didn't look promising. No doubt it included a reference to the Charity Walk incident and my tendency to lie. But he must have been prepared to give me a chance because there would be another term before I was asked to leave. It was also clear that Jill and Michael were determined that I shouldn't give up. There is a disturbing picture in the album taken that summer, of me dressed in a surplice and holding a missal. The underlying message was clear: the religious life would be my salvation.

Junior novice.

My last term at the novitiate was the lowest point of my childhood. I returned to the Lodge fearful that I faced both gossip
about my behaviour in the Charity Walk and, worse, the loss of
my one close friend. As it turned out no one, apart from Brother
Laurence, seemed to remember the hint of scandal from the
previous summer. It was a new academic year and after a long
summer holiday everyone was thinking about the term ahead.
But the loss of Alan Marston was painful and made life seem
empty.

There was nothing deliberately cruel about his withdrawal of friendship. Alan was a kind-hearted boy. It just ended. For a while we still roller-skated together but now as part of a group. We no longer had much to say to each other. The shared jokes and the simple delight in each other's company were over and because Alan was lively and popular it was apparent that he had new and better friends than me. I tried hard to shrug it off, but the loss made me miserable.

On the rebound, and probably just to show I didn't care, I made friends with a day boy called Keith Baines in the year above, who had hovered on the edge of the summer roller-skating crowd. The friendship didn't progress very far – some energetic table-tennis as the colder weather drove us off the playground and slouching around the recreation hall where a new coffee-making machine had been installed – but it led to the terminal act of misbehaviour and my removal from the Lodge at the end of term.

The one passion we shared was cinema: our first conversation had been about *The Bridge on the River Kwai*. Baines had over-heard me telling Alan, who hadn't seen it, that Alec Guinness played the main character 'Colonel Warden', and corrected me. I had the name wrong, Guinness had played Colonel Nicholson and Jack Hawkins had played Major Warden. We got to talking about other films we had both seen and it turned out that Baines was a film buff, with an encyclopaedic memory for detail.

Baines lived in nearby Boscombe and, as a day boy and the only child of dedicated ballroom dancers, was able to go to the cinema at least once a week, a privilege also allowed to senior borders but not to Lodge boys whose minds were supposed to be fixed on spiritual things. Each Monday Baines would describe in detail what he had seen over the weekend, which for me, lonely and missing Alan, rekindled my old passion for the flick-ering smoky half-light and the thrills of *The Alamo* and *Exodus*.

151

One of the major releases of the year had been *The Guns of Navarone*, an epic wartime adventure, which Baines had missed because of an outbreak of measles. When he told me that one of the smaller local cinemas was bringing it back for a special Sunday screening, temptation was too strong to resist. Sunday afternoon was recreation time and Lodge boys could go for walks. The screening started at 2.30 and lasted two and a half hours so there would be just enough time for me to get back to the Lodge in time for supper at 5.30.

Everything went almost according to plan. I arrived a little late but Baines had kept me a seat at the back of the stalls. The film was one of the most exciting I had ever seen and, thanks to Baines's generous pocket money, we stuffed ourselves with popcorn and ice cream as the motley crew of allied partisans led by Anthonys Quinn and Quayle and Gregory Peck sneaked across the Aegean under moonlight to attack the impregnable Nazi fort of Navarone.

All would have been well if the bus had come at a quarter to five as it was supposed to. A ten-minute ride from Boscombe to Southbourne would have got me back in time for supper and the hope that, in the dark, no one had noticed I had been missing. But the bus didn't come, and after twenty minutes of waiting it was clear that I wouldn't get back in time.

Baines, who had loyally stayed with me, had a bright idea.

'Why don't I give you a lift on the back of the bike? It's not far.'

There wasn't much choice. Someone in the queue had telephoned. The bus had broken down and because it was Sunday there was no alternative driver for a replacement.

All could still have been well. We set off in fine form, me sitting on the saddle and Baines vigorously riding the pedals. It was simply bad luck that the battery in Baines's back light was flat and that a policeman patrolling on his Velocette was waiting at the traffic lights at the junction with Southbourne Road just as we passed in front of him.

He sounded friendly and firm when he overtook and stopped us with his little blue flashing light.

'Well, boys, you're breaking the law twice over. Two on a bike and no back light.'

We apologised profusely, explaining that we were in a terrible hurry and hadn't realised that the back light was no longer working.

But he must have been in a mean mood because he nodded and said mournfully, 'Sorry, boys, but I'm going to have to book you. Too many kids today think they can get away with breaking the law with some footling excuse. What are your names and addresses?'

And that was it. The end of my life as a novice. I got back just in time after running hard the last two miles and was the last in the refectory queue. The Brother in charge merely raised his eyebrows when I explained my flushed appearance, saying I had been playing table-tennis. But after lunch the following day I received the summons to Brother Laurence's study and this time it was clear that I was in big trouble.

'I had a telephone call this morning, Caradoc, from the Boscombe police station. They told me that you were apprehended yesterday evening at a quarter to five with Keith Baines riding two on a bicycle without a back light. Can this be true?'

I nodded, looking at the floor.

'And may I ask what you and Baines were doing riding illegally through Boscombe yesterday evening?'

For once my flair for lying failed me. I knew that Brother Laurence hadn't believed my denial of having taken a lift during the Charity Walk. There seemed no option but to tell the truth.

'We had been to the cinema.'

'To the cinema?' Brother Laurence sounded shocked. 'But you know that's strictly forbidden for Lodge boys.'

I nodded again.

'And what did you see?'

'*The Guns of Navarone.*'

A moment's heavy silence, then swift execution.

'Well, Caradoc, I'm sorry to say this because you seem a good-natured boy and I know you have problems at home – but for some time I have had serious doubts about your vocation and general behaviour. You seem bored and somehow disconnected from the rest of the Lodge community. Do you really want to be a De La Salle Brother?'

This time I hesitated but only for a second, then shook my head.

'I don't think so.'

'Nor do I,' said Brother Laurence, 'and nor can I accept your deliberate flouting of Lodge rules, as well as the shame you bring upon the novitiate by breaking the law. Do you realise that you and Baines have been charged with a criminal offence and will have to appear in the juvenile court?'

I hadn't.

'I telephoned your mother this morning and told her what has been going on.' He paused. 'I have asked your parents to remove you from the Lodge at the end of the term. You can call her on my phone when we have finished this meeting.'

I was now close to tears. The horror of having to speak to Jill and Da about my bad behaviour appalled me. I remembered Jill's chill silence when I ran away from Nowton. Expulsion was infinitely worse – a punishment for mortal sin.

Brother Laurence, embarrassed by my tearfulness, started talking about how important and courageous it was to face one's shortcomings honestly. Many boys turned out to be unsuited to the religious life, and God would certainly not hold it against me. But at that moment it seemed like the end of the world.

It wasn't – quite. Brother Laurence was skilled at sorting out the chaff from the wheat, and I was one of three boys who left the Lodge that term. There was no stigma in leaving, just a little envy and the warm good wishes from the boys left behind and the promise of prayers from the Brothers.

At home though it was very different. Although I was relieved to leave the novitiate, and Jill couldn't criticise me for losing my vocation, I was clearly in disgrace. Jill and Da had the urgent problem of finding me a new school in the middle of the academic year. It was now December. I had O levels in June so it was vital that I should be back at school for the January term. Fortunately Father Michael was again on hand to help out by calling in favours with his contacts in the Catholic hierarchy. However, his first choice was a dud.

Laxton was a small and seedy Dominican public school that has long since closed down. The headmaster, Father Thomas, had insisted that we visit the school before the end of term, so on 17 December, the day after my return from Southbourne and two days before my fifteenth birthday, Jill and Da borrowed Alan Maskell's van and the three of us drove the ninety-odd miles to Northamptonshire. The visit didn't go well.

Our meetings were separate. Jill and Da went off for a chat with Father Thomas and I was sent with a sixth former on a tour of the school. There was an end-of-term atmosphere of excitement and mild chaos with boys running in and out of classrooms and masters shouting for attention. My round tour ended up in the sixth-form classroom where my guide and his friends, after interrogating me about St Peter's and why I was leaving in the middle of the year, offered me a cigarette, which I didn't accept because I was scared that Jill and Da would smell it.

As soon as I returned to Father Thomas's study, I knew that I wasn't being offered a place. The three of them were polite and friendly, but Father Thomas's goodbye and good luck to me gave no sign that he was expecting to see me again. On the way back to Strood House in the van Jill told me there wasn't a vacancy at Laxton at present. This struck me as odd. Why had we driven all that way if there was no place available? It wasn't until two years later that I found out why the vacant place at Laxton had disappeared so quickly.

Christmas that year wasn't very happy. Jill didn't try to conceal her disappointment. Her plan for the De La Salle Brothers to be my salvation and take me off her hands had failed. The last thing she wanted was to have her callow adolescent and adopted son living at home.

It is easy, because of what happened later, to exaggerate Jill's callous indifference towards me, and her failings as a parent. But a swift look at the photograph album is enough to remind me of how difficult and unlovable I must have been. There are pictures of me on a family picnic at West Mersea, sitting with Father Michael, playing trains with Quentin, which trigger memories of a lanky, sullen, awkward and troublesome adolescent; silent, unapproachable, and spending as much time as possible in his bedroom.

The only solution to the Caradoc problem was another boarding school and this time happily, like Nowton, the choice was good. I don't remember exactly how it happened, probably again with Father Michael's help, but just after Christmas, without even a preliminary visit or interview, I was offered a place at Belmont Abbey, a small Benedictine public school near Hereford, to start in early January. There was no time to buy the full uniform from Selfridges but in any case most of it was transferable from the Lodge uniform. My house tie arrived by post direct from the school the day before Da deposited me at Paddington Station to catch the afternoon school train to Hereford.

On my last night at home, and for the first time in months, I tried to steal some money to fund my perilous journey into a new world. But this time there was nothing to steal. Jill's bureau in the living room was locked and on Da's dressing table there was no sign of his wallet or even loose change. At last, though the silence continued, temptation had been removed and my thieving career was over. Very soon my childhood and membership of the King family would be as well.

FOUR

A Glass of Red Wine

X

I was a bit of a snob as a teenager. I would lie that Da was a doctor instead of a dentist because it seemed more impressive. I also hankered to go to a smart public school, a snobbish aspiration perfectly conveyed in Denholm Elliott's put-down to Alan Bates in the 1964 comedy gem *Nothing But the Best*. The upstart working-class Bates wants to marry the boss's daughter and asks the superbly supercilious Elliott, his upper-class colleague at the family bank:

'Didn't we go to school together?'

'Which school?' says Elliott wincing slightly.

'Um ... Repton, actually.'

'Oh' – a pause – 'I don't think so.'

Snobbery was normal for prep school boys and I had been infected at Nowton. The Roll of Honour in the hall eloquently conveyed the hierarchy of premier-division schools – Eton, Harrow and Winchester (Neville's); second-division schools – Charterhouse (Charles's) and Radley; and third-division East Anglian schools for the majority of Nowton boys – Felsted,

161

Gresham's and King's Ely. For me at least the snobbery was induced by real loss: the dishonour of taking the eleven-plus instead of Common Entrance, and the summary dispatch from Nowton to a Catholic day grammar school no one had heard of. So the move now to Belmont Abbey, a real public school, was an exciting if intimidating prospect.

My first Belmont encounter matched my expectations. Da and I arrived at Paddington in good time for the 2.15 p.m. Hereford train. A tall, good-looking young man with a furled umbrella and embroidered waistcoat detached himself from a group of chattering boys in Belmont uniform and introduced himself with a long double-barrelled name. There were several reserved compartments allocated to different age groups and Mr Taniewski-Elliott ushered us to a fifth-form compartment where, after lifting my overnight case onto the luggage rack, Da shook my hand, then gave me a quick hug before hurrying off the train.

Although first into the compartment, I was too nervous to bag a window seat, so settled into a corner corridor seat and took out a book. Soon the compartment filled with noisy boys greeting each other loudly and exchanging holiday gossip. At first no one paid any attention to me and it wasn't until the train had left the station and everyone had settled down that a dark-haired boy leaned across and asked, 'And who are you?'

'Caradoc King.'

'Cadarock?' another boy said to immediate laughter. 'That's a funny name. Where are you from?'

I told them that it was a Welsh name but I came from Essex. Then came the next question.

'So, why are you coming to Belmont in the fifth form? Where were you before?'

I answered almost truthfully, that I had been at a De La Salle novitiate but had been expelled because I didn't have a vocation, information which was met with shrugs and frowns but clearly wasn't of much interest to my new fellow fifth formers. They quickly switched to their own conversations, leaving me to read my book and watch the thickening afternoon through the windows.

At Reading the elegant Mr Taniewski-Elliott returned, with another man, thickset and less good-looking but also wearing an embroidered waistcoat. The fifth formers cheekily greeted the two men with compliments about their clothes, but shut up when Taniewski-Elliott spoke to me.

'Are you all right, King? Are these ruffians being friendly?'

'Yes thanks, sir.'

The other boys laughed and Taniewski-Elliott smiled.

'Not "sir", King. Elliott is fine. "Sir" is just for members of staff, except of course the Belmont monks whom you should address as Father.'

'Yes, sir ... I mean um, Elliott.'

More laughter then the other boys were butting in with questions about rugby teams, house prefects and something called CCF and whether we could go to the buffet car.

When Elliott and his friend had moved on to the next carriage and several boys had gone off to buy refreshments, I asked the boy opposite me, who looked quite friendly, whether Elliott was the head boy. Clearly the fifth formers, despite the cheek, were in awe of him.

'No, just a house captain and school prefect, but he doesn't half fancy himself.'

'Are the waistcoats part of school uniform?'

'No, they'll have to take them off before we get to school, but Elliott's a bit of a toff, likes to think Belmont is like Eton and that he's in Pop.'

I laughed. I knew all about Eton and its exclusive society, Pop. At Nowton an ex-head boy who had gone on to be an Eton King's Scholar, as inscribed on the Roll of Honour, had come back to lunch in my last year and Charles had embarrassingly asked him to tell us what the school was like. I rather shared Elliott's envy.

'And who was his friend?'

'Baggott. He's the rugby captain and a bit of a bastard.'

The boy, who introduced himself as Butler, went on to tell me a little more about the school; that in addition to my own house, Cantilupe, there were two other school houses: Kemble, to which he belonged, and Vaughan, all named after Catholic martyrs. He said the new headmaster, Father Roger, was OK, that his housemaster, Father Aelred, was a sadist and that the best master in the school was a man called Jenkins.

It was dark and very cold when we arrived. All I could see was the outline of ancient buildings lit up by moonlight, and feel underfoot the slip and crunch of rutted snow. Inside was a hubbub of loud voices and hurrying boys clutching suitcases and games gear. Butler showed me the boot room and found my peg and locker then a bell rang and I followed the crowd into a large panelled dining room with long trestle tables where some boy asked what house I was in and pointed me to one of the Cantilupe tables. A monk said grace and welcomed us back for the new term and then we tucked in to a supper of cold meat, salad and bread with mugs of cocoa. I sat at the bottom of the table unnoticed until at the end of supper a small boy with big glasses and about my age came down the table and asked if I was King.

'I'm Tony Aitken,' he said. 'I've got to take you to Father Martin. He's the Cantilupe housemaster.'

Father Martin was a frail little man who looked much older

164

than he actually was. His study also looked antiquated, with a cracked lino floor, a saggy sofa and utility armchairs with wooden arms like the ones at Strood House. He shook my hand warmly and said he hoped I would be happy at Belmont.

'I've asked Aitken here to show you the ropes and generally keep an eye on you. It can't be easy to start a new school in the fifth form and in the middle of the school year.'

He had a soft lisping voice and coughed a lot, puffing on a hooked pipe which he smoked non-stop except in church, class and the refectory. I liked him immediately and, despite the fact that during my two years at Belmont he had to beat me more than any other Cantilupe boy, that feeling didn't change; his kind welcome was a balm to my buttoned-up dread and loneliness.

That night was my first ordeal. Tony took me upstairs and showed me where to sleep in the Cantilupe dormitory, a vast vaulted room with forty black steel-framed beds in four rows, one along each wall and head to head down the middle. There was a polished wooden floor and high arched windows, and though there were a couple of ancient radiators, it seemed colder than my unheated bedroom at Strood House. The communal bathroom and toilets were on the floor above which meant a long public walk up the creaking staircase if you wanted a pee in the middle of the night. Prefects were nominally in charge of the dormitory but Father Martin occupied a partitioned cubicle in the corner, from which tobacco smoke wafted from his bedtime pipe and occasional gruff barks of reprimand could be heard if there was noise from the dormitory.

For the first couple of weeks Tony Aitken was my guardian. He explained the timetable, escorted me to classes, and briefed me about etiquette, rituals and jargon, of which Belmont, with its public school aspirations, had plenty. He was a cheery, talkative boy whose father ran the family jewellery firm in Solihull near

Birmingham. With his big glasses he resembled a mini version of the Shadows' lead guitarist Hank Marvin, and also had aspirations to be a rock musician. Although we were not best friends – adolescent boys are more tribal – I owe him a lot for helping a new boy with a problematic background settle into a tough competitive boarding school two years behind his classmates, many of whom had known each other since prep school.

Tony is the trigger of many memories in this chapter. He has had a long career as an actor and producer and we met each other recently, the first time in forty years, for a bottle of wine at BAFTA. He told me many things which are part of this story just as I told him many things he had forgotten, drawing on suppressed memories of events we hadn't thought about for decades but just needed someone else's memory to match and reclaim. One thing he told me was that Father Martin had asked him to 'look after me' because, as Tony put it, I was clearly a very unhappy boy when I joined the school.

The Belmont Abbey School I woke up to on that extremely cold 1962 January morning had just over two hundred boys, mostly first-generation public school sons of stolid Midlands Catholics – farmers, teachers, shopkeepers and solicitors, who wanted to give their kids a better start than they'd had. There were also a few day boys from Hereford, Catholics who would have otherwise gone to Hereford Cathedral School, Belmont's fierce rivals at sport and in pursuing local girls.

From the outside Belmont looked like a fine old public school – a group of Victorian gothic buildings and extensive playing fields, handsomely overlooking the countryside four miles outside Hereford, and dominated by a fine abbey designed by Pugin, built in 1859 on land gifted to the Benedictines by a local Catholic landowner, Francis Wegg Prosser. The non-monastic school had been an afterthought in 1929, and the community of an abbot

166

Belmont Abbey.

and around fifty monks and lay brothers still occupied most of the buildings in an enclosed area strictly out of bounds to Belmont boys. Just before I arrived, a new building had been erected housing modern classrooms and labs and Vaughan dormitories, but Cantilupe and Kemble boys occupied the old monastery buildings with two common rooms used mainly for table-tennis and two enormous all-age dormitories, hot houses, despite the freezing winter temperatures, for bullying and furtive sex.

All boys ate in the refectory and attended morning assembly in the Old Gym, a vast ramshackle windowless room lit by a giant skylight, between the refectory and the green baize doors leading to the Cloisters and the Abbey. There was a stationery cupboard presided over by Father Iltudd and known for romantic assignations between senior boys and junior 'flowers', a tuck shop, and a sixth-form common room with a billiard table and beaten-up leather armchairs.

The Belmont day started at seven with Father Martin walking round the dormitory clapping his hands. After a grumpy wash we dressed and made our beds and, when the house prefect decided we were ready, went down to the Abbey for morning mass. This was followed by a good cooked breakfast and morning assembly taken by the headmaster Father Roger in the Old Gym. Then there was class, hours of it.

Belmont was quite unlike St Joseph's and St Peter's. The De La Salle Brothers were a tough teaching order with academic success built on discipline and hard work. The Belmont Benedictines had a mellower and more eccentric approach, allowing boys to find their natural level of achievement and teachers to be more idiosyncratic and often inspired.

In that fifth-form year I was lucky to have some very gifted teachers. The saturnine and fussy Father Lawrence taught us the melody and grammar of the English language. He also introduced Jane Austen's subtle irony and Shakespeare's dramatic poetry through our O-level set texts *Pride and Prejudice* and *Macbeth*. Father Aelred, with his camp parrot squawk, nagged us into understanding pi-squared and simple equations. Father Robert intoned Herbert F. Collins's part III *French Courses for Schools* about 'la grande bouche de ma tante'. But my first Belmont muse was a lay master, David Jenkins, who taught history.

Jenks, as he was universally known, although always called 'sir', was one of those inspirational teachers every child needs at least once during schooldays. A rumpled, chain-smoking whisky drinker in his early thirties, although seeming much older, he was the owner of several battered tweed jackets, red and yellow waistcoats and a green Morris Minor convertible with the numberplate PDP 123.

Jenks was passionate about history. Like Charles Blackburne his teaching was anecdotal and freewheeling, but he had a deeper knowledge and intellect. Sadly I only had one term with him in the sixth form, but his O-level teaching of modern European history made a deep impression. I can still list four of Jenks's six 'causes of the First World War' and have a vivid memory of the contributions of Cavour, Garibaldi, Metternich and Bismarck to the unifications of Italy and Germany.

Although I did well enough in class I was a dud at Belmont's other major winter activity. I had successfully skived off soccer at St Peter's and St Joseph's, but rugby at Belmont was compulsory for all fourth and fifth formers, played twice a week on Wednesday and Saturday. Father Roger, the headmaster, was a keen ex-fly-half and, for a school of limited academic achievement, success at rugby was rated very highly.

I hated the game. Waiting around goal on Nowton's muddy soccer pitch for a soggy, stinging football had been bad enough, but rugby was much worse. The idea of flinging myself knee high against an opponent's flailing boots seemed daft and dangerous, particularly in January when the playing fields were arctic. After a couple of compulsory games I knew I had to escape.

Injury was the only solution. A bad tackle at a Colts trial match did the trick. Anguished groaning and a theatrical limp transformed mild muscle strain into a seriously sprained ankle which, according to Matron's probing figures, would take a fortnight at least to recover. I was now 'off games' – and quickly up to my old trick of sneaking off to the cinema.

A boy called Ashridge started it. He was one of the twenty-odd day boys who lived around Hereford and was already in the sixth form, so not someone with whom I would have had much contact. But since the first assembly I'd admired him from afar, for his greased rocker hairstyle, winkle-picker shoes and drainpipe trousers. So when I bumped into Ashridge and a local friend by chance in Hereford High Town, on an afternoon exeat available to fifth and sixth formers, I was very chuffed when he suggested going with them to the matinee at the Gala even though I had been told that cinema visits for fifth formers were strictly prohibited without special permission.

'What's on?'

'*Psycho*,' Ashridge said casually.

My God. Hitchcock's horror classic had been the most talked-about film since its release two years earlier but, after my first scary X experience of *Peeping Tom* at the Colchester Empire, I had been too scared to see it on my own.

'What time does it start?'

'Quarter to three.'

Hardly time to see the film and get back to Belmont in time for tea by five. The latest possible bus was at twenty to. It was high risk. I had been thrown out of the novitiate for an illegal cinema trip only five months earlier, but this invitation by a sixth former was a challenge I couldn't refuse.

The Gala was in a narrow back street parallel to Broad Street and out of sight to casual passers-by. It had (and still does as a Gala Clubs bingo hall) an imposing Victorian frontage with small gothic windows, but the inside was more rudimentary with a single-storey sloping auditorium, threadbare carpet, wall-mounted lamps with scorched lampshades and rows of creaky sagging seats. Like the Colchester Empire and Mr Spendlove's Playhouse it was one of those small, shabby independents run on a shoestring by a movie buff with eclectic taste and out-of-date programmes, soon to be engulfed by the giant Odeon and ABC chains.

Ashridge must have been a regular. He greeted the old lady in the box office by Christian name and assured her I was over sixteen. He exchanged cheeky banter with the busty blonde ice-cream lady who, he told me as we slumped into our rear-stall seats watching the Pathé News, would give you a hand job for ten shillings and a full feel up her skirt for a pound.

I was never brave enough to sample these tempting extras. Nor did I become a Gala regular because my first visit nearly went badly wrong.

Psycho was brilliant. Like *Peeping Tom,* it preyed upon my deepest fear – violent sexual killing – but with Hitchcock's gothic motel setting, and surreal blend of cross-dressing, decomposing dead body and psychopathic craziness it was even more frightening. I was totally gripped and there was no way I wouldn't stay to see it all. After dead Marion's sister Lila discovers Mrs Bates's decomposing body in the cellar I glanced at my watch. It was only 4.20, but when I raced out of the cinema at the end, emotionally gutted, and reached the bus stop the bus was disappearing down Broad Street.

I got back to Belmont half an hour after tea, knowing that I was in serious trouble. Elliott was the prefect on duty and immediately demanded to know why I was late when I slunk into the refectory. He wasn't impressed by my feeble answer that I had missed the bus and gave me an immediate 'Note', a serious bad-behaviour penalty which reported miscreants directly to their housemaster.

At nine that evening, the normal execution time for punishment, I reported to Father Martin's study in my pyjamas and dressing gown and had to wait outside listening to the thwack of the cane as one of my housemates received a beating. With extraordinary good fortune Father Martin decided to show me the same clemency shown by Charles all those years before, but this time without the sadistic preliminary.

'So why were you late, King?' he asked in his mournful lisping voice.

'I missed the bus.'

'And what caused you to miss the bus?'

It was the critical moment. Should I confess, as to Brother Laurence only four months earlier, that I had been to the cinema against the rules and face probable immediate expulsion?

'Um ... I lost the way, Father. I don't know my way round Hereford yet.'

'Then you should have allowed more time and returned on an earlier bus,' Father Martin said solemnly.

'Yes, Father.'

He watched me closely through clouds of pipe smoke. I could tell he didn't believe me. Then he smiled.

'Well, it's the first time you have been up before me with a Note so I am inclined to show a little clemency. You will be banned from all exeats until the end of term.'

'Thank you, Father.' I was hugely relieved. There was only four weeks to the end of term.

It was a close escape and enough to shock me for a while into good behaviour.

There were other school activities to which I could contribute with much greater enthusiasm than rugby. CCF was one. The Combined Cadet Force was (and still is according to its website) a junior paramilitary organisation which aims 'to provide an opportunity for young people to exercise responsibility and leadership in a disciplined environment'. In simple terms that meant playing soldiers.

In 1962 the world was in dangerous military mode and the Cold War loomed. But in England it was a relatively peaceful period. Suez, Korea and the Mau Mau struggles were over. The British colonies in Africa were moving towards independence. The Irish Troubles wouldn't erupt until later in the sixties. National Service conscription had ended in 1960 and the last National Service man was discharged in May 1963.

The Belmont CCF reflected a spirit of *Dad's Army* obsolescence. The CO was the Kemble housemaster, Dom Aelred Cousins, a fanatical enthusiast who adored strutting round in his major's uniform and taking the Thursday afternoon parade accompanied by his Labrador. Major Aelred's number two was Brother Wilfred, a jolly lay brother who, despite being an ex-Gurkha NCO, played the role of Captain Chadwick as a deadpan comedy, deftly mimicking the CO behind his back. There was also a real live Company Sergeant Major from the Hereford Regiment who earned spare cash bawling us out on the parade ground and teaching the basic elements of drill.

Prefects played the junior officer ranks and fifth formers the NCOs. I was lucky because Father Aelred took a shine to me and, even though I was a new boy without any military training, promoted me at once to the rank of corporal which put me in charge of a platoon of fourth formers.

Drill and kit inspection were the main CCF activities, which involved a lot of blancoing of belts and gaiters, polishing brass buckles, and shining boot toecaps until, with the help of hot spoons, they became like black mirrors. Failing to be properly kitted out would mean being put 'on a charge', with the usual penalty of being run round the parade ground several times carrying a rifle above your head. There were also blistering route marches round the local lanes urged on by Major Aelred on his bicycle or a hectoring sergeant-major prefect pretending he was from Sandhurst.

The high spot was gun practice on the rifle range in one corner of the playing fields. Aelred's predecessors had amassed a large stock of infantry weapons and the Armoury beside the school library, a chapel-like building known as Bleak House, was stuffed with dozens of Lee–Enfield .303s, some of Great War vintage, and a wide assortment of Bren and Sten guns. These had been collected during the war for the training of teenage boys, who could be called on to protect the Home Front. Now the guns, although regularly stripped and cleaned, were ceremonial props for parade and drill. Just occasionally we were allowed under the CSM's instruction to blast off at targets against straw bales at the firing range, a shoulder-shattering business which, with my wonky left eye, I was hopeless at.

The one school activity at which I did excel was drama. This was surprising since the peak of my stage performances until then had been playing the four-line part of Curio in the Nowton production of *Twelfth Night* four years earlier. But the influence of that devoted thespian Charles Blackburne must have run deep because, when I diffidently attended auditions for a special Easter production of *See How They Run* which Father Roger and Jenks decided to put on that year, I was amazed and excited to be offered the leading role of Penelope Toop.

See How They Run is a classic English wartime farce of clerical deception and mistaken identity. Penelope, an ex-actress, is married to the Reverend Lionel Toop, vicar of Morton-cum-Middlewick. One of her stage friends, Clive, now an army lance corporal but disguising himself as a visiting vicar to avoid the Military Police, turns up at the vicarage and the two of them are seen re-playing one of their shared scenes from *Privates Lives* by the village busybody and do-gooder who thinks she has caught them in adultery.

I must have been more extrovert than I remember to play a female lead that involved speaking in a throaty theatrical falsetto and appearing on stage in nothing but a blonde wig and a bath towel. Even more surprising was that Father Roger allowed me to act at all in the term before my O levels. But *See How They Run* was a big success and a major breakthrough in my troubled adolescence. It drew me into the mainstream of Belmont life and boosted my popularity. It also made me several good friends. Tony Aitken hammed up the busybody Miss Skillon, a tall good-looking rugby player called Stephen Ferris played my husband the Reverend Lionel, and Lance Butler, the witty, clever boy I had met on my first day at Belmont, played Clive and Elyot to my Amanda in the nostalgic re-run of scenes from *Private Lives.*

Father Roger and Jenks were the joint producers and an inspired couple to work with. A member of the Belmont community since leaving the school in 1948, Father Roger was in his first year as headmaster, at the remarkably young age of thirty-one. Though his first love was rugby he adored theatre. Directing meant he could take off his habit and let down his hair. Outside rehearsals he was the tough headmaster but working on the play he was funny and irreverent, with the quick wit of a stand-up comic, and an infectious enthusiasm to get the best performances from his cast. Jenks was the sidekick and straight man, brilliant at extracting the maximum laughs, gags and double-entendres from Philip King's skin-deep text.

The production opened the week before the Easter holiday to a riotous reception, and ran for two nights. The *Hereford Times* gave us a rave review and at the cast party I got tipsy for the first time at Belmont on a mix of authorised Bulmer's cider and some bottles of smuggled Ansell ale. Father Roger told us that he was planning to take the production on a summer tour, a first for Belmont drama. For two days I basked in the congratulations and the back-slapping then, before my head got too big, it was time to go home to the cooler response of Jill and Da. They had been too tied up with other children and animals to come and see my star performance and thought that I should have spent the time concentrating on O levels.

In fact exams weren't a problem. I felt confident and, although I didn't get the results until August, passed nine out of ten with high grades. For English grammar and literature I got the highest grades in the school.

But Jill and Da had something more important on their minds than exam results, which was finally revealed on the Speech Day weekend, three weeks before the end of term. To my surprise, and anxiety, Jill wrote and said she was coming on her own. Normally Da came to my school functions because Jill was tied up with Quentin and one of them had to stay to look after the animals. That was fine because Da had an easy friendly manner, was good at chatting to teachers and other parents without causing embarrassment. But Jill was different. Her natural shyness made her uneasy in crowds and seem bad-tempered. Also the thought of having to look after her on her own made me anxious. Since my shameful exit from the novitiate our relationship had become even more distant and I was uncertain how the two of us would get along.

All parents embarrass their children after a certain age and Jill was no exception. Instead of staying at a Hereford hotel like other parents, in order to save money she had arranged to stay at a farmhouse bed and breakfast in the nearby village of Clehonger. Of course there was nothing wrong with that. Jill liked the simple rural life so it was a natural choice, and Clehonger was much closer to the school. My embarrassment was simply because she behaved differently from other parents.

On the morning of Speech Day, as the drive and playing-field car park filled up with gleaming Fords, Vauxhalls and Jaguars, Jill arrived at Belmont looking smart in her floral summer dress but riding an ancient black bicycle she had borrowed from the Clehonger farmer's wife, which she dismounted and parked on its stand outside the Cantilupe front door, to the clear amusement of the boys and parents nearby. Or maybe I just imagined it.

Otherwise the day passed without problems. We cheered on the house athletic team, listened to the monks chanting compline in the Abbey, toured the art exhibition where my painting of a wintry elm tree with roosting birds silhouetted against a setting sun had earned a silver medal and at the speeches I was awarded an English prize. During the reception on the lawn which followed, Father Martin made a special point of talking to my mother and Tony Aitken's parents were very friendly, full of enthusiasm about our performances in *See How They Run* and the planned summer tour, which surprised Jill since I hadn't yet asked for her permission.

Afterwards most parents took advantage of the Speech Day exeat, either driving their children home for the night or out to high tea in Hereford. I had expected Jill to take me out, at least to tea at the nearby Grafton Arms, which was within walking distance of the school, although I wasn't much looking forward to it. I knew she would talk about little else than what Quentin was up to, and news of my sisters, the animals or of Da's latest DIY project, all subjects she covered regularly in her weekly letters to her boarding-school children and were the main preoccupations of her life. But she surprised me.

'Well, time to say goodbye, Caradoc,' she said briskly, 'I've got an appointment with Father Roger. Then I must return the bicycle to Mrs Partridge, collect my suitcase and catch the 5.15 Hereford bus in time for the six o'clock to Paddington.'

Before I could ask why she was seeing Father Roger, she gave me a swift peck on the cheek then disappeared up the stairs leading to the headmaster's study.

*

Not until the following afternoon did I find out the reason for her visit. Father Roger stopped me in the refectory passage and asked me to come and see him. I was immediately fearful it was because of drunkenness the night before. Father Martin had given a cider party for Cantilupe boys not on exeat. I and a few others had later topped up from a half bottle of whisky someone had smuggled into the dormitory. The taste was disgusting and the effect was worse. After a few gulps I had been suddenly sick all over the dormitory floor and had been discovered by Father Martin frantically mopping up. At the time he had seemed quite sympathetic, assuming perhaps that I had just overdosed on his cider. Now, hungover, I was fearful that he had changed his mind and had issued a headmaster's Note. But as soon as I entered Father Roger's study it was clear from his kind voice and sympathetic manner that I was not in trouble, at least not in the normal sense.

He gestured to an armchair and came straight to the point.

'Caradoc, as you know your mother came to see me yesterday. She has asked me to tell you something very important.'

I nodded dumbly, but with immediate foreboding.

'I am afraid this may come as a shock because no doubt you have always assumed that Jill and Eric King are your natural parents?'

I nodded again.

'Well, I'm very sorry to tell you that they're not. You are, in fact, their adopted son.'

I stared at him, unable at first to take in what he was saying. His words were so unexpected as to be, for a moment, incomprehensible. Despite all my fraught feelings of love, anger and hate about Jill, I had never once doubted that she was my real mother.

'The adoption laws don't allow adopted children to trace their natural parents but I can tell you what she told me,'Father Roger said in a gentler voice.'Both your parents are English and middle class but they separated soon after you were born.'

I couldn't take that in. My only immediate thought was that I didn't actually belong to the King family.

'What about my sisters? Are they adopted too?'

'No, you are the only one in the family,' he said gently.

There was silence between us. He waited. I didn't know what to say, couldn't really grasp what he was telling me, even though I realised suddenly that I felt no surprise.

'Why didn't they tell me sooner?'

It was a question Father Roger must have asked Jill because he answered without hesitation.

'They didn't want you to feel any different from the rest of the family when you were growing up. So they decided to tell you when you were about sixteen and old enough to understand.'

'So why didn't Jill tell me herself? Why did she ask you to tell me?'Why had she said goodbye to me with just a peck on the cheek after fifteen years of pretending to be my mother?

Father Roger must have picked up anger in my voice, although I felt perfectly calm. Just for a moment he hesitated, unsure what to say. Then he smiled reassuringly.

'I think, Caradoc, she was just very anxious about telling you and worried about your response. I suggested we might tell you together, but she said she had a train to catch.'He checked himself then went on.'I think she also felt that as your headmaster and as a priest I would be a good person to share this news with you and help you to adjust to it.'

I felt a sudden surge of rage listening to Father Roger's explanation but forced myself to be calm. So much of adult life is spent containing anger, forcing ourselves to be reasonable and under-standing about other people's behaviour that I guess, as an

179

adolescent trying to be adult, I was already suppressing what I felt, to excuse Jill.

She was a strong woman, not afraid to speak her mind. She must have come on her own to Speech Day with the firm intention of telling me that I was adopted, and had planned carefully with Da when and how to tell me. So why hadn't she? How could she have just left it to my headmaster to tell me?

Father Roger was talking again. He knew that I had been through a difficult time at home, in trouble with my parents, but this was very common in teenage boys, he said, part of growing up. He too had been through similar problems, a troublemaker at home and Belmont, difficulties that only improved in his final year at school when he discovered that he had a vocation and wanted to become a Belmont monk.

'Not that I am wishing the same fate on you, Caradoc,' he said with a smile. 'But I want you to focus on all the good things in your life, your academic achievements, your excellent acting and increasing popularity in the school. We are proud to have you at Belmont and I know your parents share that pride. They love you and, once this small hurdle has been cleared, and your adoption is at last in the open, I am sure you can build a new and stronger relationship with them and your sisters. Believe me, blood ties in families can sometimes be troublesome. They assume an automatic bond which sometimes doesn't exist because it is based on obligation. Nothing can be stronger than relationships built on love, trust and choice.'

I was half listening to Father Roger's words, touched by their sincerity. But I started to feel something much simpler – relief. Relief that if Jill and Da were not my natural parents and if I didn't behave like them, and didn't love them, or one of them, it wasn't unnatural and nor was it my fault. I wasn't their child.

Father Roger was watching me closely.

'How are you feeling?' he asked.

'Fine. Thank you,' I said slowly. 'But what should I do?'

'I think you should write to Jill and Eric straight away,' said Father Roger, who must have already thought about this. 'Tell them that even though you are not their natural son you love them both, it will make no difference to your relationship and you understand why they are only telling you now.'

'But they didn't tell me. You did.'

'No need to mention that. I've explained why.'

So I did what he said.

Father Roger.

XI

Jill and Da answered and their joint letter echoed mine, saying they loved me and the fact that I was adopted made no difference to our relationship and to my place in the King family. In fifteen months they would each write separate letters saying the opposite.

On her visit Jill had given Father Roger permission for me to go on the July tour of *See How They Run* at the end of term. The tour was to be led by Father Roger and Jenks and involved five one-night stands in village halls and schools around the Midlands and one gala performance at the Birmingham Theatre Centre. To carry the stage sets between the different venues Father Roger borrowed a Bedford truck from a local farmer and invited Tony Aitken and me to go with him to pick it up and have a trial run on the deserted Madley aerodrome.

It was a thrilling afternoon. Once Father Roger had got the hang of the controls he gave us both turns at the wheel and we had a wild gear-jerking time driving the three-ton lorry at top speed round the disused runways. It was the first time that

Father Roger, not known for favourites, marked me out for special attention. It was the beginning of an unusual friendship.

The tour was huge fun. Father Roger drove the lorry with a different boy in the cab each day. Father Robert, in charge of make-up, drove the school Dormobile and Jenks came in his Morris Minor, the two of them sharing boys and personal luggage. The routine was the same each day. We would arrive mid-afternoon after stopping en route for a picnic lunch; the first hour was spent erecting the scenery and furnishing the stage. Local ladies served us an early high tea and we were made up and into costume for curtain-up at half past six.

The village performances were hilarious. The audiences of mainly women and children were clearly deprived of live entertainment and laughed uproariously at every possible joke and particularly at my falsetto performance as the skimpily dressed Penelope Toop. Lance Butler and I couldn't resist hamming it up, to the irritation of Father Roger who told us we were behaving like typical amateurs, even though the audiences clearly loved it.

The best moments were the trips to the pub afterwards. It was a hot week and Jenks and Father Roger chose pubs with gardens so that we could sit outside drinking cider and shandy while he and Father Roger hit the whisky. The conversation was a freewheeling mix of silly and serious – school gossip (within limits because even off duty Father Roger was headmaster), porky jokes mainly from Tony, the imprisonment of Joe Orton and his boyfriend for obscenely defacing library books, Pope John's excommunication of Castro which Jenks, who would soon join the monastery, vehemently defended. It was great to be treated as adults and to be one of a group bonded by a shared adventure. Even our mild hangovers when we woke up in sleeping bags in a village hall added to the pleasure of playing like grown-ups.

Returning to Strood House after this excitement was an anti-climax, with some anxious adjustment to my new role as the adopted sibling. On the surface, things were better. Jane and Janet, who were still at home, made special efforts to make me feel loved and welcome. Caroline and Priscilla had still not been told and I must have complied with the secrecy. Quentin was still too young to understand.

For Jill and Da the disclosure of my adoption began a period of wary uncertainty in our relationship. Initial relief that it was out in the open meant they welcomed me home with unusual warmth, hugs and sincere chats as if to confirm that nothing was different. Jill apologised that she hadn't had the courage to tell me herself. Da told me he was proud to have me as his older son, and I knew that he meant it and that he loved me for my own sake. They told me briefly the circumstances of my adoption, but said they knew nothing about the identity of my natural parents.

And what did I feel? The mixture of anger and relief on first hearing the news had given way to more complicated feelings. Of course I liked the warmth and care everyone was showing me; I too wanted to stand by my letter, show that I loved them and that I was glad that they had adopted me. But somehow it didn't work out that way.

It was an uneventful summer, with no family holiday and no big outings, except to a steam-engine rally near Ipswich. There is, however, in the family album one whole page entitled 'Mainly Caradoc' taken on a single day at West Mersea beach. After pages full of photographs of Quentin this is unusual. It shows special loving attention paid to the adopted son and now, looking at those pictures of me – a lanky, unsmiling, troubled adolescent – I understand better some of the problems that lay ahead.

Adolescence.

That summer seemed a long interlude of suspended time. We swam in the creeks, took Madam and Eve for walks along the sea walls, had picnics on Ray Island. There's a photo of the skeleton of a canoe which Paddy, Janet's new husband, and I were building in the loft, another of Quentin and me playing trains. I hit a tennis ball monotonously against the wall of the house by the kitchen door. We went on bike rides. Caroline, Priscilla and I helped at the farm and Alan Maskell let me drive the tractor with trailer. We did all the things we had always done, but that year they seemed empty and repetitive. My O-level results arrived in mid-August with ten good grades but without special celebration.

The ennui was due partly to my age. I was now fifteen and

a half, a discontented and secretive adolescent. I would have rebelled against Jill and Da's strict discipline and isolated rural lifestyle, adopted or not. But now I had the lurking thought that my life didn't have to be like this. I didn't have to be a member of the King family if I didn't want to.

Religion was also an issue. I liked all the chanting and ritual of Belmont Abbey and admired the monks much more than I had the De La Salle Brothers because they seemed friendlier and more human. But Jill's religious fervour was a wedge splitting us apart. Years later she would renounce the Catholic Church like the rest of her devoutly converted family, but in 1962 she was a zealot. Riding the eight miles to Colchester for Sunday mass and the pious observance of night and morning prayers were compulsory. Jill was still openly disappointed that I hadn't remained at the novitiate. Transferring me into the arms of mother church had been the ideal solution to the errant cuckoo child and a balm to her conscience. But the novitiate had had the opposite effect. Its rigid discipline and earnest piety had curtailed my religious yearnings and the longer I stayed at Belmont the more irreligious I became. A year after leaving school I abandoned the Church completely, as a final renouncement of my adoptive mother.

Father Michael was a critical problem. There is a photograph of him that summer standing with Da outside Strood House, rather a nice picture of two middle-aged men who seem good friends. But the picture, like most pictures in family albums, conveys only part of the story. After six years Father Michael was another adopted member of the King family. Jill said jokingly that he was her spare husband and, though there was no hint of sexual infidelity, she clearly adored him. Father Michael had inducted her into the Church after she had almost died giving birth to Quentin. He was her spiritual counsellor, her saviour from inner demons,

Da and 'spare husband'.

her one close friend. But to Caroline, Priscilla and me, he was a creep, somehow too friendly, an infiltrator with wandering hands and a fondness for helping at bathtime; and Da must have felt the same, even though he didn't show it. Jill always got what she wanted and Da always indulged her.

As for Father Michael it is difficult to say. He certainly loved Jill and they would continue to be friends into old age, long after Jill had stopped being a Catholic. Maybe celibate and lonely, Michael was simply content to have a woman who adored him and a home and family he could spend his holidays with. And the wandering hands? Years later, Caroline and Priscilla agreed he was relatively harmless. Janet remembers her acute embarrassment seeing him watching her try on a new nightie Jill had bought her. In me he showed no interest. His failing would be disinterest, or connivance, in how Jill and Da would end up treating me.

It was a relief to return to Belmont in September. I was now in the first year sixth with new privileges, keeping hands in trouser pockets, using the sixth-form common room with its billiard table and battered leather armchairs, and a term later, when I was sixteen, being allowed to smoke there on weekend evenings.

One special privilege was the close contact with Father Roger. I am not sure how it started, probably with a request for me to see him to discuss A level options. I suspect his decision, that I should opt for only two A-levels and to take one of them, English, after only a year, indicated that he knew early on that my parents might remove me from the school before the end of the sixth form. It also explains why he went to such trouble to help and counsel me when I seemed to have adjusted easily to my adoption and had returned to school happier than the previous term.

My chats with Father·Roger took place in his study after evening prep once or twice a week and lasted for that one term. They were deeply important for me. What exactly we talked about I don't remember and that was one of the pleasures of our conversation. It was free-flowing and without agenda; I had never talked to an adult in that way before. We must have discussed my problems with Jill and Da and Father Roger's own family and childhood in Nelson, Lancashire. We would have talked about books and storytelling; it was Roger's passion for Dickens and Shakespeare that liberated my imagination and taught me to think and criticise. We also talked about religious faith and the celibate life.

It was Father Roger who introduced me to wine, which for me, coming from a family in which the only alcohol was an ancient bottle of Cherry Heering behind the cellar door and a case of Adnams Pale Ale for Da's solitary Sunday treat, seemed wonderfully sophisticated. At our second meeting, he produced a bottle.

'This wine is called Beaune,' he said, showing me the label and then extracting the cork. 'It comes from the Burgundy region of France.'

He poured small measures into two glasses, swirled, sniffed and tasted and asked me to do the same. It was delicious, a mixture of bottled plums, raspberry and blackcurrant. We had one glass each, then two nights later finished the bottle, a ritual which Father Roger repeated the following week, this time with a bottle of Bordeaux.

This was the beginning of adult civilisation.

Our friendship lasted only till the beginning of the Easter term, ending not out of boredom or fear of gossip, but because Father Roger felt that it had fulfilled its purpose and helped me through a critical period. Other school activities made a private relationship difficult.

Father Roger was also now my principal teacher. He normally taught the upper sixth but because of his recommendation that I do my English A level in a single year I joined his English classes. The set text for that term was *Hard Times* and Father Roger's teaching of Dickens was an inspiration. Thanks to Grandpa and the well-stocked libraries at Nowton, I had already read several of the popular novels – *Oliver Twist*, *Nicholas Nickleby*, *Great Expectations* and, Grandpa's favourite, *The Pickwick Papers*. But *Hard Times* was shorter and bleaker, set in the

Lancashire mill town of Coketown and featuring among a number of morally repellent characters the dictatorial Gradgrind, principal of Coketown's school, and the millowner Joseph Bounderby, a self-made man who loved telling stories of his brutal childhood. No doubt influenced by his own Lancashire working-class childhood, Father Roger was able to transform this 'sullenly socialist' novel into an enthralling story about the struggle between imagination and 'hard facts', and between wealth and morality. He also lent me his copy of Edgar Johnson's masterly *Charles Dickens: His Tragedy and Triumph*, the first literary biography to fire my interest in the relationship between a writer's life and work.

Drama was my other main activity that term. Each year Father Roger and Jenks put on a Christmas as well as summer production and that year they chose Arnold Ridley's 1923 comedy thriller and amateur-dramatic perennial *The Ghost Train*. The play is set in an isolated Cornish railway station where a group of passengers is stranded overnight. The station is reputedly haunted by a mysterious ghost train, the sight of which causes terrible misfortune. The train of course isn't at all ghostly, but carrying illegal shipments of arms and explosives, which in the last act is finally exposed. This time I got the lead role – the irritating, facetious Teddy Deakin who in the second act whips out his revolver and announces that he is in fact Inspector Edward Deakin of Scotland Yard.

The production was another theatrical triumph, not only for the excellent acting (according to the *Hereford Times*) but also the special effects of the recorded express train racing through the station with carriage lights projected through the waiting-room window and the rattling of metal thunder sheets. I was now an established star of the Belmont stage and *The Ghost Train* photos on the Belmont Association memorabilia site show a cocksure young rebel rather than the lonely and troubled new boy of twelve months earlier.

This rebellious streak would lead to a major confrontation with Jill during the Christmas holidays over a pair of chisel toes and some tapered trousers. In 1962 the Mods and Rockers rivalry was under way. Mod fashion had lopped off the toes of Rocker winkle-pickers to produce chisel toes which, with Chelsea boots and tapered trousers (fourteen-inch minimum at Belmont), were all the rage.

Jill and Da were oblivious to new fashions and my clothes were regulation school uniform – twenty-inch flannels with turn-ups and black Oxfords. But to be fashionable was essential. My mentor was Ashridge, the wild day boy who had taken me to see *Psycho* and had recently swapped his winkles for chisels and changed his haircut from Rocker sideburned quiff to a Beatles crop-top, following the band's first number 1 'Love Me Do' and their television debut in October. It was Ashridge who persuaded me, on a Christmas shopping trip to Hereford, to take my spare pair of flannels to Sketchleys the dry cleaners for tapering and to spend the last of my pocket money on my first pair of chisels.

I don't know why I took them home as I certainly couldn't wear them. But both shoes and trousers went into my trunk and then secretly into my wardrobe and the week after Christmas it was there that Jill found them.

Christmas had started well enough with the usual foraging for holly and ivy in Peldon Wood on Christmas Eve morning, the King's College carol service on the radio in the afternoon and a cold, frosty moonlit bike ride to Colchester for midnight mass. But on Christmas Day things fell apart. Quentin was taken sick after nibbling a chocolate soldier made of cow's milk. I was caught tippling from a bottle of sherry which Jill had marked with a pencil line. Then Father Michael arrived the day after Boxing Day, which put Jill in a better temper but the rest of us on edge.

I don't blame Father Michael for Jill's sudden outburst and I believe he even tried to calm her down. But her discovery in my cupboard of the chisel-toe shoes and tapered trousers provoked sudden and irrational anger. For the first time she confronted me with the accusation she had bottled up for years – and this time was wrong.

'So how did you buy these revolting shoes, Caradoc? With stolen money again?'

'No, from money I saved out of pocket money,' I said, furious because I hadn't stolen a penny since I had been at Belmont, but also guilty because I knew the Christmas presents I had given the family that year had been cheap because of the shoes.

'And what about these trousers?' She held up the offending fourteen-inch semi-drains. 'What right do you have to mutilate an expensive pair of trousers *we* paid for?'

'But everyone's wearing them like that,' I said feebly.

'Well, *you* won't. Come with me.'

Her punishment was exact and immediate. Da had been clearing out the loft and there was still a smouldering bonfire in the Wilderness. Jill cleared a space in the embers, threw on the offending shoes and trousers and watched with a stony face as they caught fire.

Caroline and Priscilla ran out of the house eager to see what was going on, Da more slowly. Father Michael stayed indoors, acknowledging that this was just a family affair. They stood solemnly round the fire, watching the trousers catch light and the cheap plasticated shoes melt in flames.

I felt humiliated. Jill's cold anger was too strong for defiance. I glared at her in silence, then turned away and walked sullenly back to the house.

The shoe-burning wasn't the official reason for my sudden return to school a week early. Quentin's allergic reaction turned out to be measles, which I hadn't yet caught. Belmont was consulted and they agreed that I should leave the Strood House infected zone immediately, surprising as the incubation period of measles starts before the actual illness. The real reason was that the shoe crisis had caused silent and mutual hostility between Jill and me and she wanted me out of the house.

My week at Belmont was solitary but happy. The school was empty and several monks, including Father Roger, were away on holiday. The weather was incredibly cold and I spent each morning huddled close to a gasfire in the school library studying. I ate alone in the school refectory. In the evening I was allowed to watch television in the monastery's guest sitting room, a great treat as there was no television at Strood House and I could catch up on the programmes my friends talked about, such as *The Saint* and *The Avengers*. I slept alone in the vast and freezing Cantilupe dormitory with the companionship of Father Martin's pipe smoke and wheezing from the corner cubicle.

The most perfect moments were skating alone each afternoon on the frozen ponds on Grafton Lane across the main road from the school. I was a skilled roller-skater from my days at the novitiate and the transfer to ice, using skates lent by Father Martin, was easy. Despite the fierce cold the weather was clear and sunny and racing around the ponds and mastering the art of skating backwards was an exhilarating antidote to the depression triggered by my confrontation with Jill.

The night before term started I drank my last glass of wine with Father Roger. When he asked after my holidays and I told him the story of the burnt chisel-toe shoes, he laughed; then explained gently that we couldn't go on meeting in this way. He was headmaster and had to treat everyone equally. He was very fond of me and if I needed help I should just ask.

It was the kindest break-up I could have had. I told him that I understood, and meant it. We went on to talk about Dickens and a planned trip to Stratford to see Paul Scofield in *King Lear*.

It was a cold bleak term. The frozen snow ruts took weeks to melt. Darkness from morning mass and through afternoon class dominated each day. The bitter cold and the emotional vacuum left by Father Roger may have prompted my first and only Belmont crush. Desmond Gilligan was a fourth former, disparagingly referred to by sixth-form connoisseurs of potential 'flowers' as 'the dumb blonde' because he rarely spoke, but to me he seemed a creature of enchanting silent beauty.

Gilligan was two years my junior in a different house so the entrancement was at first distant. I brushed cassocks with him as fellow altar boys and we smiled at each other afterwards as we de-robed in the sacristy. I then 'ran into him' a couple of times by lurking near the Vaughan junior common room during recreation periods and managed to exchange some shy pleasantries about school events which must have made it clear I was trying to chat him up.

Then I had the chance. Tony Aitken ran the Kemble Press, which printed school and Abbey stationery from an outhouse near the kitchens. It was Tony who told me that Gilligan had joined the press as a printing assistant and, aware of my stricken condition, suggested I come and help out. It was a golden opportunity but unfortunately I was too tongue-tied to take it. Instead I smoked furtively with Tony, watched Gilligan out of the corner of my eye, and replayed the *Everly Brothers Great Hits* album on the press record player, and particularly 'Crying in the Rain' which, with its poignant refrain about pride, pain and a broken heart, caught my feelings perfectly.

It was sad. I had already fallen in love three times at different schools and learned to manage turbulent feelings with reasonable self-assurance. But Gilligan was different. His dumb beauty floored me. My other crushes had been triggered by words, flirtation and chat-up – but Gilligan had a Mona Lisa silence and beauty which made me speechless. There was also a new and disturbing problem – sex. My other crushes had been just intensely romantic but now my hormones were humming with powerful new messages. I seriously fancied Gilligan and didn't know what to do about it.

Then two things happened, one which made it all possible, and another which snatched it away.

Cross-country running was the one sport I did well, after my training at the novitiate. In my first year at Belmont I won a Colts silver medal for Cantilupe. Now, in the sixth form, my target in the race at the end of the Easter term was senior gold for the out-right winner, a huge challenge because I would be running against second-year sixth formers.

The master in charge was the hyperactive Father Aelred who decided, although I wasn't in his house, that I had the potential to be the Belmont star for the inter-school cross-country championships in April. It turned out that Gilligan, as well as his outstanding beauty to which Aelred was clearly susceptible, also had running skills and after the preliminary trials we were both chosen for Aelred's elite school squad.

Training was intense, involving muddy slogs round the local tracks, but it was done by house so I did not see much of Gilligan. Then, to motivate the school squad, Aelred had a more original idea – a trip to the cinema to see *The Loneliness of the Long Distance Runner* at the Gala in Hereford, a gritty 'kitchen sink' story starring Michael Redgrave and Tom Courtenay about a borstal governor who spots the running talent of one of his bad boys and trains him to run in a boarding-school cross-country tournament.

Aelred was excited by his bold plan and a matinee trip was arranged with Brother Wilfred. Unfortunately he had overlooked that the film had an X rating which meant that Gilligan and the other fourth formers in the squad should be refused entry. The ticket lady looked doubtful peering at them through the kiosk window but was overawed by the two clerical collars and Brother Wilfred's earnest assurance that the two of them were 'almost sixteen' and relented.

The film enthralled me. I closely identified with Colin Smith, the rebellious borstal boy who, in protest against conformity, stops running when he is in the lead against the posh boy from Ranley.

In the real race I didn't deliberately stop running. I just tripped and fell two hundred yards from the finish. I sat there in the mud with a twisted ankle as the other runners pounded past. It was Gilligan, well back in the field, who stopped and helped me to my feet. Afterwards, I saw in the shower just how beautiful he was and sensed, from the smiling ease with which he stood naked in front of me, that if I really wanted him I could have him.

But love is blind and I was wrong. Two days later something happened which stopped it all. At assembly in the Old Hall Father Roger made a solemn and shocking announcement:

'There has been an outbreak of homosexuality in the school ...'

The story was a bad one. A prefect called Madley had been prowling the Vaughan dormitories, targeting junior boys and trying, with some success, to have sex with them. He hadn't been caught, but one boy complained in tears to his housemaster. Then as the word spread, other boys had reported the same. Madley's parents had been told; he would be leaving the school a week before the end of term. Homosexuality was a sin, Father Roger gravely informed us, and the exploitation of young boys by older ones was unforgivable.

One of the young boys was Gilligan. He told me about it that evening, struggling not to cry. I was shocked that I hadn't guessed the reason for his silence, a secret he didn't want to share. I knew without Gilligan telling me that our friendship was impossible.

I got into other sorts of trouble that summer term – drinking, smoking and absconding, normal stuff for a bright and problematic adolescent and no doubt a reaction to claustrophobic family life at Strood House.

Da said later that I got into 'a bad crowd' at Belmont, but it wasn't true. My two main buddies were twins, Jim and Pat Murphy, whose family farmed at Balbriggan just north of Dublin. Pat was in the first rugby XV and his quieter brother Jim was a popular house prefect and keen lighting technician, which is how I got to know him. On the theatrical/literary side were Kieran Lyons whose father ran an art college in Wiltshire, the clever Lance Butler and my old mate Tony Aitken.

My first drunken misdemeanour was on a sixth-form English trip to Stratford to see Paul Scofield in Peter Brook's *King Lear*. A legendary performance, it was the first stage production to amaze and excite me. It was also one of our A-level set texts and it was largely thanks to Peter Brook that I got the B pass in English required to sit the Oxford entrance exam at the age of sixteen.

However, the excitement must have gone to my head. During the hour we had to wander around Stratford after the performance I drank three pints of bitter in a pub and returned to the coach clearly inebriated. Even worse, I had to ask the coach driver to stop en route to Belmont so that I could puke up beside the road. Father Roger's chilly anger only thawed when I produced a very good essay on the play a week later.

Most of our bad behaviour stemmed from 'pranks' and 'escapades' rather than 'moral turpitude', schoolmasterly phrases I recall from the time. One of the best was heisting cars outside the Abbey during Sunday mass. Surprisingly, even in the early sixties and on a quiet country road, there were two regulars who always left their cars unlocked and the keys in the ignition. Pat and I would take either the Austin Cambridge or the Hillman Minx for 'burn-ups' around Clehonger and return them to the same parking place. Also surprising, given our limited driving skills, was that we never had a prang or were found out.

A murkier scam involved a cupboard door with a faulty lock, which provided secret access through the back of the tuck shop. I wasn't involved in the actual thefts, masterminded by two brothers in Kemble who had got hold of a spare key and then sold on the sweets at bargain prices. But I was caught in possession of some stolen Coca-Cola after a surprise stake-out by Father Aelred and was one of eight boys seriously beaten for the offence.

As the term passed our escapades got wilder. A second major beating followed the summer sixth-form dance. Pat and I were found with two girls from Bredwardine Convent School in the monastery garden. We had danced and drunk cider with them all evening; it was easy to entice them outside for a walk. Mine was a pretty dark-haired girl called Susan with very pale skin. After the Gilligan fiasco I wanted to neck with a girl, from pride as much as desire. My first clumsy kiss of clashing teeth and squashed lips was suddenly interrupted by the familiar lisping voice of Father Martin, out with his dog and wielding a torch.

'No, no, *no*. Stop that at once.'

We were ordered to make an immediate apology to the

Bredwardine nun in charge. Pat was given a note to his house-master and Father Martin told me to come to his study before bed. I arrived as normal in pyjamas and dressing gown and, after a doleful and lisping lecture on my unacceptable behaviour, he gave me six of the best.

Pat and I committed an even more serious offence a fortnight later on the night before Speech Day. It started as a brag, repeated too often not to do it – we would ring the Abbey sanctuary bell in the middle of the night.

We met in the Cloisters at two in the morning after waking our-selves with alarm clocks under our pillows. The Cloisters were eerily lit by moonlight. The Abbey was dark, with just the red glim-mer of the tabernacle light and Pat's torch to guide us to the bell-tower. The boom of the bell resounding through the Abbey and over the neighbouring countryside was awesome and we rang it for several minutes until lights and the sound of voices meant we had to escape swiftly through a side door into the graveyard.

At assembly the next morning Father Roger solemnly demanded that the perpetrators of this sacrilegious act own up. It had been a thoughtless disruption of people's sleep and led to several phone calls from Belmont neighbours wanting to know whether the single bell in the middle of the night was a warning of air-borne attack or possibly the imminent end of the world.

There was a moment's silence to absorb this news. Then someone laughed and quickly everyone joined in. Father Roger frowned, then he too started smiling. It was a harmless jape and we had got away with it.

Father Roger was probably feeling sorry for me. He had just had a phone call from Da to say that neither he nor Jill could after all come to the prizegiving; Quentin had had another bad allergic reaction. So they missed my award of the sixth-form essay prize for my critical appreciation of *King Lear.*

That night I got extremely drunk. It started with an authorised party in the sixth-form common room with bottled beer and a firkin of cider for the few senior boys who had nowhere else to stay over the exeat weekend. It ended with me and the hard core sharing a bottle of Scotch in the Abbey graveyard, staring up at the stars.

Drinking landed me in plenty of trouble during my last six months at Belmont. The worst incident happened during the first week of the summer holidays on an expedition for the Duke of Edinburgh's Award scheme, introduced into the school by Father Aelred to perk up interest in his Combined Cadet Force which, with the end of national service, was losing its appeal. My drunken behaviour on the expedition turned Aelred's general support into vindictive hostility and almost led to my expulsion from Belmont the following term.

The expedition was a three-day trek through the Brecon Beacons sleeping under canvas. The mobile HQ was an old Bedford bus driven by Brother Wilfred and carrying heavy equipment. We were divided into four groups of five boys; I was one of the group leaders. Each day there were different group assignments involving timed treks and navigational exercises with compasses between target points. The weather was terrible and, even though it was July, we were wet and cold during the day and slept under damp canvas at night. Aelred was in his element, roaring round the mountain lanes in his Land Rover like Montgomery at Alamein, ticking off group performances on score cards.

The showdown happened on the last day in a pub outside Brecon. Our group's assignment was to navigate without maps a ten-mile circular route from the campsite to a ruined castle near Talgarth, round a lake, through a village called Talybont and back to the campsite. We reached the castle but lost our way in the mist coming down the hillside and by late morning were a couple of miles off route on the main Abergavenny road. We stopped at the pub to ask for directions, but it was now pouring with rain, a fire was lit in the saloon and the landlord took pity. Although we were under-age he invited us in for a warm-up of bread and cheese and a round of cider, followed by another.

By the time he found us in mid-afternoon Aelred was hopping mad. We were happily playing darts and snooker and pretty well pissed. As group leader I took full responsibility and received a furious dressing down from my commanding officer. Aelred then turned on the friendly publican, when he tried to take my side by blaming the bad weather, and threatened to report him for allowing under-age drinking.

That evening we struck camp and returned to Belmont with me under a deep cloud. According to Aelred, my drunken and irresponsible behaviour had sabotaged the Duke of Edinburgh's Award.

XII

The summer holiday led to the final breakdown of my relationship with Jill and Da, although at the time nothing was actually said.

As I was now sixteen they had decided that I was old enough to go away to stay with friends, a relief to us all. So, after a fortnight working in the garden for extra pocket money and mooching in the mud creeks, I left to stay with the Murphy brothers on their family farm north of Dublin. It was an exciting journey on the Empire's Best coach to London, the boat train from Euston to Liverpool and the overnight ferry to Dun Laoghaire, which started well with beer and cards in the saloon bar with a group of jolly Paddies but followed with a cold night on deck throwing up over the side.

Staying with the Murphys gave me my first glimpse at other people's happy family life. Not that there was anything very wrong with the King family, apart from general eccentricity, reclusiveness and an unbalanced mother. All my sisters have grown up as balanced, loving people leading the simple rural lives they enjoyed as children. My problem was that I now knew I was an outsider and no longer felt part of the family.

The Murphys were very different: funny, welcoming and, despite the early death of the father, they seemed to me very happy. They lived in a ramshackle Georgian house on a large arable farm. Mrs Murphy was small and down-to-earth with a sharp tongue and a warm heart. There was an older sister called Moira, seriously courted by a local young farmer, but flirtatious and pretty enough to add spice to my holiday. An uncle, the local teacher, and his wife lived nearby and regularly popped in for cups of tea, and two farm workers lived in adjacent cottages, their large families adding to the jovial community of the Murphy farm.

I loved my fortnight there. It was harvest time so we worked hard from early morning to dusk, combining, baling, and stacking the barns, for which Mrs Murphy insisted on paying me the same wage as she paid her sons. I got a great kick from driving the farm equipment, which Jim and Pat had been doing since their early teens. After work there was a big family supper, then we watched westerns and thrillers on the TV before I went exhausted but happy to my attic bedroom with its view of the sea.

It wasn't all work. There were trips to the Drogheda cattle market where Jim impressed me with his skilful bidding for heifers against keen competition from rival farmers and the auctioneer's machine-gun lingo, and trips to the beach, driven by Pat at breakneck speed along the country lanes in the family's battered Mercedes.

The high spot of my trip was the party given by the actor Cyril Cusack at his Dublin house. The Murphy boys had known the Cusack family since they were kids, and said that *all* Dublin would be there.

It was a grand affair with plenty of champagne, a band and the garden lit by torches. Mrs Murphy had kitted me out with a dark suit from Mr Murphy's wardrobe; Jim had lent me a white shirt and tie. I thought I looked the bee's knees and, after a couple of drinks to steady my nerves, moved in smoothly on three girls chatting to each other and asked the prettiest one for a dance.

We were dancing the twist which suited me fine. I was a clumsy dancer with little grasp of steps or rhythm. But my French twist was neat enough and after a few drinks converted into a wilder shake style of my own. Then the music tempo slowed and two smart couples, men in dinner jackets, started jiving and everyone picked it up. I was now back with the blonde beauty of my first dance who immediately grabbed my hand. I was hopeless; I couldn't pick up the beat or work out when and which way to turn. She tried to take the lead, but after several tangles we agreed to stop for a drink and go out into the garden.

The girl's name was Clare. She was a year ahead of me and starting at Trinity in the autumn. She was also clearly more experienced and, without any more chat other than asking about my funny name, we were necking under the trees.

I knew a little about sex from the bragging stories of more experienced Belmont friends like Pat and Tony. I'd also been taught the normal Catholic stuff about the difference between the venial sin of light petting and the mortal sin of heavy petting or 'going down there'. So a move to unzip Clare's dress and undo her bra seemed the natural next move.

The first steps went smoothly. I unhooked the hook, slid down the zip without protest. But when I moved my hand round and cupped her naked breast she pulled away suddenly.

'Hey! Stop that. What do you think you're doing?'

I said something stupid like 'Oh, nothing', and swiftly pulled my hand away as if I'd burnt myself.

'Well, do me up again, please,' said Clare crossly. Sex siren had swiftly transformed herself into older sister.

My fingers fumbled with the bra, much more difficult to do up than undo until, with a tut of irritation, Clare pushed me away and did it herself.

'Now zip me up, please.'

I managed that, and we stood looking at each other, me sheepish, Clare cross as if she might at any moment slap me. Then abruptly her face changed into a smile.

'Better luck next time,' she said, teasingly.

I left Ireland after two weeks on the overnight ferry and to save money decided to hitch home from Liverpool. After patchy lifts across country it was already evening when a man picked me up on the A1 outside Leeds. He was driving a Volvo estate car and seemed a friendly bloke. He said he ran a sports equipment firm and talked a lot about his mountaineering adventures and a sailing boat he kept at Burnham-on-Crouch, not far from Mersea.

I should have guessed when he stopped at one of his favourite pubs just off the main road and, over a steak and chips supper, kept plying me with beer, but he was easy to talk to and seemed genuinely interested in me. After a second pint and a candid chat about my problems with Jill and Da, I was too pissed to worry. When he said cheerfully that he was in no state to drive and suggested that we should camp overnight in one of his firm's new tents it seemed like a good idea.

At first everything was fine. We lay side by side in the tent fully clothed, still chatting before we both fell asleep. It wasn't until early morning in dawn light that he finally made his move.

I was desperate for a pee and thought that was why I had woken up. Then I realised a hand was at my crotch trying to unzip me. I froze, hoping desperately that if I feigned sleep the hand would go away. It didn't. I felt the man's fingers probing gently into my trousers. I twisted away suddenly. The man now lay completely still, pretending to be asleep as if to convey that only in his sleep could such a thing have happened.

We lay like that for several minutes, in frozen silence. Then I knew I had to move. My bladder was bursting. I had to have a pee and get away. I inched towards the tent flap, less concerned that he would make a sudden grab for me than that he would say something, would want to discuss what had happened. I picked up my rucksack and carefully unzipped the tent flap. At last I was out, standing in a field covered with dew by a gate to a lane. Only then did he speak, very quietly as if to himself:

'Bye, Caradoc. Take care. Nice to have met you.'

That encounter shocked me, more because of my own brazen stupidity than fear of the man in the Volvo. I knew all about homosexuality from my time at Nowton, from the man in the Ipswich cinema, the celibate yearning of some Belmont monks and my own infatuation with Gilligan. Now I felt ashamed. Had I led him on? Was I just a little cock tease?

Something worse happened that summer – the missing watch.

Strood House was empty when I got back. Jill and Da were still on holiday in the Lake District with Quentin and Priscilla. There was a letter from Lance Butler inviting me to a party he was giving with his brother in London on Saturday. As Jill and Da were not due back till Sunday evening, I phoned to accept.

I remember those two days very clearly. It was the first time that I had stayed alone in Strood House, normally full of family and noise. Apart from feeding the animals and milking the goats morning and evening, I was free to do whatever I wanted and spent the time going for long walks with Madam and Eve along the sea walls, swimming in the creek, riding my bike to the local shop for provisions and sunbathing in a deckchair with a book.

These were things I did normally when at home and often on my own, but to do them without asking anyone and coming back to a silent empty house stirred a disturbing mixture of pleasure and sadness, and the feeling that I didn't really belong in this place, that I was an interloper, not part of the family that lived there.

The watch was a gold Patek Philippe given to Jill by Grandpa on her twenty-first birthday and by far the most expensive thing in the house. Jill rarely wore it, preferring her cheap Smiths Empire wristwatch, and kept it in one of the small drawers behind the lid of her bureau in the living room.

I wasn't looking for money this time. My thieving days had finished when I left the novitiate. What I wanted was information about my adoption. I had blanked this from my mind after she and Da had told me that they knew nothing about my natural parents. Now, alone and brooding in the empty house, the wish to know who I really was kept nagging at me. I had a rare chance to find out, and Jill's desk was where she kept her secret papers.

There was the usual stuff in the main drawers of the desk, letters from us children, school reports, bank statements, Quentin's vaccination certificates, knitting patterns, the Electrolux washing machine handbook, old photographs of people I didn't recognise, but nothing about me, no sealed envelope with my name on it enclosing my adoption papers and details of my real parents.

I tried the drawers inside the lid, too small for papers but full of knick-knacks. Then, still in its display case, I found the gold watch, a slender round disc with black Roman numerals on a white face with a pigskin strap. It was the most beautiful thing I had seen, and when I tried it on it fitted my wrist perfectly. I knew I would have to borrow it for Lance's party. Apart from school uniform I had no smart clothes and didn't even own a pair of denim jeans. I would have to wear ordinary flannel trousers with wide turn-ups and my Marks & Spencer charcoal-grey jersey over a white shirt. The watch would transform the dullness of my costume. Jill and Da weren't due back until Tuesday so I could safely return it to the drawer before they arrived home.

Lance's party was in his family's large Kensington mansion flat. I don't remember much about it because I got drunk too quickly. There were a couple of other Belmont boys in the second year sixth I didn't know well but most of the guests were friends of his brother, who did something in the City. My strongest memory is of feeling awkward and badly dressed amongst a lot of London people much smarter than me, an awkwardness which would recur often over the next few years.

When I got back to Strood House I was out of luck. Jill and Da had returned home a day early. I felt immediate anxiety about returning the watch in my pocket to the drawer before being found out.

That night I tried creeping down when everyone should have been asleep. The watch was in my dressing-gown pocket. Just as I reached the living-room door Da appeared on his way back to bed after a pee. I had to pretend I needed one as well and then was far too nervous to try again.

The next day was worse and the day after that. I knew I had to return the watch to the drawer but anxiety froze me. I was sure they had already found out that it was missing and were waiting to trap me as I put it back.

They did find out but not for several days. I was there when Jill opened the drawer, after a family tea. I saw the frown on her face when she turned round and looked quickly away, not wanting to catch her eye. She didn't say anything. I guessed she must have thought she had put it somewhere else because she left the room and went upstairs to her bedroom, while I helped clear the tea things.

I was now caught. I couldn't return the watch to the drawer and had no idea where else she might have hidden it and might have already looked. I knew she would tell Da that evening when he got back from work and once they had looked in every possible place, they would realise the watch had been taken, and I would be the obvious suspect. My room could be searched and I would be found in possession. I had to transfer the watch from my sock drawer to somewhere it couldn't be found.

Later that afternoon, when everyone was out in the garden I hid the watch in the most unreachable place in the house, a hiding place I would not be able to check for another thirty-five years.

It took several days for Jill to say something and, although I guessed she knew, she didn't accuse me.

'Oh, by the way, has anyone seen my gold watch?' she asked casually, after Sunday lunch. We shook our heads.

'Have you lost it?' Caroline replied, not very interested.

'No, but I think someone might have taken it,' said Jill firmly, not looking at me. 'It was certainly there before we went on holiday.'

There was a moment's silence. Quentin and Priscilla looked bemused, but Caroline immediately picked up on what Jill was saying.

'You mean someone has stolen it?'

'Possibly ... or borrowed it perhaps.'

Of course I should have said something, but I couldn't. Nor could I sit in silence because that would have been even more suspicious. So instead I turned into duplicitous accuser.

'So who could it have been? Who's been in the house?'

Only two people apart from me. Our neighbour Alan Maskell and Mrs Puxley, the cleaning lady who would have been given keys.

I was expecting Jill to challenge me, make the accusation which I might have first denied, but in the end would have owned up, faced the punishment and been restored to her trust. But, although she glanced at me, she didn't try to catch my eye. She merely shrugged and said slowly, 'I don't know. Maybe Mrs Puxley found it while doing the housework and hid it away somewhere safer. I'll ask her on Monday.'

That was it. The question was never asked. Why didn't she accuse me? Was this, for her, the final confirmation of my depravity, the breaking point, the justification of the action which Jill and Da were already planning to take? If so there was no point in confronting me with it. Or perhaps they were both too scared of me to do so, just as I was too scared to return the watch and ask for forgiveness.

There is a photograph of Jill sitting on a rock in the Lake District during that summer holiday, in a moment of sad reflection, with a caption which she wrote herself, 'That fools should be so deep contemplative'. Very soon I would find out what was worrying her.

The rest of the summer holiday passed calmly enough. Janet and her husband, Paddy, came down with their two children which always cheered us up. Quentin had his first communion. I got a B in my English A-level, not bad for a sixteen-year-old, and to celebrate I went with Da to a traction engine rally and afterwards drank shandy in a pub garden. We swam in the marshes, went on bike rides and picnics to East and West Mersea.

At last I returned to Belmont. Da and I shared a bus to Colchester and at the bus station, where I changed for the number 7 to the station, he pressed a five-pound note into my hand, gave me a kiss on the cheek and told me to work hard. I would never see him again.

*

'That fools should be so deep contemplative.'

I received their letters in the same post in early October, after breakfast in the normal way. There were two, one from Jill and one from Da, odd because the weekly letter, written on Sunday and posted on Monday, usually came from Jill. Just looking at the familiar neat handwriting on the envelopes made me anxious.

I opened Jill's letter first.

Dear Caradoc,
After long and painful thought we have decided that we can no longer accept you as a member of the King family. We have worried for a long time about your dissolute behaviour and the effect it might have on the rest of the family. Father Thomas told us after our visit to Laxton that it was clear that you were a degenerate boy from a bad family and although we have tried hard

over the years to give you our love and full support, we no longer feel able to do so. We are therefore writing to Father Roger to tell him that we will stop paying your Belmont school fees at the end of this term and after that you must make your own way in the world. Aunty Molly has kindly offered to provide a home for you and we shall also arrange for a sum of money to be placed in a bank account in your name. You will no longer be welcome at Strood House and we wish to have no further contact with you. It saddens us deeply to be forced to reach this decision and we will always remember you in our prayers. Da is writing to you separately.

Jill.

Da's letter echoed hers.

I must have expected it. After the shock of being told I was adopted I didn't feel surprised, but I was very angry at Jill's reference to Father Thomas. How could the headmaster of a shabby little school, whom I had met for only twenty minutes, say something so cruel? Why did they believe him?

Father Roger must have received his letter in the same post as the next day I was summoned to his study. I showed him my letters and, although our old closeness had gone, he was very sympathetic and clearly upset.

'I telephoned your parents as soon as I got their letter, Caradoc. I told them how highly you are valued here at Belmont, that I strongly disagreed with Father Thomas's view of your character. I also told them that you were a very clever boy and could go far, and that curtailing your education in this way might be harmful. But I'm afraid their decision is final.'

He paused, as if expecting me to say something, but I was dumbstruck. Then he smiled.

212

'But there's good news as well. I have acted swiftly on something I have had in mind for some time and your excellent A-level result makes possible. I spoke today to Ken Wheare, the Rector of Exeter College, Oxford, whom I know personally. He has agreed that, even though a year earlier than normal, you can take the Oxford entrance exam at the end of this term.'

I was stunned. Although Father Roger had talked generally to the upper sixth about university applications, he had said nothing to me until now about being a possible Oxford candidate. Belmont's cleverest boy, Lance Butler, was being specially tutored for the Cambridge scholarship exam at the end of term but this was a rare exception. Belmont's academic record was mediocre and boys opted for red-brick universities. The last boy to go up to Oxford was an old Belmont friend of Father Roger fifteen years ago.

To celebrate this exciting news Father Roger produced a bottle of wine and we had a chat, like old times. He was keen to know how I felt about Jill and Da's letters, but seemed reluctant to discuss them. I got the impression that his conversation with Jill had not been easy and all he would say was that they were wrong and misguided in their decision. So we talked about the future, about Aunty Molly and the Blackburnes, who had maintained a strong interest in my welfare, and about how I should tackle the Oxford entrance. He told me to ring Aunty Molly which I did the next day and also to write a letter to Charles telling him what had happened. He said this time there was no need to reply to Jill's letter.

I was happily pissed by the time I left his study, both from wine and the strangely intoxicating thought that I was now free. I had been banished from the King family and the future was up to me. I felt reckless optimism, and a fortnight later I got into such serious trouble that I was nearly expelled from the school.

Breaking into the abbot's cocktail cabinet was a crime close to sacrilege. Normally boys were not allowed behind the green baize door into the monastery and it must have reflected the deep importance to the school of a Cambridge scholarship that, while the abbot was away in South America, Lance was allowed to spend a couple of hours a day working quietly in his study.

The same privilege hadn't been offered to me because it was felt that the two of us would distract each other and I had to do my extra study in a quiet corner of the school library. But the shared status of being Oxbridge candidates had drawn Lance and me together and I got into the habit of slipping behind the green door and joining Lance for a fag when he was studying.

Smoking in there was bad enough, but our crime was much worse. In a corner of the study was a small walnut cupboard which, judging from the silver tray of glasses on the table beside it, was clearly a drinks cabinet. The cupboard was locked but after several days of being tantalised by what was inside, I had the bright idea of picking the lock with the paper knife on the abbot's desk. It was surprisingly easy. After some prods with the sharp point of the knife I had opened the door to reveal a mirrored interior with a bottle of gin and decanters of sherry and whisky.

For several days Lance and I had a ball – discussing the finer points of English literature over evening drinks and cigarettes. Our exposure was sudden and hysterical. One evening the door burst open and there stood Aelred, quivering with excitement.

'Ah, ha! King and Butler!' he said in his familiar falsetto, jabbing a finger towards us. 'Got you now!'

He had, well and truly; it turned out that he had been targeting us for several days. The consequences could have been

214

catastrophic, not only for us but for Belmont as well. The crime was so serious that expulsion, plus possible excommunication, was the inevitable penalty and Belmont would have lost its first Oxbridge candidates for many years.

That sobering thought, plus the excuse of my upset emotional state, must have saved us. The punishment finally decided, after a telephone call to the abbot in Buenos Aires, was a severe head-master's beating. It was a gala occasion with boys clustering on the stairs leading to Father Roger's study as Lance and I arrived for punishment dressed in pyjamas. Lance went first so I had the extra torment of waiting outside, listening to the massive thwack of ten strokes and watching Lance totter out, pale with shock and struggling to hold back tears.

For me Father Roger's displeasure was worse than the pain.

'I am disappointed in you, Caradoc,' was all he said. It was much worse than anything Jill and Da had written in their letters. I had ignored the special effort he was making to help me. I had betrayed his trust.

'I'm sorry. It was stupid,' I mumbled.

Father Roger shrugged. Then he beat me so hard that, accord-ing to the boys waiting outside, blood was showing through my pyjama trousers and for several days sitting down was bloody painful.

Things then settled down and, suppressing all thought of family problems, I started to work hard for my Oxford entrance exam.

In early December I went by train to Oxford. I had to stay two nights in Exeter College for a written exam and inter-views, occupying an undergraduate's study and bedroom suite on a front-quad staircase, looked after by an elderly male scout in a brown overall coat who called me 'sir', and eating with other tongue-tied candidates on lamp-lit polished tables in the panelled College Hall, benignly overlooked by generations of college rectors whose portraits lined the walls. At night it was so cold that I slept on the sofa in front of the gasfire in the sitting room wrapped in my long army surplus overcoat.

All candidates for English Literature sat the same exam, a frightening ordeal for several hundred candidates sitting at rows of desks in a vast exam room called Schools in the High Street. I was lucky: there was a general question about the nature of tragedy for which I could rehash my prize-winning essay on *King Lear* and another one on the role of the narrator in fiction, which allowed me to compare two recent set texts of *Wuthering Heights* and *Tess of the d'Urbevilles*. I thought I had done all right.

The interviews were more of an ordeal. The first one was with Mr Hall, the sub-rector and law fellow, a tetchy figure who made me nervous. He asked me why I wanted to read law and instead of saying that I didn't, because it seemed better to grab every opportunity to impress, I said I was fired by the intellectual challenge of law in deciding between innocence and guilt. He then asked if I wanted to be a solicitor or barrister, which was disconcerting because I didn't want to be either. But I had to say something.

'Barrister.'

'Why?'

'Because I have done quite a bit of acting and I could apply my theatrical skills to performing in court.'

Mr Hall clearly wasn't impressed. Only then, seeing his frown, did I explain that I hadn't planned to study law and thought that my subject was going to be English. He looked puzzled. Checking a list, he said he should have been interviewing me as moral tutor. Without explaining what that meant, he shifted the conversation to general issues, like the spread of communism,

President Kennedy's recent assassination and whether I believed in God.

The English tutor, Jonathan Wordsworth, was more affable. A descendant of the poet, he was young, handsome, and wore a three-piece tweed suit. He asked me vaguely what were my favourite works of literature – and I rattled off Shakespeare and Dickens and expanded on what I'd written in the exam. He then asked me about poetry and, sensing it was better to keep off Wordsworth, I volunteered Keats and particularly 'Ode On a Grecian Urn'. He asked me why I liked the poem, and to compare its themes to 'Ode to a Nightingale'. I waffled nervously about nature, death and beauty; Mr Wordsworth nodded and smiled. It seemed clear to me I was talking nonsense. Later he would remark crushingly that he had only offered me a place because of my handwriting.

My last interview was with the rector, Kenneth Wheare, a genial older man who asked about the origins of my name and then about Belmont Abbey and whether I had enjoyed my time there. He said Father Roger had mentioned that I had some family problems, but without prompting me to talk about them. He asked me what hobbies I enjoyed and when I mentioned acting told me about OUDS and Exeter's John Ford Society and moved the conversation to Gilbert and Sullivan, whose operas he greatly admired. Somehow we then moved on to the Kennedy assassination and the recent resignation of Harold Macmillan as prime minister. I knew he was testing me, but he did it in such a friendly way that I stopped worrying about how to impress. It was like talking to Father Roger.

When I left he shook my hand and said, 'I enjoyed our chat, Caradoc, and hope we can find you a place, although that's not really up to me but your admissions tutor. Whatever happens, good luck. You're a bright chap and deserve to do well.'

It was a gesture of support and friendship I badly needed and which Ken Wheare would stand by during the two difficult years ahead.

I returned to Belmont desperately wanting a place at Oxford but adopted my normal defence mechanism of telling Father Roger that I had performed so badly I didn't stand a chance. That last week of term was a strange and sad time. I was the only boy leaving the school and because I preferred not to talk about what had happened to me, only close friends like the Murphy brothers, Kieran Lyons, Tony Aitken and Lance Butler realised it. So I slipped away from Belmont with few farewells. Father Roger gave me an unlikely hug, wished me luck and told me to come back whenever I wanted. I missed saying goodbye to my housemaster Father Martin, who was somewhere else when I knocked on his study before the school bus took the London boys to Hereford station. I didn't return to the school for over forty years.

My last visit to Belmont was three years ago, to attend the Belmont Association Annual Dinner with Tony Aitken. About twenty-five old boys came to the dinner, although the school had closed down in 1994. We were an odd mix from different decades – provincial solicitors, teachers, small businessmen and civil servants.

There was a lot of talk over dinner about Father Roger, who as headmaster had transformed Belmont as both an academic and sporting school and then abruptly resigned and left the monastery. Afterwards, as the whisky flowed, Tony, who has stayed in close contact with him, told us what had really happened. In 1968 Father Roger had fallen in love with his secretary, Joyce, who was already married to the school bursar and the mother of a boy in the school. After a year of secrecy and anguish, he had left the school and monastery to live with Joyce. They were together for thirty years, the last eighteen of them in Las Vegas where Father Roger worked as a medical counsellor. But the two of them had never married because Father Roger was still bound by his priestly vows which he refused to renounce. In 1996 Roger was struck down with a fatal kidney cancer, and his old friend, Father Mark Jaboulet, then Abbot of Belmont, was finally able to resolve Roger's problem with the Catholic Church and by special dispensation he was allowed to marry his long-time partner shortly before his death.

It was a moving story. Father Roger was a hero of my childhood, a role model of kindness and leadership, my saviour from Jill and Da's rejection and the damage it caused. It pleased me deeply that he had found happiness and spiritual redemption after the emotional upheavals of his own life.

My other hero Jenks, or Dom David Jenkins, had also died young, in 2003, aged seventy-one. A decade earlier, after being headmaster for six years and a teacher there for thirty-four years, he had been responsible for the closure of Belmont Abbey School. He had devoted half his life to the school and clearly adored it. In the valedictory issue of the *Belmont Magazine* he published a moving farewell message which said 'When I came here ... what I felt was the naturalness and the normality, the honesty and directness, the genuineness which every monk, master and boy related to and was related to by every other ... It has all been very worthwhile.'

I feel the same. I was only there for a short time, again arriving in the middle and leaving early, but this very average school, and its two inspirational teachers, was for me exceptionally worthwhile.

FIVE

Growing Up Is Good for You

XIII

It was strange not returning to Strood House after leaving Belmont. Instead, after reaching London on the school train, I took the suburban line from King's Cross to Enfield and a new home with Aunty Molly. My arrival, lugging a Revelation suitcase stuffed with my school clothes, must have been even stranger for her. Aunty Molly was then a spinster in her early fifties who had lived alone since Grandpa's death in 1958 and, from the spacious Hermitage in Forty Hill, had moved a mile away to Archway, Gentleman's Row, an elegant but decrepit Georgian house she had converted and lived in the ground-floor flat. She now had to share this with an adolescent nephew in whose company she had probably spent no more than a fortnight. We both felt apprehensive.

But on 15 December, I got a letter from the Rector of Exeter which changed my life and made my first Christmas away from home a very happy one.

'I am very pleased to tell you that, subject to you obtaining a second A level in order to matriculate, we can offer you a place to read English Literature, starting in the Michaelmas Term 1964.'

Two days later, just before my seventeenth birthday, a trunk full of my childhood belongings was delivered to Archway – a last joint Christmas and birthday present from Jill and Da. It badly upset me and that evening, when Aunty Molly was out playing bridge, I went on my own to the pub at the end of Gentleman's Row and got slowly drunk. Next day, with a hangover, I wrote them a sarcastic Christmas card thanking them for my childhood and education and announcing that I had got a place at Oxford. Then I tore it up.

My childhood was over and I realised for the first time that I was now without both family and blood relations. As the seasonal good cheer ebbed into the bleak, empty days of early January I felt lonely, and anxious trying to adjust to my new home, and formidable adopted aunt.

Aunty Molly, Malaya, 1946.

Aunty Molly had led an exciting life. During the war she worked first as an ambulance driver and then joined the WRACs and after training was posted to the Far East. The second woman to land in Singapore after the Japanese surrender, she was sent to the notorious Changi Jail to assist in the rehabilitation of POWs. In January 1947 she had left the army and joined the Malaysian Civil Service as a Welfare Officer. She was posted all over Malaya during the attempted Chinese takeover and there she first met the man she would finally marry forty-five years later.

Unmarried, gregarious, well travelled and independent, she smoked, drank, partied, drove rakish cars, had boyfriends. A vivacious, good-looking woman, she wore bright lipstick and smart clothes, the epitome of the worldliness her sister so despised. Molly was the scarlet woman. Jill was the devoted, self-sacrificing housewife and mother who had given up a brilliant musical career for the sake of her children.

Despite their different lifestyles, the sisters shared a sharp tongue and Celtic stroppiness. Molly also could be difficult to live with, fussy and bossy, with elaborate protocols about cutlery etiquette and good table manners, derived from an inflated conviction that her family were really 'top drawer' while most other people, including her more affluent neighbours in Gentleman's Row, were rather common. She was not at all intellectual, but an avid reader of middlebrow fiction and the *Daily Telegraph*, staunchly right wing and not afraid to tell people that the end of capital punishment was a bad mistake. But that was only a side of her, the stock attitudes of her class and generation.

She also had a natural gift for friendship and a rebellious streak, which enabled her to have a long and unsuitable affair with a Caribbean builder called Carter and include a couple of waspish queens, Simon and Elliot, among her closest friends. She would be very good for me at just the right time – proud of my Oxford place, supportive and understanding about what I had been through with the Kings, but also tough and unsentimental, with a firm belief that socks were for pulling up and life was for getting on with.

But Molly wasn't happy. She still missed her father, and nine months earlier had suddenly lost her brother Sidney, who had abruptly sold his partnership in Weld & Beavan and moved with Effie and family to Cornwall, where he had bought some land and seaside cottages which he planned to rent out to holidaymakers. Soon after he arrived he had died suddenly from a heart attack while out working in the fields.

Molly also missed the affluent Hermitage lifestyle and found it difficult to accept that she now had to work for a living – as a dental nurse. Holidays and travel were limited. Her one-third share of Grandpa's estate had been enough to buy and renovate the house but, apart from a small portfolio of shares in oddball businesses like Malayan Tiger beer and Pifco Electrics on the Great Cambridge Road, she had modest private means. Like most of the wartime generation she lived thriftily. All lights had to be switched off when not in use, a paraffin heater was carried from room to room and I have chill memories of frost on the inside of the bathroom window and too little hot water in the bath to cover my body.

Her cooking was also thrifty and not very good. Meat rolls, mince, spam, milk puddings, macaroni cheese and over-cooked vegetables were at that time family staples and Aunty Molly's fridge was crammed with tasteless leftovers which had to be enlivened for cold suppers with generous helpings of piccalilli, Branston pickle and tomato chutney.

There were treats as well. Breakfast was the best meal, starting with a neatly cut half of grapefruit followed by bacon, eggs and fried bread every day, white toast with hand-rolled butter balls and home-made marmalade, accompanied by large cups of percolated coffee and, with the last one, a companionable du Maurier tipped cigarette, the first of Aunty Molly's daily dozen.

The other indulgence, after Strood House austerity, was alcohol, which Aunty Molly enjoyed keenly but drank sensibly. We had amontillado before dinner and usually a glass of wine with the meal, preferably Beaujolais (pronounced Beaujolly), carefully re-corked each night, and on special occasions a bottle of Nuits-St-George or a good Bordeaux from the cellar inherited from Grandpa. Her main tipple was whisky, always a cheap brand mixed half and half with home-made soda which she drank after supper, chatting by the fire or listening to the radio, and sometimes before weekend lunch.

Soon after my arrival I asked her, over a fireside whisky, whether she knew anything about my natural family. Aunty Molly was surprisingly informative.

'Your father was an opera singer who left your mother. He went off with someone else when you were born. Your real name is Barton,' she said matter-of-factly. 'You also have two brothers who were at the Leys School in Cambridge.' She went on to tell me that after I was adopted a strange woman, possibly my mother although she thought more likely the family nanny, had arrived out of the blue at Strood House to try to take me back. There the story tailed off. She said that was all she knew, but I sensed also that my natural family was something she didn't particularly want to talk about, part of my life which had nothing to do with her.

We never talked again about my past. I respected her unspoken wish that she didn't really want to know. Also the idea that my father was a philandering opera singer must have satisfied my curiosity because for the next three decades I made no effort to find out anything more, even though only a year after our conversation, the law changed and adopted children were allowed to see their original birth certificates and other records of their natural families.

Aunty Molly was more concerned about my future plans than digging over the past.

'You'll have to get a job, Caradoc, while you study for your A level because I can't afford to keep you. Jill has sent a cheque for a hundred pounds to deposit in a new bank account in your name, but don't spend it too quickly because Jill said that's all you are going to get.'

This was my pay-off. Mean by modern standards but £100 in 1964 was almost the amount of one term's fees at Belmont, so a substantial sum for a seventeen-year-old. I spent £30 of it three days later, on an ugly second-hand Zündapp Bella motor scooter.

Molly's friend Elliot helped me find the job. He worked in the hotel business and heard that the Berkeley in Piccadilly (now demolished) needed a temporary night waiter in its staff dining room. The pay was good because it was night work and there seemed to me a touch of glamour about working behind the scenes in a great London hotel. I scootered up to London on the Zündapp and after a short interview with Mr Prentice, a snooty under-manager with a pencilled-in moustache and wearing a black jacket and pinstriped trousers, I was offered the job.

It only lasted three weeks, but that was enough. Riding there and back again in the dark was hard, and to call the job waitering was a misnomer. Most of my time was spent washing up in a steamy windowless kitchen and acting as general kitchen boy for the bad-tempered staff chef. But I worked hard and got to know the night-staff regulars who spent most of the time playing cards, drinking Scotch served in teapots because alcohol was banned, and bickering about whose turn it was to answer the bell from guests.

There were long periods in the early hours when there was nothing to do. I kept awake reading history books. Sleeping on the job was strictly forbidden. It was reading that got me fired. Drinking, playing cards and gossiping about the guests were fine but Mr Prentice, who according to gossip had been dismissed from a royal household for pilfering, took great objection to my reading. The first time he dressed me down loudly in front of the other staff who, as soon as he had gone, told me to pay no attention; Prentice was a jerk. So I did it again and Prentice went ballistic, called me an insubordinate puppy, and told me to pick up my cards.

I now needed a long-term job away from Enfield. There was little chance of finding anything locally apart from work in a restaurant or shop and living for too-long periods with Aunty Molly might lead to friction. The obvious solution was to apply to Gabbitas & Thring, the well-known prep school master recruitment agency.

I was in luck. The gingery figure in a three-piece tweed suit who introduced himself as Gerald Warboys asked a few questions about my education and beamed with pleasure when I told him I had a place to read English at Oxford. He said he had just the thing for a young Catholic with a good educational background – the role of junior assistant master at Barlborough Hall in Derbyshire, prep school for the Jesuit college Mount St Mary's, which had a last-minute vacancy because of sudden illness. An interview wouldn't be necessary because his recommendation would be enough. The salary was the standard rate for this position – £400 per annum and I could start at once. Would I please fill in the registration form, a swift phone call, and then the job would be mine. So two days later, like Nicholas Nickleby, I headed north by scooter to a small village near Chesterfield with a small suitcase strapped on the passenger seat.

Barlborough wasn't Dotheboys Hall, but a typical minor prep school of that time, with its run-down accommodation, oddball staff, many on the run from murky private lives, and an autocratic headmaster who wielded the strap on the hand with sadistic glee.

I had never been a school prefect so disciplining, let alone teaching, small boys was a new challenge. A few cheeky trouble-makers tried it on at first, asking silly questions and pretending not to hear or understand me, but once I had survived these initiation rites and learned to apply the standard teacher tricks of angry voice, heavy silences and mocking sarcasm, I settled easily into my new role of master rather than pupil. I also found that I really enjoyed teaching, communicating the enthusiasm for English and history planted in me by Jenks and Father Roger, and applying Charles Blackburne's irreverent *1066 and All That* approach to historical events.

Barlborough Hall was a fine Jacobean mansion set in spacious parkland. Junior assistant masters were expected to help with games, so in the afternoon I had to referee cold and muddy junior football games and in my last term umpire cricket, both of which I loathed. But I drew on my own more solitary sporting skills and in the Easter term trained up a cross-country squad which, with me coaching on the run, achieved such a high per-formance that the team reached third place in the Derbyshire prep schools tournament run at Barlborough just before the Easter break.

By the end of the first term my popularity rating among the boys was high, but the staff were more difficult. The three Jesuit priests and one lay brother weren't a problem. They lived sepa-rate lives as a mini-religious community with a separate refectory. Even the strap-happy headmaster Father Ambrose was friendly and full of praise for my work in the school. The problem area was the lay staff, a motley crew led, in the best prep school tradition, by two army officers, Captain Bulmer and Major Standish. These two clearly loathed each other for reasons eventually explained to me by the sour old maths master, Mr Hengist.

The problems were class and rank. John Bulmer was a Welsh Guards officer in his early thirties, forced to retire early from the army after a fall from a bolting horse which had buggered up his back. He was tall and good-looking, with a sporty beard and jovial manner which made him popular with the boys. He rode a Lambretta 200 which I envied because it was much faster and more stylish than my clapped-out ugly 100cc Zündapp. Bulmer decided to befriend me because, as he put it, we were of similar class; he was clearly impressed that I was going to Oxford which was on a par with his military training at Sandhurst. So, a couple of times a week, we would roar up the school drive on our bikes after prep and hole up in a local pub where he would tell me his army adventures, notably at Suez, and lubricious stories about his posh girlfriends who never appeared but were apparently keenly competing for his favours.

If Bulmer could just about claim to have been wounded in action, his senior officer, Major Standish, looked a poor and seedy imitation of a soldier. A decade older than Bulmer, he claimed to be an ex-member of the Royal Artillery with battle experience in Korea. But it was difficult to take him seriously. Despite the three-piece tweed suit and regimental tie there was something distinctly unmilitary about his appearance, which was unkempt and slightly soiled. He had a whining voice and a common accent, and talked interminably about his subject, geography, the wartime exploits of the Royal Artillery, of which he seemed to have encyclopaedic knowledge, and Crystal Palace football club. He clearly drove John Bulmer mad with irritation.

That Easter holiday I went to stay with the Blackburnes and had my final encounter with Jill. Charles had always kept in touch, and I had been back to Nowton a couple of times since leaving. After I had heard from Father Roger that I was adopted I had written to Charles and this started a correspondence from which I have kept several of his letters, written on the back of discarded pages of his desk diary in his familiar Parker 51 handwriting. They are poignant mementos, which show both Charles's affection and strong wish to help and also, from letters I must have written him, my troubled state of mind. He wrote in one:

My dear Caradoc, V. many thanks for your letter and vital information. I have been thinking a lot about you and your future and it is difficult to put all my thoughts down on paper without risk of misunderstandings ... I do realise – and I'm sure all do (except the Kings!) how terrible all this is for you – waiting, wondering etc. It is worth repeating that you should not think of being a nuisance to people. My experience is that however charitable people are theoretically, they don't bother about people they don't like. The fact that people seem to be bothering about you is a proof that you have qualities that are agreeable and pleasant to people; it isn't just indiscriminate charity ...

One thing, however, dear boy: You must never let the word Charity appear in thought, word or deed vis-à-vis the Blackburnes. We don't regard anything we do or did for you as anything but a pleasure. So if any or all plans break down, then you come to stay whenever and for as long as you like. If by any chance we're all away and the place is shut up of course you

couldn't; but that practically never happens! I could easily sug-
gest that we employed you as a gardener in the hols: but this
would not do as you would have a guilt complex every time you
were five minutes late; and I should feel like Simon Legree in
Uncle Tom's Cabin *whipping on the slaves! (or should feel like*
Jill King and her list of jobs: '8.22 Caradoc oils mower; 9.01
Caradoc pulls weeds'!!)

And in another:

I do appreciate how boring & embarrassing it must be for you
to be living (apparently) on other people's charity. But I think I
have said before that Blackburnes, Havers, Nightingales etc., etc.
are not given to indiscriminate charity to people they don't know
or don't like. If you go on getting invitations from the above (&
lots of others) it must be that not only do they feel sorry for you
& want to help, but they actually like you a good deal & have
pleasure in your society. I really do mean this & hope that it is
a paragraph that will come to mind in moments of black depres-
sion, when you feel like 'Oliver Twist'!

As well as offering friendship and advice Charles's letters were
also full of news about Nowton and the Blackburnes' life.

I was just about to write to you: not about anything special –
but just a letter, when yours arrived. My dear, the gaiety you
Catholics get up to! Neville and I have been buzzing around
recently: Wednesday to CG [Covent Garden] *to hear Figaro*
which was a splendid production. Thurs: after a happy morning
at the Zoo and afternoon at '55 Days in Peking' to SW [Sadler's
Wells] *on to hear La Belle Helene which was q. well done but*
like 'Salad Days' – so we left in the first interval! Fri: to Bristol

233

and back between 8.45 and 4.45 for a Memorial Service for our old uncle. The Havers' were back from Le Touquet by w/e – so a bottle of Campari was consumed. This w/e we're off to Glyndebourne and the following week there are 2 Handel operas to be heard at Sadler's Wells.

One letter particularly touched me when I read it again forty years later.

So let me say at once that if I personally was a free agent (i.e. had no brother or sister) and I could sort out the financial position – I would not have hesitated a year ago to adopt you; nor do I now hesitate to say that any help or advice I can give you will never be a bore or the least trouble.

The strength of his feeling would quite soon cause problems for us both, but at the time those letters were deeply reassuring in moments of depression.

He never told me whether he made direct contact with the Kings though I think he did. In his letters he tries to be impartial and writes about 'not wanting to take one side or another' but the summer before there had been a very frosty response from Jill and Da when I said that I planned to visit Nowton. So I had turned down Charles's invitation to play a part in his August outdoor productions of *Love's Labour's Lost*, with a cast of old Nowton boys and various amateur thesps and friends.

The Easter trip was my first return to Nowton since my eviction from the King family. Charles, Betty and Neville were all there, and although I slept in a spare room in the school the four of us ate together and spent evenings in the Small House. It was an exciting but scary visit, which was the effect the Blackburnes always had on me. Charles and Neville were charming, affably camp and very amusing. They were also intimidating because they were still my joint ex-headmasters. Chain-smoking Betty was her normal gruff and barking self and continued to call me 'Dog', the nickname she had created for me when I joined the school. The three of them, having lived together for years, were a formidable trio. Even though they were kind and hospitable I couldn't help feeling awkward and self-conscious while trying hard not to show it.

The idea of me making a surprise visit to Strood House came up on the first evening. Charles, who knew that the Kings had continually failed to answer letters from Father Roger, the education authorities and possibly his own lawyers, suggested it.

'My dear, I think you must,' he said over dinner. 'It is quite unacceptable that you should be just banished from their life without further contact. It may not lead to reconciliation, but at least you should have a chance to talk to them and try to reach an understanding. It's possible of course that Jill and Eric feel embarrassed by what has happened, realise they have handled it wrong but feel unable to make the first move. It's all very silly and I think it important that you make one last try to put the matter to rest. If they don't want you to live with them any more that's fine, but this cold silence can only be hurtful for everyone.'

The prospect filled me with dread. I didn't quite have the courage to say that I had no wish ever to see Jill again, that I knew how angry and obstinate she could be once she had made up her mind and that I was quite sure a visit from me would not be welcome. So I agreed with the Blackburnes that it was worth a last effort to try to break the hostile silence and two days later set off on my scooter for the thirty-mile journey to Strood House.

It was a sunny spring day, blue sky and breeze across the marshes; Strood House looked welcoming and beautiful. I rang the bell on the front door in the yard beside the house and stood back waiting. Suddenly the window above me opened.

'What do you want?' It was Jill, her tone sharp, her face expressing both anger and panic.

Having talked it through with Charles, I knew what I had to say.

'I just wanted to talk to you. To try and make peace.'

'Go away!' she shouted. 'I don't want to talk to you.'

'But ...'

'You are not wanted here. Just go away.'

Years later I found out the reason for her panic. Caroline and Priscilla were walking the dogs with Quentin in the Cow's Field when I turned up. Jill had been terrified that I would still be there when they came back, that they would be glad to see me, that her eradication of my existence in the family, the blanking of my name in conversation would be confronted and she would be forced to explain the inexplicable to her children.

I didn't stay. I got on my scooter and drove away and didn't return to Strood House for over thirty years, long after the Kings had left.

The Blackburnes were very upset by what happened. Charles felt he was in some way responsible. For the rest of my stay they did everything they could to ensure that I had a good time, a trip to the cinema to see *My Fair Lady*, a visit to a local famous author – their close friend Angus Wilson – who lived nearby with his partner Tony Garrett, the gift of a leather biking jacket which Betty bought me in Bury. There was also an impromptu drinks party for other local friends, where I met two families who both became for a short time important in my life, the Havers and the Nightingales.

Michael Havers was then a criminal barrister on the East Anglian circuit and destined for a brilliant legal career, culminating as Mrs Thatcher's Lord Chancellor. I had first met his sons

Nigel and Philip during my lunch trip to Nowton two years earlier; they were both now illustrious old boys, Philip at Eton and Nigel at acting school. Their mother Carol was charming and beautiful and the family were Blackburne favourites. Whether because they actually liked me or as a favour to the Blackburnes they took me under their wing. The impromptu drinks party led to an invitation to come and stay at their country home near Newmarket. During that visit Michael took Philip and me to Ipswich Crown Court to watch him in action. One of his cases was defending a local farmer charged with buggering a pig. Michael's witty and eloquent defence included the farmer's unlikely claim that the pig had just backed onto his 'member' when he was having a pee, but Michael's deft cross-examination of the farmer's hostile neighbour and prosecution witness achieved an acquittal.

The Nightingales, also at the party, were another happy family, not glamorous like the Haverses but also very kind and supportive. Dr Nightingale was a bluff tweedy GP with a practice near Newmarket and presided over a family of adoring womenfolk, of whom the oldest daughter, Helen, was a year younger than me and in her last year at a boarding school in West Runton in Norfolk. As a prep schoolgirl she had been at Moreton Hall, which sparked off conversation about the Olivia in *Twelfth Night* I had adored during my last summer term at Nowton, who turned out to be Helen's best friend's older sister.

She was small, pretty with an infectious laugh. I felt there was immediate rapport between us and managed to say, when it was time for the Nightingales to leave, that I hoped we would meet again. She smiled.

'That would be nice, in the summer after my exams. But you can write to me at school if you like.'

Charles, who had been chatting to the parents, must have overheard us and sensed a budding romance.

'My dears,' he said, taking Helen's hand to say goodbye. 'I do hope you both will join us. It's all been decided.'

'What has?' we said together.

'That this year we shall do a late-summer production of the *Dream.* Nigel and Philip have agreed to return to the Nowton stage after their last year's debut in *Love's Labour's Lost.* So will Tony if Angus's travels permit. So what about you two for Lysander and Hermia?'

And so it was agreed. Helen and I would be one pair of Shakespeare's muddled lovers – and as it turned out in real life as well.

At Barlborough the expected Bulmer–Standish showdown happened a week after the start of term. John must have checked the Major's military credentials during the Easter holidays. For a while he said nothing but I could tell from the gleam in his eye when he listened to Standish that he was just waiting for the right opportunity – and Standish gave it to him.

At a staff supper the conversation turned to cricket. John Bulmer had played for Sandhurst and was a deckchair coach for the Barlborough first team. Standish also claimed cricket expertise, not as a player but as a devoted Yorkshire fan. It turned out that on the previous Saturday both he and Bulmer had been at the same county match in Sheffield with Yorkshire playing John's home side Hampshire. There had been an incident, which didn't make sense to the rest of us, involving a hand injury to a Hampshire batsman from a Yorkshire bouncer which had forced him to retire from the match. The Captain and the Major both had strong views about what happened, and at some point in the heated conversation, Standish said something about falling off a horse which made John so angry that he leapt to his feet and knocked over his chair.

'Are you trying to imply that my back injury is invented, Standish?'

'Of course not, Captain,' said Standish, inflecting the word. 'But there's not much sign of it.'

In chill silence John walked round to where Standish was sitting at one end of the table.

'Major Standish, I want a word with you. Outside. Now!'

'What about?' said Standish, looking nervous.

There was a dramatic pause. Then Bulmer said slowly, 'About your impersonation of a Major of the Royal Artillery.'

Standish looked even more nervous.

'What on earth do you mean?'

'I mean that after checking military records I have discovered that you are in fact a Captain Standish of the Catering Corps who was cashiered for fraudulent conversion of army supplies. In short, you are a conman and a thief.'

There was stunned silence.

Standish at last rose to his feet.

'That's a bloody lie, Bulmer.'

'No, it isn't.'

'Well, come outside then.'

They were now standing face to face, glaring at each other. Bulmer turned and led the way to the door. There was only one solution.

It didn't last long and only Bulmer returned, pale and clearly shaken with a small cut on his cheek. Standish disappeared, apparently leaving the school the next morning with his suitcases in a taxi. Father Ambrose announced at prayers that he had had to go suddenly – for family reasons. I had to take over teaching geography.

I greatly enjoyed the rest of that term. It was only six years since leaving Nowton and I had retained rosy memories of indolent sunny days spent in a large country house set in beautiful grounds. I happily joined in with the boys, fishing in the lake and going on bike rides. Also, to relieve the tedium of cricket, I introduced the Nowton favourite Merchantmen, which was a huge success. John and I continued our pub trips and, without the threat of being breathalysed, could enjoy the thrill of racing our scooters through the local country lanes on hot evenings, mellow after a couple of pints.

I was also in a flutter of love. After a first stilted exchange of letters with Helen at her school in West Runton we started writing weekly with humorous accounts of school life and tender anticipation of meeting again in the summer holidays.

But all was not well. Whether from love, indolence or the residual shock of my brief encounter with Jill, I was finding it difficult to concentrate on A-level history. I was still fired up by Jenks's enthusiasm, mugging up A. L. Rowse's *Elizabeth* and A. J. P. Taylor on twentieth-century Europe, but without direction I found it very difficult to answer the sample questions I had been given. When I sat the examination by special arrangement at Chesterfield Grammar School I was so nervous I blanked on the questions. I knew that my paper was lousy and certainly not good enough to get the B grade I needed for Oxford.

Term ended a week later and after fond farewells to my pupils and promises exchanged and never kept to meet John Bulmer in London, I strapped my suitcase onto the back of the scooter and drove back to Enfield. I had nothing to do until rehearsals for the *Dream* starting in mid-August and no money. The only prospect was to get a temporary manual job in Enfield and spend several weeks living with Aunty Molly, a dispiriting thought. I also felt depressed at the prospect of my failed A-level.

I needed to get out of myself.

XIV

One evening the Archway phone rang. Unusually, it was a call for me.

'Hello, Caradoc. Fancy a trip to France?'

It was my cousin Tim Battle. I had seen him only twice during the last six years, because of the estrangement between our families. Tim was in his last year at Gresham's, a Norfolk public school popular with Nowton parents.

I was immediately excited by the plan. Tim's parents were driving down to stay with Jessie and Da's sister Mavis who now lived in the South of France with her new partner, Manfred, a German businessman who had retired early and was supposed to have pots of money.

Tim's plan, agreed by his parents, was that the two of us should hitchhike through France and join the rest of the family for a holiday at Menton, a seaside resort close to Mavis's house in Malbosquet, a village in the hills close to Vence. It was irresistible. I had never been abroad before. I immediately said yes

241

and was invited over to lunch the following Sunday at the Battles' house near Richmond.

'All happy families resemble each other but each unhappy family is unhappy in its own way.' This quote from *Anna Karenina*, now a platitude on family life, applied to me. Other people's happy families – the Havers, the Nightingales and the Battles – attracted me like a moth to light.

Tim's father, Dickie, was then at the top of his career as a consultant plastic surgeon and the Battles lived comfortably. They owned a substantial 1930s house with large garden next to Richmond Park, and had two cars in the garage and a cottage at Shingle Street on the Suffolk coast. It was an affluent and beguiling contrast to the penny-pinching heirloom sparseness of life at Archway.

We left London for France on the midday boat train and arrived in Calais in the early evening. I was immediately struck by the enticing 'foreignness' of everything – the babble of French, men in berets, wafting Gauloises, Pernod water carafes, and the sophistication of sitting down to *steak frites* and a bottle of *vin ordinaire* in the station buffet before heading out of town to find a field to pitch our tent in. Aunty Molly had told me that her grandfather had once been arrested at Calais for hitting a station porter over the head with his umbrella because he didn't understand his English, but I adored France immediately.

Our journey south started in pleasantly bucolic fashion. The weather was hot and the lifts were plentiful. We brought *jambon* and pâté in a *charcuterie*, baguettes in the *boulangerie* and beers in an *alimentation* for boozy picnic lunches. We made a detour to see the famous railway carriage in Compiègne where the 1918 Armistice was signed. We camped on the outskirts of small towns and stuffed ourselves with delicious but incredibly cheap *prix fixe* menus at nearby Routiers and on the second night had boozy games of *boules* with two local lads at a cafe on the outskirts of Fontainebleau.

Further south the lifts ran out and rain set in. A commercial traveller took us on a detour to Vichy and then dropped us in the middle of nowhere after deciding to visit a relative. We spent a wet and fruitless afternoon supplicating oblivious motorists and then took a bus to Lyon and headed for the rail station. There was only one train to the Côte d'Azur that evening, the daytime equivalent to *Le Train Bleu*, for which we impulsively bought tickets, blowing most of the rest of our holiday money.

At around one in the morning we reached Nice and stumbled out of the station into a hot, noisy and very foreign city. It was too late to ring Mavis and we had no money, so we walked along a street following a signpost to *Le Mer* thinking our best bet would be to sleep on the beach, but reaching a town park with benches we decided that was far enough.

The park seemed empty and, feeling dead tired, we just stretched out on two benches and fell asleep. But not for long. I woke to the murmur of voices and someone trying to open my rucksack which I had strapped to the end of the bench. My immediate response was frozen fear. I could see a second man hovering over Tim's bench. Anger took over.

'*Allez vous en*! Leave us alone!'

My shout woke Tim who sat up suddenly and fell off the bench. The men laughed and then started gabbling in French, too fast to understand but apologetic hand-waving and repeated '*Pardon, Monsieur*!' made it clear that they meant no harm. In the dim glow of a streetlamp they looked like tramps and, judging from the smell, were drunk. We had clearly fallen asleep on their normal benches. After more *pardons* the Frenchmen at last shambled off to find somewhere else to sleep, leaving me and Tim to return to our benches.

Back to sleep, but not for long. A loud new voice erupted in my dreams.

'Attendez, attendez!'

A gendarme was gabbling in French and making dismissive gestures with his hands, indicating clearly that he did not want us sleeping in his park and that we should clear off.

We hung about in the streets until eight o'clock, then called Aunt Mavis from a cafe payphone. I could hear her warm, jolly, very British voice standing beside Tim in the phone cubicle.

'Darling Tim, how lovely to hear your voice. Where are you?'

Tim described our overnight adventures.

'Poor darlings, how dreadful! Manfred will drive down straight away to collect you. Now give me the address.' Half an hour later we were in the walnut and leather comfort of Manfred's Jaguar snaking up the road to Malbosquet.

The remainder of the holiday was total pleasure. Most of it was spent by the sea in Cap Martin close to Menton. Tim and I stayed in a campsite but every day joined the Battle family at their hotel by the beach, which looked a bit like Monsieur Hulot's from the outside but was much more luxurious, with chandeliers, tables laid out on the terrace, a bar with deep leather armchairs and a garden of jewelled ladies with deep tans reclining on elegant wooden loungers, while their poodles piddled in the flowerbeds.

But the best of the holiday was our three days at Bastide d'Agrimont, Manfred and Mavis's pretty pink house covered with bougainvillea, with its tantalising views of shimmering lavender hills and distant blue sea. Tim and I slept in the pool house and we spent all day around the pool, reading, playing cards and eating simple but delicious al fresco meals in the shade of a vine-wreathed loggia. The only other activity apart from swimming was Dickie's compulsory afternoon Egyptian PT which he defined with great solemnity as lying absolutely still on his bed thinking about nothing.

On our last night Manfred treated us to dinner at a restaurant in nearbyVence which Dickie said was one of the best on the Côte d'Azur with two Michelin stars. We sat in a candle-lit garden and I sampled for the first time the exquisite taste of pâté de foie gras and syllabub, dishes of nectar after the mince, spotted-dick and rice-pudding diets of school and Strood House.

The South of France holiday was a transforming experience. I discovered the good life – sun, sea, laziness, delicious food and wine and the slow tempo of a hot climate. Eating breakfast on a sun-drenched terrace, lazing by a pool, doing nothing but reading and occasionally swimming in a clear, blue sea remain constant pleasures. It was the first indication of a life full of treats, that growing up was good for you, that swimming in the Mediterranean was a great deal nicer than icy plunges into the North Sea at Easter, that olives, courgettes and fresh-picked peaches were a life beyond over-boiled greens and sludgy swede.

But mostly I loved that holiday because for a short time I was part of a happy and sociable family. Tim and I were now good friends and Jessie and Mavis were two of the nicest women I have known, warm, generous and intensely loyal to the people they loved. They were typical of their class and generation, brought up by strict and devoted parents, whose main ambition for their 'gels' was for them to marry well, like their mothers, and devote themselves to the care of husbands and children. They were exceptionally close sisters, loyal and extremely fond of each other which years later, when Mavis and Manfred moved back from France to live just a few miles away from Jessie and Dickie's

Suffolk retirement cottage, gave them shared strength in coping with ageing husbands and widowhood. As role models when I was growing up I owe them both a lot.

Back in Enfield the news wasn't good. An envelope with my results was on Aunty Molly's hall table. I had passed my history A level but with only a grade D. It was devastating even though expected. My Oxford place, redemption from the stigma of being thrown out of home, was forfeit.

Father Roger was again my saviour. He hadn't waited for my return but, after checking the results, had immediately contacted Kenneth Wheare at Exeter to try to get an extension. Remarkably, the college agreed. After an anxious week working in Aunty Molly's garden, I received a letter from the rector saying that, in view of my exceptional family circumstances and relative youth, he was pleased to tell me that the college would give me another year to get the necessary B grade.

Another letter was waiting for me – a circular from Charles with the cast and rehearsal schedule for his adult production of *A Midsummer Night's Dream*. Rehearsals would start in early August and all members of the cast were invited to stay at Nowton.

There were urgent things to be done first – a visit to Gabbitas & Thring and on Father Roger's advice signing up with Wolsey Hall, Oxford for a history A-level correspondence course.

Mr Warboys, in the same tweed suit but without waistcoat because it was midsummer, greeted me like an old friend. When I told him my reason for needing another teaching job at short notice he seemed slightly disappointed, probably hoping that I was now eligible for the Gabbitas & Thring full-time, rather than temporary, staff list, but he produced with a magician's alacrity 'just the thing'.

Yardley Court, Tonbridge was rather different from Barlborough, he tactfully explained. It was one of the top prep schools in the Home Counties, a staunchly Anglican establishment with a close connection to Tonbridge School. The school had opened before the First World War and was run by the third generation of Bickmore headmasters. Its urgent need for a junior master was because the appointee for the job had decided instead to travel before going to Cambridge, behaviour that from Mr Warboys's tone was by G & T standards quite unacceptable.

I said yes immediately. A swift phone call led to an interview at eleven o'clock the next morning at Yardley Court. It was a school that didn't take junior masters on spec, despite my good reference from Barlborough.

I met both the Bickmores, brothers and joint-headmasters. It was swiftly clear that they would offer me the job. Both of them were friendly, John soft-spoken and earnest and Michael brisk and no-nonsense. They were pleased that I already had two terms' experience because this was normally a straight-out-of-school pre-university job.

After Michael had gone, John took me round the school, a rambling Edwardian building with huge grounds. He explained that two thirds of the pupils were day boys and that he, the junior master and the matron Miss Armitage, were residents in charge of boarders. Then, after showing me a small room in the attic that would be my bedroom, he offered me the job for £600 per year, a large increase on my Barlborough salary.

A week later I was off to Nowton. Charles had enclosed a paperback edition of the play with his letter and asked us all to learn our parts before we met, so I spent the week sitting in the Archway garden mugging Lysander's lines and dreaming of fair Hermia while Aunty Molly was busy being a dental nurse.

The three weeks at Nowton were the usual mix of excitement

and anxiety. Charles had gathered most of the cast from last year's *Love's Labour's Lost*, many of whom were my contemporaries: the Millmans with David playing Oberon and Martin my rival Demetrius, Nigel Havers playing Puck, Tony Garrett playing Bottom. The production would be Victorian with a fairy masque set to Mendelssohn's incidental music. Presiding over the star-crossed lovers and 'rude mechanicals' were Charles and Betty playing Theseus and Hippolyta as Albert and Victoria.

The weather was perfect and it was wonderful to be back with old schoolfriends reliving a halcyon Nowton summer, sharing the Green dormitory next to Charles's bedroom, eating at the top tables in the empty dining room and, during gaps in rehearsals in the rose garden, fishing in the lake and lazing in deckchairs under the giant cedar on the South Lawn. I also made a new friend, a languid blond boy called James de Quincy, introduced by Charles as Nowton's cleverest old boy.

Charles was an inspired director and a delightful, witty host. Neville, with Sadie Sedgwick and snuffling Pekinese in support, was artistic director in charge of costumes. Chain-smoking Betty bossed everyone around and played Hippolyta in the same way, gruffly speaking her lines with the earthy poetry of a school laundry list. The Haverses, Tony's partner the famous Angus Wilson, the Nightingales and other close Blackburne friends enhanced the country-house party atmosphere.

The Blackburnes were in their element and treated me as a favourite; but I felt self-conscious as one of a group who knew each other much better and had shared the golden period as Nowton sixth formers. The oddity of my early exodus to St Joseph's was now emphasised by my recent expulsion from the King family.

I was also in a feverish flutter about Helen Nightingale. Thanks to Charles's deft casting, it seemed natural that our on-stage love affair as Lysander and Hermia would play out in real life as well. But Lysander's generally feeble lines were right in one respect – 'The course of true love never did run smooth.' Although she didn't fall for Demetrius, Helen/Hermia was clearly hesitant about Lysander as well. It took me several months to discover that she was keeping her options open for someone more eligible than an infatuated adolescent with an odd family background. But for three weeks she played her *Dream* part to the full and off-stage we flirted intently.

The *Bury Free Press* described the production as 'sheer magic' and Lysander and Hermia as 'totally enchanting'. The two performances left vivid memories – the smells of make-up, pump-action mosquito repellent and the dusky rose scents of the floodlit garden, along with the sweatiness of the Victorian costumes and the enchanting closure of Puck's epilogue:

If we shadows have offended
Think but this, and all is mended,
That you have but slumber'd here
While these visions did appear.

The applause, congratulations and excitement were intoxicating. So was the on-stage picnic supper for cast and friends, and sleeping drunk on Pimm's under starlight on the Small House lawn.

There are two other poignant memories.

One is kissing Helen Nightingale for the first and only time on a rainy afternoon in the study of her family home near Wickhambrook. Her parents must have decided that I was an acceptable suitor and had sweetly asked me to lunch on the Sunday after the closing night. We spent the afternoon listening to records and while playing the Beatles album *Revolver* we finally kissed, and sunk onto the sofa until the door was opened by her little brother who looked at us accusingly and asked what we were doing.

Back at Nowton, after the rest of the cast had left, Charles persuaded me to stay an extra night before returning to Enfield. We had supper in the Small House with Neville and Betty and watched Laurence Olivier and Joan Fontaine in *Rebecca*. Charles walked me back to the empty school. He leant forward to kiss me goodnight on the cheek, his moustache brushing my skin. He then looked at me searchingly and I knew he wanted to kiss me properly and even more that I should kiss him. He said something sweet about my performance and how much he would miss me. There was a wistfulness in his voice and I sensed how strongly he felt about me but also knew it was impossible and not what I wanted. My hesitation was enough. He shrugged, and gently patted my cheek. There was nothing to be said, and although Charles gave me a warm hug when I left the next morning and told me to come and visit whenever I wanted, something had shifted and ended between us. I made a couple of daytime trips to Nowton but never again stayed the night.

Yardley Court was very different from Nowton's rural bohemia and the second-rate shabbiness of Barlborough. It was an old-fashioned and heartily hetero school, proud of its three-generation antiquity. The Bickmores' father, Miles, still did a bit of senior Latin coaching and both he and his ex-joint headmaster brother, Maurice, lived close to the school and regularly attended first XI games. The new headmasters took after their predecessors. Michael was married with several children and John, who lived in the school and reminded me of Jenks, was a confirmed bachelor, like Uncle Maurice.

Yardley, like most prep schools, was the self-absorbed and smug fiefdom of its headmasters, preoccupied with getting its boys into decent public schools, and out of touch with the adult world. There was a good staffroom story about Uncle Maurice bumping into an old boy called Gilbert Harding, with a television crew in Tonbridge High Street, and asking him what he was up to these days, blithely unaware that Harding was one of the BBC's most famous presenters and a household name.

This distance from the modern world suited me well and I had no problem settling in. Most of the staff had worked at the school for years. There was none of that Bulmer–Standish feuding in the staffroom and everyone was very friendly. Mr Crompton, who taught maths, was genial and jolly, and good friends with the tall and more ascetic English teacher Mr Tutton; Mrs Winter was tweedy and imposing, married to the editor of *Country Life*. They all seemed to get on well, respected the Bickmores and were content with the limited horizons of teaching at a second-league prep school in a small provincial town.

The Yardley routine was much the same as Barlborough – assembly, class, break, class, lunch, afternoon school, twice-weekly games – but as most of the boys went home each day around four o'clock the evenings were cosier. The thirty boarders were looked after by Mr John, the matron Miss Armitage, and the assistant matron Susan, a hearty but lonely spinster, who enjoyed having a drink at the local pub on her evenings off, and in my second term let me practise driving in her Triumph Herald.

Despite my clear recall of Nowton and Belmont friends I only remember two boys at Yardley Court, Edward and Tom Brown, whose mother Shirley was a junior mistress at the school and lived a couple of streets away. Tom was in the infant class and too young to be taught by me but Ed, two years older, was in form 2, which I taught for English and history. He was a gifted, funny boy, who responded with cheeky enthusiasm to my *1066 and All That* history lessons and my retelling of the English classic

251

stories I had mugged up from the *Oxford Companion to Literature*. Edward's enthusiasm sparked the friendship between me and Shirley, which started with an invitation to family Sunday lunch in my second term and has lasted a lifetime.

Mrs Winter's introduction to the Theatre and Arts Club was my first-term entrée into Tonbridge social life. The club was already rehearsing its autumn programme – a duet of Harold Pinter one-act plays, *The Collection*, and *The Lover*, which is about clandestine afternoon lovers who turn out to be man and wife. This was a big scoop for the club because the plays had not yet been released for amateur performance, and were very different from the club's traditional autumn fare of Rattigan and Coward, and summer musicals or costume drama. The mastermind of this coup was a camp ex-actor called Julian, an English teacher at Tonbridge School, who claimed to be a friend of Pinter's agent, and was rumoured to have joined the club because of his crush on Peter, a young club member, who worked in the town library.

My role was only assistant stage manager but watching rehearsals swiftly dispelled any impression of Tonbridge as an emotional backwater. Julian directed and cleverly cast himself as Harry in *The Collection*, playing opposite Peter, as his young interior designer partner. But the real drama was the blazing passion of the couple who played the Lovers.

I don't remember their real names and as a newcomer didn't foresee the looming scandal – until at the cast party the off-stage wife of the Lover got drunk and threw a glass of red wine over his stage wife and called her a slut. Several club members blamed Pinter, saying his work was sinister and subversive. Julian, turned down by the librarian, resigned petulantly. Soon afterwards a less challenging summer production was announced – Bolt's *A Man for All Seasons* in which, after a tough audition, I was given the part of Thomas Cranmer.

Meanwhile my summer romance was fading into wistful memory. Helen was now in her final year at West Runton and although we still wrote loving letters to each other, it was difficult to find new words to say the same things; the gossip and jokes about school life were wearing thin. I thought about Helen a lot, though I was still too inexperienced to transform her into erotic fantasy. But being 'in love' with a girl was hard work, particularly so far apart and after only a fortnight together.

I was beginning to lose heart when the invitation arrived. 'Helen Nightingale and Pippa Newcombe request the pleasure of your company at a party in honour of their eighteenth birthdays to be held at the Angel Hotel, Bury St Edmunds. Black tie optional.' The date was early December, just after the break-up of the Yardley Court term. Helen had mentioned Pippa as one of her oldest friends though I hadn't met her.

The invitation made me excited and apprehensive. The either/or dress code was the first hurdle. I didn't own a black tie and my only lounge suit was my threadbare Belmont charcoal flannels, unmistakably a school suit. Susan, the assistant matron, explained that 'black tie' was the codeword for dinner jacket and kindly took me in hand. We went to Burton's in Tonbridge High Street, where I bought a tasteful dark-blue and black pinstriped suit with large lapels and big shoulders in which I looked, according to Susan, gorgeous.

The next problem was finding somewhere to stay. A note with the invitation said that Mrs Nightingale would be glad to help with accommodation so I phoned her. Unfortunately help was not a bed for the night chez Nightingale because of a family full house but details of Bury hotels.

'Though surely the Blackburnes would be glad to give you a bed at Nowton,' Mrs Nightingale added. 'It's only two miles outside Bury.'

She sounded surprised when I explained that as it was so close to the end of term I wouldn't want to be an imposition. I didn't add that after the embarrassing encounter in the summer, this was just not an option. But she had a better solution – a room at the Angel where they had been given a low price on a block booking, sharing with Charlie Bentham, a close friend of Helen and a house captain at Rugby. She was sure we would get on. I thanked her, feeling doubtful.

The end of the Yardley Christmas term followed tradition – carol service, a satirical review produced by Mr Michael in the school hall, mulled wine and mince pies for parents and staff. Then suddenly the school was empty except for Mr John, me, and the two spinster matrons waiting to depart to relatives for the Christmas break. I rode the Zündapp back to Enfield, a bulging suitcase strapped to the back seat. Then, after an overnight stay with Aunty Molly, who was full of plans for a merchant-ship voyage to South Africa she had booked for early February, I set off for Bury wearing my new suit under my biking jacket and rain trousers to stop it getting creased.

Charlie Bentham was already in occupation when I arrived, sitting on his bed drawling to someone on the bedside phone. He waved a nonchalant hand without looking round; I knew at once that we weren't going to like each other. A leather suitcase embossed with the intials C.J.M.B. was open beside him on the bed and his double-breasted dinner jacket was draped over the wardrobe door. Our conversation, when eventually he ended his call, went something like this.

'Oh, hi, I'm Bentham.'

'Hi, I'm Caradoc. Good to meet you.'

'Ya, Helen's told me about you. Funny name.'

'Welsh.'

'Ah, never been there.'

Pause. I dumped my rucksack on the bed.

'Hear you're a prep school master. On your way to Oxford.'

A small tinge of respect in his voice.

'That's right. What about you?'

'Last year at Rugby. Then Sandhurst.'

'Ah.' A military man, probably from a line of General Benthams.

'Where were you?'

'When?'

'School, I mean.'

'Belmont Abbey.'

'Where's that? Never heard of it.'

I'm sure he wasn't really that bad and my minor school chippiness no doubt exaggerated his drawling disdain. Maybe he too had seen *Nothing But the Best* which had come out that year and was deliberately playing Denholm Elliott to my Alan Bates. But I felt increasingly inadequate as he casually donned his studded dress shirt, monogrammed cufflinks and cummerbund, expertly tied the black tie and chatted about his responsibilities as head of house and captain of games while I slipped into my Burton's off-the-peg pinstripe, Marks & Spencer drip-dry poplin shirt and old Belmontian tie. He gave a raised-eyebrow smile listening to me phone Charles and ask whether I might come over to lunch the next day.

Things didn't improve in the ballroom. As soon as Helen and Pippa made a demure double entrance down the stairs, it looked clear that my presumed status as 'the boyfriend' was to be claimed by C. J. M. Bentham. It was nothing obvious and, like much to do with love, perhaps mostly my imagination. Helen kissed both of us enthusiastically and said how glad she was that at last we'd met. She and her mother made a point of introducing me to friends and relatives, most of whom Bentham clearly already knew. I also met James de Quincy again.

After dinner I danced with Helen several times and, fortified by plenty of wine, had stopped feeling self-conscious about my lack of black tie and was showing off my wild French twist. Then the band's tempo changed and Bentham moved in with a tap on her shoulder. His jive was effortlessly cool. Mine was pathetic. Anna, a schoolfriend of Helen, took my hand but I didn't know the moves and had lost my rhythm. While people admiringly made space for the birthday girl and her dashing partner, I tangled, tripped and bumped until Anna laughingly suggested that we should sit this one out and told me endearingly over a drink that Bentham was a complete prat.

It was worse at the end of the evening when the lights dimmed and the music slowed. Bentham moved in swiftly and I watched over Anna's shoulder as he and Helen glued themselves together for the smooch, his hand possessively resting on her green silk bottom. Fortunately I was too pissed to care. Tipsy Anna was now pressing her body distractingly into mine and making it clear from the closeness of her lips to mine that she wouldn't mind if I kissed her. Why not?

The next morning I woke early with a bad hangover and the memory of Helen's last words before she left with her parents.

'Caradoc, I really like you and I want us to be friends but ...' Taking hold of both my hands, she had given me a deep, bleary look and a swift peck on the cheek.

Luckily Bentham was deeply asleep so I packed my bag, put on my suit and left him snoring. I had a quick solitary breakfast in the dining room then hit the road into a cold clear sunny morning. At half past ten, when I knew Charles would be presiding over Matins in Nowton Church, I phoned the Small House and spoke to the housekeeper. I told her I had to go back urgently to Enfield and unfortunately wouldn't be able to come to lunch. One jilted lover was enough to cope with.

XV

Christmas that year wasn't very happy. Aunty Molly had found me a temporary job in the stockroom of Pearsons the department store, which lasted until Christmas Eve. We spent the holiday period playing whist and rummy, and going to boring local drinks parties. It started snowing on New Year's Eve and went on for the first ten days of January 1965. I sat huddled in front of the fire in the otherwise freezing house mugging up history and losing myself in the romantic mysticism of Lawrence Durrell's *Alexandria Quartet*.

I was relieved to get back to Yardley Court. My young and exuberant pupils were the perfect antidote to depression. Shirley Brown was my other saviour.

She was thirteen years older than me, a lifetime ahead in wisdom and experience. Her life hadn't been easy. Brought up by two stepfathers she was already divorced from one husband and had had a love affair with a married and much older 'public figure', the father of her second child, whose identity was a closely kept secret. But Shirley was fun, funny and generous, and the first person since Father Roger I could talk to honestly about love, life and bad times with the Kings. She had moved from London to Tonbridge because her sister Chloe and young family lived round the corner. Her two children, Ed and Tom, seemed happy to accept me as a quasi uncle and for the next three years Shirley's small Victorian terraced house in Ashburnham Road was my second home. When I felt lonely and rootless, Shirley provided stability and happiness.

Our age difference then was about right, too much for us to become lovers – Shirley a beautiful thirty-year-old mother, me a spotty and gangling seventeen-year-old – but close enough to become very good friends. She helped me to *like* women rather than lust after or fall blindly in love with them, which I had found difficult after my hostile relationship with Jill. More charming, gregarious and worldly wise than anyone I had met close to my age, Shirley helped shift my adolescent self-preoccupation to a curiosity about the world at large; to value people's special qualities, however different they were.

My other close Yardley friend, Susan the assistant matron, was very different. She was a blunt Yorkshirewoman with thyroid and drink problems and no time for arty-farty nonsense, who gave her time, and Triumph Herald, generously while I practised for my driving test. I failed the test twice, then in the last week of the Easter term passed, despite turning on the right-hand side of a keep-left traffic bollard and then reversing out into a main road. I took Susan out for a thank-you steak dinner in a country pub and she drove us back, well over the limit before it was against the law, singing drunken rounds of 'On Ilkla Moor Baht 'at'.

My other memories of Yardley Court are limited. In January the whole school watched Winston Churchill's funeral, the Thames dockers dipping their crane jibs as the naval cortège carried the coffin downriver from Westminster to the state funeral in St Paul's. There was other international news flickering on the black and white screen in the school refectory – the civil rights marches in the American South, the first US deployment in Vietnam and the arrests of Myra Hindley and Ian Brady. But most evenings I spent re-studying my set texts and writing essays for the Wolsey Hall A-level history course. The thought of failing again and being stuck for ever teaching in prep schools and refereeing muddy football matches filled me with gloom.

The bleak Easter term at last ended, clocks changed to summer time and the Yardley Court gardens were full of daffodils. Aunty Molly was still on her travels to South Africa and, as there was little point in returning to Enfield, Mr John, who lived in the school with a housekeeper, allowed me to stay on in my room and join him for supper in the private dining room.

The summer term was happy like all prep school summer terms – the thwack of cricket ball, lawnmowers droning through open classroom windows, doves cooing, boys in white scampering along grass running tracks to the crack of the starter pistol, cheering parents. There were drab rainy days as well, boys quarrelling in an overcrowded assembly hall, masters tetchy because of lack of concentration, Mr Michael on the warpath for noise and wild behaviour. But my overall memory of that term was of innocence, happiness and the glow of my popularity with the boys.

In early June I was allowed to sit A-level history on my own in the private dining room under Mr John's supervision. I knew as soon as I had finished that my answers were good and that this time I had done it. I remember, on a Sunday after the exam, being allowed by Susan to borrow her car for the first time on my own and a long trip driving fast through sunny Kent lanes to the coast, swimming and lazing the afternoon away on a beach near Rye and eating Cornish pasties washed down with shandy in a pub garden on the drive back.

The good times didn't last. I had one more exam to do at the end of term but, as there was no way I could revise for it, this didn't interrupt rehearsals for the role of Thomas Cramner in *A Man for All Seasons*. The Oxford Use of English exam was taken by all students at that time and intended to assess the literacy of science and maths students at the university. It should have been a doddle. I was going up to read English and had got a B-grade English A level at the age of sixteen. But a fortnight before the exam something terrible happened.

Tom was hit by a car crossing the main road on his way home from school. Shirley heard the squeal of brakes and the sound of skidding and a collision. With a mother's fearful instinct, she raced up Ashburnham Road to find her unconscious child lying in the main road surrounded by strangers.

Tom had broken bones and a head injury. For several days he was unconscious and in intensive care at the local hospital, while doctors tried to stabilise him and assess the extent of the damage. Ed stayed at his Aunt Chloe's house. Shirley camped at the hospital desperately waiting for news. At last Tom opened his eyes, recognised his mother and began to talk to her. The doctors were swiftly reassuring that there should be no long-term damage.

Even though Shirley and I were not yet very close friends, the accident shook me badly. Tom had regained consciousness two days earlier, but I remember sitting in an exam room at Tonbridge School with a small number of other Oxford hopefuls, staring blankly at a paper full of easy questions, then writing in nervous haste against the clock several answers which I discovered, on re-reading the exam paper later, were completely wrong.

I left Yardley Court at the end of term flattened at the prospect that yet again and for the last time I would fail to get into Oxford. During the second half of term I had watched the BBC series *The World of Wooster* with Ian Carmichael playing Wooster and Dennis Price playing Jeeves. I remember imagining – ludicrously as Bertie was too fatuous to be a Varsity man – that Oxford would in some way be a cross between the hothouse intellectual world of the bow-tied A. J. P. Taylor, whom I also watched avidly on television, and Bertie's blimpish upper-class world, and that my college scout, like Jeeves, would offer me each day a choice of Lovat tweeds or white flannels and blazer, buff my brogues into mirror-like brilliance, and in the evening serve cocktails to my amusing friends when they visited my college rooms. It was bleak to realise that this glittering world would finally escape me.

Putting on a brave face I returned to Enfield because I hadn't seen Aunty Molly since Christmas. Again I turned to Father Roger for help. He offered to write to Kenneth Wheare to explain the circumstances of Tom's accident just before the exam but advised me to wait first for the A-level history mark which would be considered before the Use of English results. It would be another summer of suspense.

My first holiday adventure wasn't a happy experience. After getting tipsy together at Helen's birthday party James de Quincy had written to invite me for a weekend at his family home in Aldeburgh. After putting it off for some time, I eventually phoned him and accepted the invitation for a date a long time ahead. I hardly knew James and had grown shy about accepting invitations from families I didn't know. But James was charming and clever and as I had no close male friends at the time his invitation intrigued me.

The de Quincys lived in one of Aldeburgh's grandest houses, an Edwardian pile on the gated Park Road estate. Apart from James, the household was entirely women: two adult sisters, Eliza and Lucy, a housekeeper, a cook, and the formidable Mrs de Quincy, who seemed old enough to be James's grandmother and was frightfully grand and very snobbish.

The weekend was like a hunter trial course of very difficult jumps, which I failed miserably. The first was the Friday night dinner, with several courses of dull food served in the formal dining room by the ill-humoured housekeeper, with enough changes of plates, cutlery and glasses to make Aunty Molly's table arrangements seem primitive. The conversation, little aided by thin supplies of wine, was as indigestible as the food. Mrs de Quincy held forth on current affairs – mainly about the 'very common' Edward Heath who had just taken over as leader of the Tory Party replacing 'dear' Alec Douglas-Home whose family she knew well – then subjected me to searching questions about my family, education and social connections, and told me that the man whose portrait hung on the wall was James's father, a diplomat who had caught malaria in India and died when James was too young to remember.

The second ordeal was bridge which, Mrs de Quincy announced, they always played on Friday evening. I knew the basics of the game from Aunty Molly, but was no match for the fiercely competitive Eliza, who partnered me against her mother and James. I tried to conform to the bridge 'conventions' which Eliza had urgently whispered to me before the start of play but became hopelessly confused, not helped by Eliza's muttered commentary on my play, along the lines of 'But why on earth two clubs?', 'Oh, my God, not the king', and 'Funny time to trump!' until at last Mrs de Quincy told Eliza to keep quiet because she was spoiling her concentration.

Saturday was even worse. In the morning we played golf at the famously crusty Aldeburgh Golf Club, my first time on a golf course. This time I was the target of Mrs de Quincy's irritation as she nagged me with ironic 'bad luck's as I regularly sliced my ball into the rough and finally boiled over into 'Oh, really, Caradoc!' when I excelled myself by extracting a chunk of immaculate turf with a vigorous putt at the 16th hole.

Sailing in the afternoon was just as bad. I had told James that my sailing experience was very limited and, sympathetic about my earlier embarrassments at bridge and golf, he offered me a private lesson in the family's eighteen-footer.

From the jocular greetings from other sailors as we rigged up the boat at the jetty it was clear that the de Quincys were prominent members of the Aldeburgh Yacht Club. We started well enough, going upriver with a good following wind towards Snape. But the return journey against the wind was much more difficult. On summer weekends the Alde is crowded with sailors. So as well as tacking problems we had to deal with lots of other craft on the river.

James took the helm and, after some initial fumbling, I got the hang of his shouted commands, 'Ready to go about' and 'Going about', switching the jib sheet and ducking the boom when it swung across as the boat changed course.

Then James handed over control of the tiller and mainsail sheet. I followed his instructions carefully and at first all was well. We changed tack smoothly twice. Then, just as I was about to go about, there was a sudden surge of wind. I pulled tighter on the sheet instead of letting go. The wind caught the mainsail, there was a lurching plunge, and we were both tipped into the water as the boat went over.

When I had extracted myself from the sail above my head I spluttered my apologies. James was reassuringly calm. He grabbed a rope attached to the top of the mast and tried to pull himself up on the upturned side of the hull. I clung onto the side to add my weight. But a clinker-built eighteen-footer with a big sail and carrying a lot of water is more difficult to right than capsize. As we were struggling another boat cruised close by.

'My God, James, how did you manage that?' It was the drawling voice of a man who had greeted us on the jetty. 'Want a hand?'

James was sweet about it. As we showered at the Sailing Club, he told me it could have happened to anyone. Nor did he mention it to his mother, whose vigilant gaze we managed to avoid when we returned to the house in borrowed dry clothes. But Mrs de Quincy was in close contact with the Sailing Club grapevine. By dinner time she knew all about 'the incident this afternoon', waved aside James's claim that it was entirely his fault, and listened to my account of it with raised eyebrows and an ironic smile, clearly indicating that she was not in the least surprised.

Nor did it surprise me. I was clearly gauche, boring and socially inept. Posh and clever people made me very nervous.

I had to get another job and, although Aunty Molly and I got on fine, the prospect of more shop or gardening work in Enfield was irksome. Mr Warboys of Gabbitas & Thring helped out once again. A family called the Ransomes, who lived in Tunbridge Wells not far from Yardley Court, were looking for a summer tutor for their thirteen-year-old son Alec who had failed his Common Entrance exam to his father's old school, Radley. Could I help out?

The Ransome family were friendly but distinctly eccentric. On the surface they were conventional enough. Mr Ransome was a well-known estate agent in Tunbridge Wells, and the family lived in a large, plush house on the prestigious Neville Estate. The eccentric member was Mrs Ransome, a handsome and exuberant woman who managed to run two parallel marriages – with Mr Ransome her legal spouse and with a Mr Metcalfe, who worked in advertising and lived in a beautiful farmhouse on a large Sussex estate thirty miles from Tunbridge Wells.

It took me some time to unravel the family secret. The first hint came on my first night at the Neville Estate house. Mr Ransome said that at least half my time would be spent at Haningford Farm, the home of a family friend. Sure enough, three days later, Alec and I with Mrs 'but just call me Laura' Ransome set off to Sussex in her convertible Sunbeam Rapier. Alec and his mother settled in at the farmhouse as if it was their second home and Laura cooked dinner for the three of us and the family friend, David Metcalfe, when he got home from his job in London. Laura greeted him with a loving kiss just as she had with Mr Ransome on my first night with the family and later that night, when I visited the bathroom downstairs from my attic room, I saw through an open door that Laura and David shared a bedroom and a large double bed.

Alec was a cheeky, cheerful small boy and we easily settled into a pleasant routine of maths and English lessons in the morning and free time in the afternoon, most of it spent driving Alec's latest toys – a go-kart and an old Austin 7 cabriolet – at perilous speed along the concrete strip of driveway which ran for a mile and a half between the farmhouse and main road. We had great fun together and it didn't seem right to ask Alec about his extended family, so I put the question out of my mind, happily accepting Laura Ransome's double marriage as perfectly normal.

Everything changed when Alec's nineteen-year-old sister, Kate, returned from a holiday in France. Kate was at drama school in London and disturbingly beautiful, with blonde hair and blue eyes like her mother's, a curvaceous figure and honey tan. She treated me with friendly indifference as if to underline my role in the family as a paid employee. She also called me 'Cradock', saying my full name was too much of a mouthful.

Her brusqueness, it turned out, was not much to do with me. It was soon clear that she didn't share her brother's relaxed feelings about David Metcalfe as a surrogate father and had a difficult relationship with her mother. Outwardly they behaved more like sisters than mother and daughter. Laura, who had once been an actress (a season at Windsor Rep before being literally swept off her feet by Mr Ransome on a skiing holiday), was gushingly loving and Kate tried to imitate her mother's theatrical exuberance. But beneath the surface there was a great deal of tension.

Mostly it was normal domestic mother–daughter squabbling which I remembered from Jill's angry relationship with Janet. Laura would complain about the state of Kate's room, her unwillingness to help out, her unsuitable clothes. But one day it flared into something serious and there was a major row. Kate had driven back very late at night from Haywards Heath in the Sunbeam which, after Kate's nagging complaints about being imprisoned in the countryside, Laura had lent her on the strict condition that she didn't drink.

The row simmered in sulky silence for most of the day and then erupted over the dinner table, exposing the real reason for Kate's hostility. I don't remember who provoked it but suddenly Kate said furiously:

'Oh, why don't you just shut up, Mum!' which provoked an immediate angry response from David, who normally kept out of family arguments.

'That's enough, Kate,' he said loudly. 'Don't speak to your mother like that!'

Kate response was explosive.

'And you can shut up, too, David. What's it got to do with you? You're not even a member of this family.'

There was a tense silence which, from Kate's furious expression, was a prelude to a torrent of recrimination.

Then David said calmly: 'Well, Kate, as long as you are a guest in my house I would just ask that you show reasonable politeness.'

'In that case I'll leave tomorrow.'

The next day it was all over. Kate didn't leave. Mother and daughter had clearly made it up and Alec, when I asked him what the problem was, shrugged. 'They're just too alike.'

But curiosity made me push him further.

'But isn't it something to do with your odd family arrangement?'

'What do you mean?'

'Having two homes, with two fathers. It must be strange for you and Kate.'

He shrugged again.

'You mean because my mother shares a room with David?'

'Um ... yes. It's a bit unusual.'

'We're used to it. David and my dad are old friends. They were at school together. David was Mum's boyfriend before she met Dad.'

It was Kate who explained it all several days later, when our relationship had changed. It started at a birthday dinner for Mr Ransome for which we all returned to Tunbridge Wells. The dinner was in a smart restaurant in the Pantiles with some other family friends. David had remained at the farm.

Kate paid attention to me for the first time, asking questions about my family and Yardley Court where two of her old school-friends had brothers. She was wearing a little red dress and after a couple of glasses of wine I couldn't keep my eyes off her. That night I discovered that Mr and Mrs Ransome slept in separate bedrooms.

A few days before I was due to leave the farm a letter arrived, forwarded to me from Enfield, with the news that I had got an A-grade pass in history. Then two days later a phone call from Father Roger who had heard from Exeter that I had scraped through my Use of English with a pass.

I felt huge relief and excitement. My Oxford entrance in October had been confirmed by the college. The next stage of my life was now fixed. I was no longer a junior prep school master between jobs. I was 'going up' to Oxford and to hell with Jill.

The Ransomes seemed delighted. Mother and daughter cooked a family dinner in my honour. And we drank champagne and then red wine. Washing up together afterwards I knew Kate was flirting with me but by the end of the evening I was too tipsy to do anything about it.

The next day I got lucky. Laura took Alec to an afternoon dental appointment in Haywards Heath. Laura asked me if I would like to come too, possibly anxious about leaving Kate and me alone together, but I said I wanted to pack because I was leaving tomorrow and also had some reading to do.

I was just drifting off by the pool after lunch when there was noise above me and I looked up.

'Hi, Cradock. Having a good time?'

Kate stood laughing at her bedroom window. She said something else which sounded like 'Come up and see me some time!', but disappeared before I could respond.

It happened very easily. I waited a couple of minutes, in case she was about to come down, then put on some shorts and went into the house and climbed the stairs. Her bedroom door was open. She was gazing at herself in her wardrobe mirror and must have seen me behind her because she twirled round suddenly, smiling but startled.

'So what do you think?' she said, gesturing to her pretty floral skirt. 'Mum bought it for me and I'm not sure I like it.'

'It's beautiful.'

'Do you really think so?'

I stood by the door looking at her.

'So are you,' I said nervously.

She smiled. For a moment everything was still. Then she moved towards me, reached up and touched my cheek.

'Would you like to kiss me?'

I did, hesitant and clumsy. Then she kissed me, her tongue to mine, hands sliding up my back and pulling us close, my hands sliding down onto the curves of her bum, and our legs stumbling back towards her bed.

We didn't actually do it. Helen let me touch her pointed breasts and nipples, then the exquisite caressing trail up her legs to her thigh to the soft, damp patch in her knickers, then I felt her hand over mine holding me back and her lips on my ear.

'We can't, Cradock, I've made a promise. But ...'

Her hand was on me, unbuttoning my shorts, stroking me with skilled assurance, kissing me open-mouthed, smiling into my glazed eyes. Then it was all over, a moaning Chesil Beach moment, Kate holding up her sticky fingers, me gasping like a just-caught fish, she laughing, then hugging me in tender consolation ... and soon after came the sound of a car, Laura's voice calling, the two of us frantically putting on clothes, giggling nervously, me slipping along the corridor back to my room while Kate went downstairs saying breezily that she had been sorting out her clothes and had last seen me by the pool.

Sweet Kate. She told me later, smoking outside in the dark after dinner, that we couldn't do it again, that we should never have done it, she already had a boyfriend, and had just got carried away. She also told me the truth about David and her father, that Laura and her father had nearly split up a couple of years ago, and Laura had told Kate and Alec that she loved David and wanted to be with him and didn't want to go on being married to their dad. But somehow, she said, they had worked things out so that the two of them could share her.

I sensed the anger in her voice. I also realised that I had been used a little, just for fun and probably to defy Laura. But I didn't care. What had happened that afternoon, my first spluttering steps towards sex with a woman, had been wonderful.

The start of the Oxford term drew near and Aunty Molly's growing enthusiasm matched my increasing anxiety. She was proud of my achievement; it appealed to her snobbery. Although successful solicitors, the Beavans and the Welds had not gone to university and she enjoyed bragging about my success at Enfield drinks parties. She also read my copy of *Brideshead Revisited* and was convinced that Oxford would be full of 'top drawer' people from good families and the grander public schools.

Her 'going up' gift was a new bespoke suit which, despite my Burton two-piece navy pinstripe, she was convinced I might need for 'smart luncheon parties'. We went to Hepworths in the high street, and after close study of the cloth book, we opted for a three-piece Prince of Wales-style salt-and-pepper worsted tweed which she breezily informed the manager had to be tailored in time for my departure to Oxford the following week.

On the big day Aunty Molly drove us 'up' in her Vauxhall Victor which I had washed and polished the day before. She wore a green silk suit in honour of the occasion and I was resplendent in the Hepworth tweeds with a red knitted silk tie which I had bought in the Oxfam shop for half a crown. Unfortunately the suit shoulders didn't quite balance and one seemed to stick out a bit more than the other, but Aunty Molly didn't notice and said I looked very smart, so I didn't mention it.

We reached Exeter College at the earliest freshman check-in time of three o'clock and I joined the queue at the porter's lodge while Aunty Molly waited in the car. A bowler-hatted porter informed me that my room was on Staircase 11 in the back quad with access from the Broad Street entrance. The room was in fact a suite, with a sitting room overlooking the Broad and an airy bedroom facing the back quad. The rooms were bare and shabby, with empty bookshelves, a battered red leatherette three-piece suite in front of a gasfire, frayed carpet, and picture-frame outlines on the yellow painted walls, but it was the largest space I had ever exclusively occupied and seemed extremely grand.

Aunty Molly gave me a bracing 'good luck' hug and a ten-pound note for 'bits and pieces', then said she had to leave to get back to Enfield in time for a Bridge Club party. I escorted her down into the quad, which was filling up with cars of excited freshers and parents, clutching tablelamps, cushions and record players. Molly reversed the Victor under the arch, waved, and disappeared up the Broad.

Standing alone, watching the bustle of activity around me, I felt sudden anxiety, a fleeting memory of Jill and Charles outside in the rose garden at Nowton. I also felt a bit of a prat in my lopsided Hepworth tweeds. None of the other freshers were wearing suits. A few were dressed in jackets and flannel trousers. Most of them were in jeans.

I followed the drifting crowd, round the front quad, into the junior common room, then hung around outside the porter's lodge, reading the announcements pinned to the noticeboard of freshers' welcome meetings – the college rowing club, the John Ford Society, soccer and rugby trials – and found my name on a list of English first-years, announcing a meeting the next day, signed by Jonathan Wordsworth. A tall boy with long hair in jeans and a navy poloneck stood beside me in front of the notice-board. We nodded to each other.

'Are you on this?' he said, pointing at the English list.

'Yes, I'm King.'

'Hi. I'm Philip Pullman, but Nick to family and friends.' We shook hands and I sensed his appraising eye on my three-piece suit. Then he smiled. 'Fancy a drink? I met up earlier with a chap called Richard from our year. We arranged to meet in the Buttery at six.'

There was time to swap my suit for jeans and a sweater. Although I had no idea to what extent, I knew that my life had changed.

SIX

Grown Up

XVI

The last part of this story is mostly about finding my natural mother. I have added what I learned about Jill, after a reunion with my adoptive sisters following a thirty-year gap. The last chapter is about my return to Strood House and a surprising and poignant story from its then owner. I wrote it all as part of a journal, several years before I decided to write a childhood memoir and have kept it in that form.

For many years after childhood I was too busy being an adult to feel more than mild curiosity about my natural parents. But in my mid-forties I had a mid-life crisis of tangled love affairs and leaving my wife of twenty years. In the aftermath, when I had returned home and was trying to repair the damage, I realised for the first time I had no idea who I really was. I had achieved plenty in my life but, abandoned by two sets of parents and without known biological roots, I seemed a self-made artefact. I needed strongly to find out more about the links between my origin and my behaviour as an adult and as a child.

A friend and solicitor working in the family division told me about Ariel Bruce. She specialised in tracing missing families for adopted, orphaned or abandoned children. Her office in Bloomsbury was only two streets from mine which seemed auspicious so I made contact.

I liked Ariel immediately. She was about my age, forthright, friendly and attractive. She gave me tea and we sat in her book-lined office and I told her about myself, my adoptive family, about not finding out that I was adopted until I was fifteen, and being banished from the King family eighteen months later. Then she asked me if I knew anything about my natural blood parents.

I told her what Aunty Molly had told me years before, that my real name was Nicholas Barton. Listening carefully Ariel explained what she could do.

The first step was for me to apply for a copy of my original birth certificate rather than the shortened post-adoption form that confirmed my name and date of birth. Until 1964 an adopted child could not apply for his or her original birth certificate; the official view was that the privacy of the birth parents should be protected. Since then all adopted children have been able to apply to the National Records Office. After a brief counselling session by an official counsellor to ensure that the adopted person is stable and sensible enough to receive the information, a copy of the birth certificate is handed over with an explanation of its contents.

The birth certificate, Ariel explained, will give the place and date of birth, and the mother's full name and address at the time of the birth. It will give the same information about the father if the application is made jointly. If it is made only by the mother she is entitled to give the name of her husband if she has one, whether or not he is the actual father, but if she is unmarried the father's name will be recorded as unknown.

Ariel's search would start from the birth certificate and any other information I could give her. From this, using a network of local researchers, she would search for birth certificates for the mother and/or father registered on my birth certificate. Then from wedding certificates, sibling birth certificates, death and probate certificates she would try to trace my family history, to find out which of the family were still alive and where they lived. When the information was found, Ariel said, there was no certainty that blood relations she had traced would want to admit to or talk about the past or have any contact with the adopted child. Building up the contact and connections between the searcher and those found was a crucial part of her job.

The search turned out to be surprisingly easy. Aunty Molly was right in some respects but also mysteriously wrong. A few weeks after our first meeting, having sent her first a copy of the birth certificate, I went to see Ariel again. My name was indeed Nicholas Barton and my birth, on 19 December 1946, was registered in Poole, Dorset. My mother's name was Joan Barton, née Richardson. My father's name, according to the certificate, was James Barton whose occupation at the time of my birth was 'Food Distribution Officer' for the Allied Military Government.

It was a warm evening and Ariel opened a bottle of white wine to celebrate my family news, or maybe to offset the shock. She had in front of her a file of copied certificates, which she used to take me slowly through the family history. According to my mother's birth certificate her father had been a seed merchant living in Sidcup when Joan was born. She had married James Barton in 1933 and divorced him in 1947, soon after I was born, and in 1951 had married again to Owen Beckett. From the first marriage there were four sons, Simon, William who died in infancy, Julian and myself. From the second marriage, one daughter, Jill, born in 1953. My mother had moved to different parts of southern England when married to James but when Jill was born she was living at the address registered on my own birth certificate in Chester Road, Poole, Dorset. Her second husband, Owen Beckettt, had died in 1989, and from the will Ariel had discovered that his daughter and legatee Jill, was at that time also living near Poole, now under her married name. The name and address were in the current telephone directory, so Ariel had the phone number of my half-sister, who disconcertingly shared the Christian name of my long-absent adoptive mother.

Ariel then asked the crucial question, 'So what would you like me to do next?'

For a moment I hesitated.

'What would you do?'

'Well, if you wanted me to pursue this further, my next step would be to ring Jill and, adopting the cover of a distant relative who is keen on genealogy and putting together the family tree, try to get her into a conversation about the family history and find out whatever she is willing to tell me.' She paused, looked at me and smiled.

'So what would you like me to do?'

This time I didn't hesitate.

'Ring her.'

Three days later Ariel phoned again. 'I had a long chat with Jill. She's very nice and told me a lot about the family which I want to tell you. When can we meet?'

We met that evening. Ariel wasted no time in telling me what she had discovered.

'First, the good news. Your mother is still alive. She is in a nursing home in Dorchester. She's frail and cannot understand everything or speak very clearly because she had a stroke five years ago. Your half-brother Simon also lives in Dorchester and sees her almost every day.'

She paused, smiling, allowing me to absorb this news. For a moment I felt nothing. That my mother was still alive and well enough to meet was hard to take in.

'She came from a large family of sisters,' Ariel went on. 'She was the youngest by eight years; her mother died when she was fourteen. Three of her sisters all moved to the Poole area after they married and your mother joined them, and it was there that she met her first husband James. They divorced at the end of the war and your mother married Jill's father, an old family friend who had also been married before. Jill and her husband have two children and so do your brothers Simon and Julian, although Simon was recently divorced.'

I felt excitement and apprehension. My head whirled with divorces, remarriages, half-brothers and a sister, cousins, nephews and nieces. I had discovered my family. The mystery had been solved. But after being so long without any family the prospect of meeting a large new one was daunting.

'How did Jill respond to your questions? Didn't they make her a bit suspicious?'

Ariel smiled reassuringly.

'No, she was very friendly and responsive and seemed glad to tell me everything. She said that because the family was so extensive she wasn't surprised that someone was trying to piece it all together. Apparently her husband Barry is an amateur genealogist.'

'But who did she think you were?'

'A second cousin on James's side. I guess she wouldn't know that much about her mother's previous husband's family. James himself is dead but Jill told me that he too remarried and had another family.'

We both laughed. There was something almost mischievous about Ariel, which suited her name. I could easily imagine how her friendly, gently probing, reassuring questions would have persuaded Jill to tell her as much as she had. She had been the same towards me.

'But wasn't she at all suspicious?' I asked.

'Perhaps just a little by the end of the call. But I sense it didn't worry her, that she was partly expecting someone to get in touch at some time and ask these questions.'

'You mean . . .' I hesitated, slowly taking in what she had said. 'She knows about me and thought that one day I might get in touch?'

'I think so, but I didn't ask her.' She stopped, watching me carefully. 'Do you want me to?'

The answer was simple.

Ariel phoned me later that day and wouldn't tell me anything on the phone but asked me to come and see her as soon as possible. I was there in half an hour.

'She already knew about you,' Ariel said without preamble. 'She wasn't surprised that you were trying to make contact.'

'And what about your phone calls? How did she take the subterfuge?'

Ariel laughed. 'She had already guessed. We had a good chat.'

'And what else did she tell you?'

'Not much more, but she told me that all the family knew about you, that your mother had held on to you for several months before giving you up for adoption and that your mother's sisters and your brothers had all seen you. She said that everyone thought you'd been sent to New Zealand.'

I was silent. For the first time in my talks with Ariel I couldn't find the right words. I was close to tears. The thought of my mother keeping me for several months, showing me to the family before giving me up, was terribly sad. Why had she held on to me for so long? How could she then give me up? What had she felt about it? Was the mysterious 'nanny' who had visited Strood House to ask for me back in fact one of Mother's married sisters?

Ariel read my mind. 'She didn't want to give you up, Jill said. Your mother loved children. She just couldn't cope with another one. She was on her own. Her husband had left her. She already had two young children to bring up.'

'And who was my father?'

The question hovered between us.

'Jill doesn't know. She doesn't think anyone does. All your mother's sisters who might have known are dead now.' She paused. 'And just because James is named as your father on the birth certificate doesn't mean he is.'

I was silent, my mind and feelings empty. Ariel watched me, her face gentle.

'What else did she say?' I asked finally.

'Not much,' Ariel replied, adding, 'she wants to tell you herself. She is very keen to meet you.'

'Really?' I said doubtfully.

'Really. Call her.'

That evening I did. Jill answered the phone herself after three rings. I guessed she was waiting for my call.

Just hearing her voice was enough. It was a soft, kind voice and she sounded just as nervous as me. I asked her if she was. She laughed. So did I.

'So when are we going to meet?' I asked her.

We met a week later. Jill lived close to the family home in Poole, where she had spent her childhood. Jill had told me on the phone that half the house was now let to a family friend and the other half unoccupied since her mother's stroke five years earlier, but still full of her furniture.

Jill and her husband, Barry, met me at Poole Station. Although the platform was full of early-evening commuters Jill and I recognised each other at once. We both had the same look of apprehensive expectancy. There was a momentary hesitation, a questioning smile, then we simply hugged each other.

Jill is small with a round face, short dark hair and green eyes. It wasn't until we stood together in front of a mirror at Jill's house later that we could see our similarity. The sense of kinship was for me – I think for both of us – immediate.

It was strange – but it was easy. This small, friendly, soft-spoken woman was my half-sister. We had been born from the same mother. We shared her genes – and also, from the photographs Jill showed me of our mother, her rounded face, slightly mischievous eyes and quick smile. Jill was the first flesh-and-blood relative I had met in almost half a century of life. I liked her. I knew without question that she was a good woman, a loving mother, a loyal wife and sister.

Barry came in with tea and cake. Then he proudly brought out the extensive family tree he had been compiling and the family photograph albums. I was to be given a full introduction to my natural family – dead and alive.

My maternal grandfather was William Richardson, born in 1864 and married to Sybella Susanne Bowden, born in 1871. There was no marriage date but the first of their seven children, Marguerite, was born in 1893 when her mother was twenty-two. The births of the first six children were scattered regularly over the next fourteen years, all girls and all, except for Barbara who died aged three in 1910, given nicknames. First there was Marguerite, or Margie, then Catherine, or Kaka, born in 1897, Irene, interestingly called John in 1899, Sybil/Pardy in 1900,

Gwendoline/Bubba,1903. Joan, our mother, was a late arrival, born 11 January 1911, less than a year after Barbara's death. Four of her sisters were all more than ten years older.

Jill was born in 1953 from Mother's second marriage to Owen Beckett; she knew little about her mother's family life before that. Her half-brother Simon had already left home and Julian was fifteen when Jill was born. But she did remember the old aunts, Kaka, Pardy and Bubba, who were still living in the Poole area when she was growing up and she had heard stories from them. Old Richardson had been a spice merchant, based first in London and then in Kent. The family had also been comfortable, if not prosperous, and the pictures from the album displayed it. In one picture with his dog, Grandfather Richardson looked a stern patriarch, with his George V beard, bow tie and Derby hat. A holiday picture on a beach at Cromer showed all the sisters, pretty laughing girls in long cardigans and skirts sitting around their grandmother wearing an enormous hat with her youngest granddaughter, Joan, in a pinafore on her lap, waving her spade.

There were lots more pictures of little Joan, preening in her party dress, posing with Bubba as Pierrot and Harlequin. There were pictures of her as a young woman, including a rather rakish 1920s picture of her in shorts looking coquettishly over her shoulder as she stroked a horse. There was one picture of her as a middle-aged mother with Simon, her eldest son, in uniform beside her. Simon, now in his early sixties, worked with computers and had three children. Julian, she thought, because she hadn't seen him for several years, was a director of a national transport company with a young family and lived somewhere in the Midlands. She hadn't anything more to say about them and I guessed that the family relationships through Mother's two marriages were not close.

Jill was happier telling me about her own father, Owen

Beckett. His marriage to Joan had taken place in December 1951, although the marriage certificate showed that they were already living together in Chester Road. Owen had had a variety of jobs but no proper career but seemed to have had a busy social life. There were pictures of him wearing a chain of office for some local society next to a bejewelled and anxious-looking Joan. In another picture Joan was wearing a large hat, holding a monkey at a garden fete. The picture I liked most was Joan cooking in her kitchen, watched by ten-year-old Jill. They both looked so alike – and like me.

'Were the two of them happy together?' I asked Jill.

'Happy enough. But he wasn't an easy man.' She laughed, then added, 'A good father though.'

There was one picture I still wanted to see.

'Have you got one of Mother taken recently?'

Jill went to her desk across the room upon which was sitting a framed photograph that I hadn't noticed before. An old woman sitting in a garden at a table doing a crossword puzzle, her hair the familiar old lady's short grey perm. She was wearing glasses and looking intently at the newspaper in front of her with a pen in her hand. She could be anyone's granny.

'That was just before her stroke five years ago,' Jill said quietly. 'She looks much the same now but older.'

'Can she still read?' I asked.

'No, I don't think so. But I don't know if she really wants to. Her memory is not as good as it was, or just as good as she wants it to be. But she still talks about the past a lot.'

'Does she know about me yet?'

'Oh yes. Simon told her straight away and she seemed pleased.'

Mother with her sisters and my Grandmother, Cromer 1914.

Mother and Jill, 1960.

285

Mother, 1930s.

Mother and monkey.

XVII

I did not meet Simon and my mother until three months after meeting Jill. The delay was because of Christmas and Mother's health. She had to be in one of her good spells, Simon told me on the phone, and the cold weather had made her a bit chesty. Despite Simon's assurance that she was very keen to meet me I wondered if the prospect of meeting the son she had given away for adoption forty-eight years earlier might also upset her health. I also guess that there had to be plenty of time for the family grapevine, for Julian to be consulted as well, and for Jill to reassure everyone that I was a nice enough guy, not bitter or angry, just a thoughtful adopted child who had done well enough in life and now wanted to find out something about his natural family.

This reassurance was one of the first things Simon asked for. I went down by train and we met at Dorchester station. He had suggested we had lunch at a pub a couple of miles away, before meeting Jill at the nursing home, so that all of us could see Mother together and give me and Simon the chance to get to know each other.

'Well, Caradoc, it's good to have the chance to meet you but I do hope that you are not looking for a new family. The truth is that we are all very tied up with our own families now and fifty years is a very long time not knowing someone, even if he is your half-brother. Life has to go on.'

From a man who didn't look as kind and thoughtful, the words might have seemed unfriendly. But I understood Simon. For him, Julian and Jill and their families, and most of all for Mother, my appearance could come as a disturbing shock. For me it was a process of happy discovery because I needed to know about my origins. But for my siblings, who had known about me for years, it might be an awkward intrusion.

'It's OK, Simon. I'm very glad to meet you and Jill. And I'm very glad to be able to meet Mother. But that's enough. I just needed to fill in some gaps. If Mother doesn't know who I am – and I never see her again – I'll still be happy. I think it's probably as much for my kids as me – to be able to tell them who I am and where I came from, rather than just an adopted child of unknown parents.'

Maybe Simon sensed in my tone of voice, as I had in his, that I was honest, neither unkind nor particularly self-centred. Once we were settled by the pub fire with our pints and plates of steak and kidney pie, he seemed much more relaxed than he had been when he had stiffly shaken my hand at Dorchester Station. I liked the look of him. Taller than Jill, shorter than me, he was balding with a grey fringe of hair and a kind, gentle face. But I also sensed, maybe through the tone of voice, or his blunt opening statement, that there was a canny, down-to-earth quality about Simon – something I detected in Jill as well and recognised in myself. A family resemblance. Simon must have recognised the same in me and realised that I was someone he could trust because the story he began to tell me was honest and very moving.

'I suppose that you could say that we are an eccentric family. Mother has four living children and all of them have different fathers. Two long marriages and two illegitimate children. Unusual for a woman of her class and age.' He smiled ruefully.

'Two illegitimate children?'

My mind worked fast. Simon, Julian and William, the one who died, sons of James Barton; Jill, daughter of Owen Beckett; and me, father unknown.

'Who is the second ... illegitimate I mean?'

'Me.'

He took a long sip of beer, then he told me.

'I only found out four years ago when Mother had her stroke. I think she wanted to tell me before she died after keeping it secret for sixty years. She had an affair with a neighbour's son when they were living in Highgate, North London.'

'Your father?'

He nodded.

'It could have caused quite a scandal. She was only nineteen, not long out of school, living at home with her father. All her sisters had left home and got married. So grandfather sent her off to Poole, where two of the sisters, Bubba and Pardy, lived. They could take care of her and grandfather could avoid the scandal.'

Simon's story was extraordinary. He had spent almost sixty years of his life believing that the wrong man was his father. But also extraordinary was that my mother had lived in Highgate, two miles from my present home.

'Mother was lucky, always has been. She met James in 1932, when I was still a baby, and he married her in April 1933. I thought he was my dad because he had been around as long as I remembered and they never told me the truth. I was always James's son – and he was a wonderful father. Then, six years later, my brother Julian was born and we became a proper family.'

'What happened to James?'

He was after all the man named as my father on my birth certificate, a married woman's right, as Ariel had explained, even though according to Jill, the marriage had come to an end more than a year before my birth.

'He's dead,' said Simon quietly, 'died in the late sixties.'

So even at the time of his death Simon had thought James was his natural father.

'The divorce must have been tough for you and Julian. What happened?'

Simon shrugged.

'Oh, a usual wartime story. He was away on active service. He met a girl in Greece, came back and left. But I don't think they had been happy for a while.'

'And my mother? At home alone in wartime England with two young children? Had she met someone else? My father perhaps?'

'He didn't bring the Greek girl home,' Simon said, 'but when he got back to England he met another woman on her own with young kids. They married and he went to live in the North. They had more children and I didn't see him much after that.'

What a mixed-up wartime story. Father of two young children has love affair overseas then comes home, leaves his wife, and moves in with someone else's wife, or maybe widow, and her young children.

'The sad thing,' Simon went on, 'was the last time I saw him – or rather didn't see him. We were both coming to London for the day, Dad from the north and me from Poole. We arranged to meet for lunch in a restaurant near King's Cross, but he didn't come. I waited there for half an hour then left, assuming that he had forgotten or couldn't be bothered. Stupidly I never phoned him and he didn't phone me. I think we both must have thought that it was the other's fault, but were too proud or upset to ask. I only found out a couple of years later at his funeral what had happened. His wife, or rather widow, told me how upset he had been that I hadn't turned up for that lunch. He had muddled the dates of course; both of us had been there, but on different days.' Simon made another rueful smile. 'It still upsets me that he died thinking that I didn't care. He died very suddenly too, just a heart attack and out like a light. And I still miss him.'

I wanted to reach out and clasp his hand. It was an extraordinarily sad story. I asked him if he would like another drink. Simon refused. But there were still questions I wanted to ask.

'And what happened to your real father?'

'I don't know. Mother had no further contact with him, but told me that he died in the war, years before I knew anything about him.'

I had one more question.

'Do you have any idea who my father is?'

Simon smiled, and shook his head. For the first time he looked straight at me, scrutinising my expression.

'Well, I suppose that's the big question. But I'm afraid I cannot really help. Mother's the only one who can answer that, if she can remember and if she wants to.'

He got up from his chair.

'Let's go and ask her. Who knows what she'll remember if she's in a good mood.'

We drove the six miles back into Dorchester saying little. I felt nervous. I was meeting my mother for the first time in fifty years, a mother who until Ariel's phone call to Jill three months earlier was an unknown missing person, blanked out from my mind. Now I knew a lot about her – a big family of older sisters, her long marriages, her two illegitimate children. I knew from Jill and

Simon's story that everyone loved her – a wayward and feckless woman but a fun and loving mother as well. I liked that. I felt glad she was my mother, but what would she be like? Had she thought of me? Did she want to see me? Would we laugh, cry, embrace, like each other?

Simon must have sensed my feelings.

'Don't expect too much,' he said. 'She is now a very old woman and although some days are better, she can't speak very much because of the stroke and her hearing is very limited – or rather she hears only what she wants to hear. I'll probably have to translate her words to you and also sometimes explain to her what you are saying. She's not very good with strangers.' He quickly realised what he had said and laughed. 'But I know she's looking forward to seeing you. The nurse told me she has had her hair specially shampooed and set this morning.'

I wonder what we would talk about – my wife, the kids, my job? I had brought photographs. Then, as we approached the outskirts of Dorchester, one thought formed in my mind, something that had been nagging at me during our conversation over lunch.

'Where did she go to school, Simon?'

'South Hampstead High, I think it's called. Two of her sisters went there as well.'

'I don't believe it!'

What an extraordinary coincidence. My daughter Flora was now in the fifth form at the same school.

I explained to Simon. He laughed.

'I told you we were a rum family. Maybe that will be just one of many surprises.'

My mother was sitting hunched in an armchair by the bed. Her hair was white, thin but carefully set in neat curls. She was wearing a pair of tortoiseshell glasses which looked too large on her lined and sunken face. On her lap was a toy furry cat, sheltered under her pale-blue cardigan.

Simon went to her first.

'Hello, darling,' he said, kissing her cheek. Then Jill did the same.

They stood beside her and turned towards me, standing by the door.

'And this is Caradoc, or Nicholas as you used to call him. He's come all the way from London especially to see you.'

Mother looked at me. She frowned as if at first she couldn't see. Then slowly, a little apprehensively, our eyes met. We both smiled. I walked towards her. Jill had told me that Mother always liked to kiss – but it seemed too intimate. Instead I placed one hand over her old woman's hand lying on the arm of the chair and squeezed it gently.

'Hello, Mother. It's good to meet you.'

She nodded her head slowly, twice. The sound of my voice seemed to reassure her. I felt her hand grasp mine; weak watery eyes blinked at me through the strong glasses. She smiled, but there was something questioning and vulnerable in that smile, a hesitation like my own.

'Can I sit down here beside you?' Still holding her hand, I sat on the bed next to her chair.

Now she was saying something to me, stammering the words. I leaned closer.

'Nice ... nice boy.'

The three of us laughed. I lifted her hand and kissed it. We had broken the ice.

We looked at the photographs I had brought of my children, Charlie and Flora, and she clucked and ah'd. I told her about our house, my job, and how pleased I was to have found her. Simon told her that Flora went to South Hampstead, the school she had been to as a girl seventy-odd years before. She didn't seem to remember that. Then Simon and Jill told her their own bits of family news. I half listened while my eyes wandered round the room. It was small, most of it filled by her bed with its pink eiderdown. There was a TV set on a chest of drawers, an armchair beside the bed and a small wardrobe crammed next to the door, but no room for anything else. There were pictures hanging on flowery wallpaper, fading tints of a Scottish loch and mountains, a steamer coming into harbour, a black terrier and a marmalade cat sharing a bowl of food. Comforting images like the furry toy that helped to make the fading world seem soft and harmless.

Then the door opened and a nurse appeared carrying a tray.

It was not until the tea things had been cleared away that Simon asked the question I didn't think he was going to ask. He must have consulted Jill beforehand for she brought out of her bag a photograph album which Simon put on his mother's lap.

'I thought you might like to see these, darling,' he said. 'They were taken about the time that Caradoc was born.' He opened up at the first page and started to flip slowly through the album, beckoning me to look as well. Leaning forward, I could see the old black and white photographs, holiday snaps of people on beaches, Mother with a horse, smiling groups standing by a car. Simon kept up a running commentary of familiar names, Mother nodding as Simon explained. Then Simon pointed to a picture of a baby in a white gown lying on a blanket under a pine tree.

'That's Caradoc, isn't it, darling? At Chester Road, about six months old?'

We all lean forward smiling as you do when looking at a picture of someone else's baby. But I felt an odd and eerie feeling to be looking at myself, fixed in a photograph album of a family who had lost track of me fifty years before. Sitting beside me on the bed Jill must have sensed it. She squeezed my hand and said, 'Long before my time.' (she hadn't been born until 1953, the year I went to prep school.) Another picture caught Jill's attention as well.

'Look, there's my dad with James. They were good friends for a while.' The picture was of two men in rolled-up trousers standing by the seashore, grinning, one of them eating an ice cream.

Her remark seemed to give Simon the cue he needed. He held the album open at that page waiting for the photo to trigger her memory.

'You know, darling, the one thing Caradoc would really like to know ...' His voice was soft and almost teasing. 'He'd like to know who his father was.'

There was a moment's silence. We all looked at Mother. She seemed puzzled at first, slowly forming the question in her mind until she understood. She looked round slowly, looking at us watching her. Her face went blank as if she might cry, then the blank look was replaced by a coy complicit smile. But she didn't say anything.

Simon tried again.

'I wish I could remember. There were a good many people around at that time.' He was now sounding playful. 'There was that army officer from the medical corps. I can remember him. And wasn't there some man with an eye patch, who played in a dance band on Bournemouth Pier and had digs above the newsagent at the end of the road?'

Mother nodded happily at everything Simon said. But she herself said nothing. Whether she remembered or not she wasn't letting on.

Simon persisted.

'Of course, there was also Owen , Jill's dad. Isn't it true that you and he were once caught together in the bedroom in Aunt

Bubba's house? I suppose he couldn't have been Caradoc's dad as well?'

We all waited expectantly. Jill and I had talked about this when we looked at the wedding certificate. She told me of a possible earlier affair – but Simon had been non-committal when I had asked him over lunch. I was surprised that he was being so persistent now. But Mother just shook her head, smiling. She wasn't saying no. Either she couldn't remember, didn't want to remember, or did and didn't want to talk about it. My father was her secret. I didn't mind. It was enough to find her. We left soon after that, when Mother's head began to nod with tiredness. We all kissed her. Simon told her he would be back tomorrow.

XVIII

The next time I saw my mother was at her funeral, eight months after our meeting. Jill had phoned with news that Mother was growing very weak. She asked if I wanted to see her again but then agreed that it wouldn't make much sense because she wouldn't recognise me. For me our single meeting had been close and special enough.

The funeral was at Dorchester Crematorium at midday, giving enough time to drive down from London that morning. I left after an early breakfast but the traffic was terrible and I started to feel anxious that I would be late. How could I be late for my own mother's funeral, a mother with whom I had shared only about eighteen months of my life in and out of the womb?

Luckily I arrived in time for greetings in the crematorium foyer where everyone had assembled before taking their seats in the chapel. I was the last to arrive and keenly expected. Jill was relieved to see me and swiftly introduced various cousins and old friends of my mother who, alerted about my recent reappearance in the family, greeted me warmly. For a funeral everyone seemed very cheerful.

This festive atmosphere continued in the chapel where a jovial local priest, who hadn't known my mother, told us we were commemorating a life which had ended in natural old age so we shouldn't grieve about Joan's passing but celebrate her remarkable achievements, the mothering and grandmothering of so many relatives gathered that day, her warmth and many friendships and endearing things I knew nothing about like her fondness for classical music and visiting National Trust houses. Although the priest was speaking carefully rehearsed lines, which only changed a little at each funeral, I sensed the collective warmth and love for my mother and even at that bleak moment of the coffin vanishing behind the curtain felt happy just to have met her and to be at her funeral.

Afterwards we drove in convoy to the house of one of Simon's children in a nearby village for a buffet lunch in the garden. Here I met my other half-brother and his wife and adolescent children. Julian was a good-looking well-dressed man, who didn't look his age which is eight years older than me, with the easy confidence of a successful businessman. He was friendly and charming but I sensed the underlying wariness and remembered that Jill had told me he was rarely in contact with the rest of the family. His chic French wife, Marie, was more forthcoming and happy to answer my questions about Joan, although it was difficult to tell from her tempered enthusiasm – about what an extraordinary and marvellously warm person she had been, but of course very strong-willed and often difficult to please – whether she had actually liked her or had found her just a difficult mother-in-law.

Joan's extraordinary nature shows well in a photograph taken at the funeral of her four children standing side by side – Simon,

Julian, Jill and me, all of us with different fathers as far as we know, but with a mother of two long marriages. I didn't know how fully my siblings shared the funeral eulogies. I had not had to live through the muddle and pain her behaviour must have caused others, including her decision to give me up for adoption; but I felt keen pleasure in knowing that she was a woman of courage, independent spirit and a strong zest for life. I sensed her genes in me and felt very happy that she was my mother.

Not long after my mother died I went to a different family funeral, Aunty Molly's. It was also the occasion for another reunion.

Her husband Raymond phoned me early on a Sunday morning in early January.

'She died, Caradoc. This morning, just after four.' His voice was broken with grief, tiredness, shock. 'She died in my arms.'

An hour later I arrived at Archway, the house Molly had owned for thirty years and had shared with Raymond for the last five. His granddaughter was there, a nurse who had driven them home from their Christmas trip to Devon the night before and, thankfully, had stayed the night. Karen, red-haired and pretty, was warm and friendly but looked shocked and tired like Raymond. She had been up most of the night as well, called the ambulance for Raymond when he woke her up, waited with him at the hospital until the doctor certified Molly as dead, came home with him without his wife, and talked to him until he fell asleep.

Raymond told me what had happened. 'She woke me in the middle of the night, saying she wanted to go to the lavatory, asking for the bedpan.' There was a register of panic in his voice. 'I told her to get up and do it herself, as I always did. It was better for her to be tough, not to give in.' His voice wavered on the edge of tears. 'But this time I drove her too far. She managed get up and with the help of her frame reached the lavatory. She even flushed. But as she walked back from the bathroom she just collapsed onto the floor.' He stopped, looking bewildered.

'I'm sorry,' he said finally. 'I got her back to the bed. I had her in my arms, talking to her but it was already too late. I think I killed her. I should never have made her get up. If only I'd thought a bit more.'

I wanted to walk over and hug him but Raymond, at eighty-four, was not that kind of man. He was strong, dignified, stiff-upper-lip, especially in grief; and we both might have cried.

'No, Raymond, you didn't kill her,' I said firmly. 'You kept her alive, you gave her something to live for. You made the last five years of her life extremely happy.'

The funeral service was at Enfield Parish Church, a cremation to follow. Like Mother's, the funeral was, for me, an occasion for greeting more than farewell. Three of my adopted sisters – Janet, Caroline and Priscilla – had come to pay respects to their elderly aunt, and maybe to meet the adopted brother they hadn't seen for thirty years. Although only a nephew by adoption, I was my aunt's closest living relative.

I saw them when I stood on the altar steps to deliver a tribute to Molly, requested by Raymond. They were sitting in the same pew and none of them had changed much in thirty years. Priscilla had the same soft, round and gentle face. Janet, married at eighteen and now with granddaughters of that age, was still blonde, youthful with the familiar outgoing friendly expression. Caroline, short, plumper and with glasses looked a kinder more cheerful version of her mother. They smiled when I caught their eyes.

My tribute described Molly's meeting with Raymond forty-four years after their first love affair.

'Molly's great change of life, her annus mirabilis, happened in 1990, much later than it happens to most people. In January that year my wife and I gave an eightieth birthday party for her, inviting many old friends she and I had known for years. Among the guests invited was someone I had never heard of, a man called Raymond.

Raymond couldn't come to the dinner, but I finally got out of Aunty Molly the identity of this mystery man and their story is probably the most romantic I know. Raymond was someone she had met and fallen in love with in Malaya in 1946. They had a passionate affair which ended when Raymond, a married man with family, had to return to England. Raymond's wife died in 1987 and, as he told me later, he had been clearing out his house in Hampton-in-Arden and discovered his old diaries, one of which went back to 1946. He had always kept the number and addresses of new friends he met each year, and there he found Molly's old Hermitage address and phone number. By extraordinary luck, although Molly had moved house, her phone number had moved with her. But when Raymond tried the number a couple of times there was no reply. A few weeks later, having tracked down her change of address, he sent Molly a Christmas card, mentioning that his wife had died and giving his own telephone number. A day later Molly phoned and a couple of days after that they arranged to meet in Hampton-in-Arden where Raymond lived.

I asked Raymond what it had been like when they had first met. Had they easily recognised each other forty-four years later? He smiled and said he recognised Molly immediately

301

when she got off the train at Hampton station. She hadn't changed a bit.

It was clear that Aunty Molly was deeply in love all over again. She was frisky, youthful and full of a new energy and zest for life which was wonderful to see. When she finally admitted she might possibly be in love I asked what she was going to do. Marry him? No, live in sin, she said cheerfully, and the next time I visited Archway I found a large double bed had been installed.

The love affair blossomed over the next few months and for me it was an enormous pleasure getting to know Raymond, whom I liked at once, seeing how happy they made each other. Eventually they decided to do something that Aunty Molly had always wanted, to return to Malaya, this time together. In November 1990 they set off on a cargo ship from Tilbury, bound for Singapore. Their plan was to drive from there up the Malay peninsula and if, as Molly told me firmly, they travelled well together they might then possibly get married.

The occasional postcard followed over the next three months and they were clearly having a good time. Then, out of the blue, a faxed copy of their wedding certificate arrived at my office on Valentine's Day, dated that day from a small town in Malaya, just a few miles from the old hill station at which they had first met forty-four years earlier.'

After the funeral there was the cremation and then a luncheon buffet at an Enfield hotel. It was time to re-meet old friends and family.

My three sisters were there, Janet and Caroline with their husbands and an assortment of children, polite, smiling teenagers, stiff in best dark clothes, shaking hands politely with older relatives who they hadn't seen since the last funeral, or wedding, and now among them me, the mysterious Uncle Caradoc they had never met before. There were cousins too, Patricia and Barbara, Sidney's children, whom I remembered from childhood when staying in their house after the Great Flood and caravan weekend visits to Mersea, now middle-aged women I could have sat next to on a long train journey without recognising.

Janet, Caroline and Priscilla not only looked the same but were the same; their voices, mannerisms, personalities unchanged after thirty years. And I to them? Probably similar – despite the much greater changes in my life than theirs. They have continued in the tradition of the King family. Caroline married her schoolteacher husband thirty and a bit years ago and now had five or six children and grandchildren and, like her parents, lived in rural isolation in the Scottish lowlands. Janet was the same – still living in the two converted cottages outside Tintern-on-Wye she bought with Paddy after their teenage marriage in 1962, now a grandmother and also a mother of divorced children. Priscilla, my youngest and closest sister, was happily living with George, her Polish partner, in a flat in Edinburgh, close to Da who moved there after he separated from Jill a decade or so ago.

Everyone was more relaxed and friendly as the wine flowed. When coffee was served we four Kings sat together, spouses and children having drifted away, leaving us to our own family reunion. This was time to try to catch up and put the past in its place. Caroline apologised for having left it so long. Janet said I must bring the family down to see them in Tintern. We all agreed to meet again soon. Thirty years of absence closed easily into the present.

We did meet again, several times. The winding-up of my Aunt Molly's estate, of which we are all beneficiaries, turned out to be a four-year legal marathon. We met in the offices of Weld & Beavan, then at Archway, now empty but for the riff-raff of furniture and personal possessions which didn't interest the auctioneers, and then over a pub lunch to air our complaints about the solicitors' dilatory behaviour. We revisited childhood memories, talked about our own kids, liked each other all over again. But it was the letters my sisters wrote to me that movingly brought back our shared past and helped me make sense of it.

Priscilla wrote:

You asked what effect your departure from the family had on the rest of us. That you could be aware of our pain in the midst of your own says a lot for you.

It was like a death, only worse. Jane and Janet had already left home, Caroline and I were at Hengrave and Quentin, I think, had already started at the choir school, so we were used to being apart and meeting in the holidays.

Quite suddenly it was announced that you would not be coming home any more, that you had been adopted as a baby and had 'inherited a bad character' and were beyond control. All traces of you were removed from the house and your name was never to be mentioned again. And that was it.

The shock was tremendous. Until then we had all had a secure and happy childhood, loved and trusted our parents. I think I grew up rather suddenly. I was fourteen then, and if my later teenage years were quiet and well behaved, maybe I thought the same could happen to me.

I saw you once. You came back to Strood House on a motor-bike. I had been walking the dogs along the sea wall and saw your arrival, Caroline's hysterics, and Jill shouting at you from her bedroom window. I came in a bit later and everyone was pretending that nothing had happened. They didn't know I had seen you. Caroline was in her room with 'a headache'. We sat down to tea. I said nothing. It was the worst meal in my life.

When Jill and Da split up I had been at home for a couple of long periods and had got to know them both well, and from an adult standpoint it became increasingly clear that Jill's behaviour was very far from normal, that her ill health, the reason for my being at home, was far more to do with her state of mind than body, although I would not dismiss the physical symptoms lightly.

I had already returned to live in Edinburgh when they announced that they were parting company. I was glad for Da's sake, Jill's behaviour towards him then was both cruel and vindictive, and often quite bizarre. I never forgave mother for what she did to you, and now she did the same to Da. She always had complete control over the house and children and made all domestic decisions. I am quite certain that it was her decision to cast you out. Da is guilty by default for not standing up to her, by accepting her stories about your behaviour and claims that you were beyond her control.

Da was seventy when he came to live alone in Edinburgh. I realised immediately that I would have to look after him, and that it would be a commitment until he died, and so it proved. Just like Aunty Molly and Grandpa.

He made a life for himself and learned all the domestic things to make himself independent. He was happy and fulfilled living alone and said so. He and mother continued to correspond and meet at weddings and family occasions. He never criticised her, only saying about her that she was 'a rather difficult woman'. Mother's attitude was very bitter and she distorted the past horribly. It took us a long time to realise how many lies she had told about everything. It was she who divided us from both the Beavan and the King sides of the family and did/does her damnedest to divide us among each other. Fortunately we ring each other up to get to the bottom of mother's wilder claims.

The last few years Da became very frail and needed me a lot, which help I was glad to give. He long ago forgot why you were no longer in the family and would follow your press cuttings with interest and cut them out for me to see. He wrote once to mother to ask about you. He showed me her reply, a stream of abuse, which said far more about her than you.

He was delighted when Aunt Mavis got in touch and I think would have liked to have gone to her eightieth birthday celebrations only he was afraid of upsetting mother because of your involvement.

Jane's death [suddenly of an asthma attack in her late fifties] was a terrible shock to him and to all of us. I won't say he never recovered nor that it hastened his death since he was, after all, nearly ninety-one when he died, but it did affect him strongly. He seemed to become smaller. I think he was glad to go. He was getting more and more frail and also more forgetful, though his mind remained clear to the end.

As for mother, I had tried, as had the others, not to take sides, so went to see her and corresponded regularly but she became increasingly difficult, particularly to me. If I did something I was interfering. If not, I was neglecting her. Whatever I did was wrong. Since Da's death she has refused to have anything to do with me – guilt because I looked after him? – accusing me (although not directly to my face) of all sorts of vile things, writing to Janet about me and to Da's lawyer. I have tried writing to her, but she simply sends the letters to the lawyer – to his acute embarrassment because he is a nice man – and the last one she sent back unopened marked 'refused –

returned to sender'. So you see. I now have some very faint idea of how you felt!

I try and tell myself that she is old and ill and probably senile, but it doesn't really help. She never forgets nor forgives. She is implacable. She and Aunty Molly both had strong characters and indeed shared the same illnesses, but Aunty Molly, though far more disabled, always struck one with her immense courage and good cheer.

Janet wrote:

Jane and I knew from the beginning that you were adopted, but also that it was one of those matters that was simply not discussed, and I don't remember us ever talking about it and certainly the parents didn't. Mother's story was that you were conceived as a last chance to hold together a fading marriage (there were two very much older brothers) but according to the matron of the Barnardo's from which you were adopted, your father was not your mother's husband. I would have put this rather less bluntly had I not known that you know the other side of this. When Quentin was born I must have queried how this affected you as mother said that she had checked with Uncle Sidney that your position as eldest son was unaffected. Funny how these old memories float to the surface.

Mother's conversion to Catholicism was the start of the rot. Jane and I escaped the worst of it as we were both too settled in our schooling to be shifted about – my shifting was due to expulsion . . . so Jane went from Endsleigh to Pipers, I from Endsleigh to Elmhurst, to the High School and, being naturally bolshie, never got caught by the Church. Interestingly, even Quentin mutters about his messed up education – always

307

changed schools without warning in the middle of a term. The parents' division was absolute: Da earned the money, Mother had absolute power of the house and children. Gamma gave her the deposit for Strood House on the condition that it was bought in her name so she always considered that it was hers. How Da also managed to buy 45 North Hill [in Colchester, where he practised as a Dentist] I don't know, only that he sold it and told Ma later. I suspect from then on everything he did was wrong in her eyes; certainly she hated him being at home all the time as she had to consider somebody else.

Mother's rejection of you did make me hang on when various of my sons went off the rails. I was quite determined never to write off one of my children. Da never knew what it was all about and when we finally plucked up enough courage to ask mother I couldn't get a coherent answer from her. 'He stole.' Yes, well so did I, and got beaten for it. 'He was a liar.' Ditto. 'He played truant.' I got expelled for that but funnily enough I don't remember getting beaten for it! I rather suspect that Ma wasn't quite sure how to cope with me – she was always terrified that I would present her with a bastard. With you she simply convinced herself that you had 'bad blood', that it was nature over nurture and whatever other fashionable whisper she heard. She had absolutely no idea that male adolescence can be pretty gruesome sometimes, for by then she had Quentin on whom the sun shone (and still does). Was mother jealous on Quentin's behalf that Priscilla idolised her big brother rather than her little one? Shall we ever know . . . She was and is an extremely jealous woman. Da trod on her patch when he retired, he loathed being forced to tour Ireland (endlessly) in the motor caravan, disliked Hofotty Wen [the house in Wales where Jill and Eric finally settled and also separated] and when Ma converted the cowshed for him to live in, she hated any of us 'visiting' him when we were staying at Hofotty. And mother wonders why Da left. With hindsight I am quite astounded that he stayed. Actually no, he was always polite and never set out to make waves. I can well understand Ma's complete disbelief when the worm turned. And was she ever bitter. Your description of her as a paranoid woman who needed to find scapegoats for her own demons is terrifyingly accurate. Quentin was never formally told that you'd been thrown out – you just weren't there and any questions were stonewalled. I knew from Jane what you were doing (up to a point) and I remember telling Ma you were at Oxford, for her to dismiss it as another lie – yours or mine? Toss for it . . .

XIX

One more story about my adoptive mother Jill, told to me just before she died, put all this in place and was another prompt to write this book.

Eighteen months after Aunty Molly's funeral, Priscilla sent me a photocopy of an estate agent's brochure with a friendly letter saying she thought I might be interested.

I didn't think so. As I started my own family and then much later traced my blood family, my adoptive family disappeared from my memory. Maybe I banished them just as they had banished me. So, having glanced through the brochure announcing the sale of Strood House and looked with mild curiosity at the black and white photographs of the old living room, I threw the brochure into the waste bin.

But impulses are transitory. The binning of the brochure must have stirred my curiosity about Strood House and the years I lived there. Memories can be compartmentalised, shelved and repressed, but never erased. Whether I chose to think about it or not my childhood stayed acutely with me. It is an imaginative resource of precisely detailed scenes and events, good and bad. It has shaped my adult self and enriched my imagination with memories and contradictory feelings of nostalgia, pain, tenderness, sentimentality and rage – emotional data that I have always carried. These memories also became strangely 'romanticised'. With no parents or siblings to share the past, and for years no family photographs to prompt memories, what consciously remained was an abbreviated and polished version of my 'unhappy childhood', referred to dismissively or occasionally expanded into familiar short stories for curious family and friends.

So I decided to go back.

It was a February afternoon. The sun was cold yellow across the water as I drove up to the house for my 2.30 appointment with Mrs Daunt. The tide was high for late afternoon and the marshes were almost covered. A couple of hundred yards down the causeway the water was already edging under the fencing onto the road. If it was still rising the road would soon be impassable and traffic would start to queue at each end of the causeway, the drivers waiting patiently for the ebb. I remembered from childhood the day trippers to Mersea Island who regularly knocked on our front door asking to use the phone or borrow a towrope after foolishly driving across the flooded causeway and suffering engine failure on the other side. If it was the weekend, Da would normally be polite and helpful – but if it was on a weekday and Jill answered the door she would just say no.

I made today's appointment with Mrs Daunt five months after I had binned the estate agent's brochure. By the time that I had acknowledged to myself that I did want to go and see Strood House I had forgotten the name of the estate agents and felt strangely uncomfortable about ringing Priscilla to ask her. But the name of Daunt was distinctive so I phoned Directory Enquiries and gave the name and address. It turned out there were only a couple of Daunts in the Colchester area phone book so I swiftly got the number. It was an eight digit number rather than the 'Peldon 267' Jill or Da would apprehensively announce when the telephone in the hall had occasionally rung. When I dialled Mrs Daunt answered immediately. I gave her an honest explanation when she told me that the house was still for sale.

'It's a spur of the moment interest, Mrs Daunt, you see I used to live in the house as a child thirty-five years ago. I heard it was for sale.'

She asked my name and when I told her she laughed.

'I know about you,' she said. 'We found your name written on the wall in the attic after we bought the house. Didn't you have a little theatre up there?' I said yes and asked her how long she had lived there. 'Thirty years and a bit. We bought it from your parents in 1966.' Two years after I had left home.

'So, why are you selling?' I asked quietly, anticipating the answer. There was sadness in her voice.

'My husband died suddenly last year. Our children have all grown up. Time to move on.'

Now, in the wintery afternoon sunlight, I waited outside the old front door in the yard at the side of the house. I had last stood there watching Jill at the bedroom window above the door, hearing her furiously telling me to go away and never come back again.

Mrs Daunt was a small, kindly woman with grey hair. She smiled warmly as she shook my hand, but I could see the grief etched on her face.

'Would you like a cup of tea? I've just put the kettle on.'

Mrs Daunt settled on the sofa at the music room end and

served tea. On the alcove shelves beside the unlit fire stood photographs of her husband, their children and their children, smiling studio shots in school uniform. I asked about her family and how they had enjoyed living at Strood House. She smiled but immediately looked tearful.

'It has been a lovely home for us for more than thirty years now. Of course we had our ups and downs like most families but we all loved it here.'

Two of her children still live close by, married with small children in local schools. Clearly the ups and downs had held this family very close together, unlike ours.

Finally she asked whether I would like to see around the house – an invitation I had been eagerly waiting for. Whatever happened to make me leave it, I remembered every detail of the house of my childhood, from the sound of the door catches, the creak of the water pipes, the east coast winds slicing through the willow tree outside my bedroom window, the sound of adult voices downstairs when I was trying to go to sleep. These were my memories and I wanted to relive them.

'Help yourself,' said Mrs Daunt. 'I'm sure you can find your way about.'

Most of the rest of the house was like the living room – very familiar and also different. There were two major changes. Upstairs a new ensuite bathroom had been added to the bedroom I shared with Priscilla. Downstairs the potty room and lobby by the back door had been re-sited to make a larger bathroom. Otherwise, apart from the different carpets and decorations, the rooms, and the sound of their doors, were still the same.

On the top-floor landing, outside my parents' bedroom, were the steep attic stairs leading up to where we performed our family plays and Mrs Daunt had found my name pencilled on the wall. But I had just one reason to look in the attic. To see if I could find something that was lost thirty-six years earlier, Jill's Patek Philippe watch.

The way I hid the watch shows how disturbed I was about being accused of theft. I had to hide it, get rid of it or, but impossible, own up that I had borrowed the watch and given it back. So I had taken it secretly up into the attic, unravelled a ball of wool in an old knitting basket that I found stored between the rafters under the eaves at the end of the house, then had wrapped the watch in the rewound ball of wool and replaced it in the discarded knitting basket. When I had left the house for the last time two years or so later, the watch would still have been hidden in the attic, but the chances of it being found would have been slight. Now I wanted to go back to the attic to see if the ball of wool might by a remote chance still be there.

But it wasn't. The attic had been re-partitioned to make an extra bedroom. The rafters were bare under the eaves. There was nothing there. Just dust.

I went downstairs and asked if I could look round the garden.

'Of course,' said Mrs Daunt. 'I'll make some more tea and leave you to your memories.'

It hadn't changed much. There were more flowerbeds around the big lawn beside the house and the poplars planted by Da along the wall between us and the Harding house were now almost as high as the willow tree. The grass track through the coppice leading towards the vegetable garden, on which my sister Caroline 'kept a shop', a large green plywood structure built lovingly by Da for one of her birthdays, was still there. The vegetable garden, Martha's Vineyard, which we laboriously dug and weeded most summer weekends, was now grassed over but the paths across it leading to the small orchard, along which I travelled on my bike and red trailer doing useful jobs for Da, were still marked. The River Nile, the small weedy creek on which we raced the two old paddleboats Da had bought from the town park, was now dried up.

The orchard was the same, apple trees and sloe bushes whose growth must have been stunted by the biting salt of the east winds, because they looked about the same height and were now bare in the winter sunlight. Standing in the orchard, I had a sudden clear memory of something else, something important, which happened when I was maybe eight.

It was a hot summer's day, when most summer days seemed to be hot and still and empty. Priscilla and I had been playing some game with Caroline which had tailed off leaving the two of us standing alone in the orchard. I'm not sure what prompted us to look at each others' naked bodies because Priscilla and I were used to seeing each other in the bath. We were already half naked and just in shorts because of the heat and I must have made the first move though I sense the thought was shared. I don't remember the words, probably just a dare – 'Will you show me yours if I show you mine?' – but I slipped down my shorts and we touched each other.

It stopped there and we never did it again. Recently I reminded Priscilla of this encounter. She didn't remember it, but said she might have told Jill, perhaps innocently wanting her to explain the male anatomy and its difference to her own. And I remembered hearing from Aunty Molly, long after they had thrown me out, that one of Jill's claims was that I had molested my little sister. Was this what Jill had told Father Thomas at Laxton, which had made him dismiss me as a degenerate and advise her to throw me out?

Now I stood in the orchard, looking out over the Cow's Field where we played and exercised the dogs, skidded on the frozen puddles in winter and wallowed in them during the summer when the water was so deep it flattened the wellington boots against our legs until water sometimes lapped over their rims. I breathed in deeply the cold marshy air, a smell which still moves me, looked at the sky's blue and orange tinting into mauve with a now visible slither of moon. The Essex marshes are an empty desolate place and I felt happy to be there.

In her sitting room Mrs Daunt had laid out clean teacups and seemed reluctant to let me leave. She was going to her daughter's the next day, but clearly many days went by when she sat alone in this large empty house looking at the photographs, the cream paintwork yellowed by nicotine and reminding her of her husband's death from lung cancer and remembering, like me, happier days.

Then, in answer to a simple question, Mrs Daunt revealed something that seemed the last missing piece in the jigsaw of my childhood.

I asked whether she had seen the Kings again after she and her husband bought the house.

'Yes, for a year they lived in Strood Cottage, which came with the house. We didn't see them much but I remember the party in the garden for your sister Caroline's wedding.'

She was silent for a couple of minutes sipping tea.

'But there was one other time, several years later, after your parents had taken Quentin to live in Ireland. It didn't work out there apparently. Something to do with the National Health your father said.' She paused. 'One day, out of the blue, we got this call from your mother at one of the railway stations in London. Geoffrey spoke to her and said she sounded upset. All she said was that she had nowhere to go and just asked if she could come down and stay for a few days. And Geoffrey, being a kind-hearted chap, said yes.

'She didn't say much, or do much while she was here. We gave

316

her her old bedroom and she just stayed there for several days, sleeping and weeping.'

Sleeping and weeping. In her old home where life had once been happy? Before all but her youngest child had left home. The old family home. Before the anger, fear and guilt she must have felt in expunging me from the family memory began to eat into her. A weeping, sleeping, ageing woman.

The phone rang. I half listened to Mrs Daunt chatting to her daughter. Then thanked her and drove back to London playing loud Mozart to repress my sadness.

Postscript

This book cannot end sadly. For the eight years since I wrote that last chapter life has been good.

Ingrid and I live happily together with our six-year-old daughter, India. I feel extremely close to my two older children, Charlie and Flora, who are doing well in their careers and in good relationships. My ex-wife Janey and I still have dinner together and I hope we can stay friends despite the damage of divorce. We are all in good health.

Early this morning, I ran round Hampstead Heath. Fearless rabbits were grazing on the Kenwood lawns before the dog walkers invaded. There was bright sun and cloudless sky, a shimmering mist above the dew-soaked grass, one of those 'good to be alive' September days before autumn's creeping cold and darkness.

We have lived next to the Heath for eight years and its semi-wildness and shifting seasonal beauty is the perfect antidote to any wistful longing for the country life of my childhood. The twice-weekly run has been an essential help writing this book, hard exercise clearing the clutter of daily worries, releasing frag-ments of memory and fusing them into story. The book is now finished and I have spent the last month reading through it, checking'what's in the box'. Today is a Friday when I work from home. I have the flat to myself, so a good day after the morning emails to write this short conclusion. There are a couple things I would like to add.

The first is about truth. Since being sent to school with 'I am a Liar' embroidered on my jersey I have always been conscious of the stigma of lying and of making up stories about myself. So here is a simple declaration. Allowing for memory loss this book is as true as I can tell it, with one qualification. It tells a story and a good story needs more than just a record of actual events. It needs shape and highlight in order to give the events it describes point and focus and make the story worth reading. So I have been selective about what I have included and very occasionally elided certain events to sharpen their focus.

Norman Mailer said shortly before his death that there is no difference between fact and fiction because they are both a pack of lies. Barack Obama has said that his memoir *Dreams from My Father* was a totally true story although some characters had been merged together. Michael Holroyd, the guru of modern biogra-phy whom I am lucky to represent, said in an interview on the publication of a recent book that'he wished people didn't make such a hard and fast distinction between fiction and non-fiction. You can't make anything up, but you have to try and recreate it.'

I hope this book doesn't upset anyone. Most of its events hap-pened around fifty years ago and, now that I have read it all, it seems more an elegy about lost happiness and innocence than about unhappiness. So I have used real names, only changing them or disguising circumstances to avoid risk of offence or embar-rassment. Several members of my natural or adopted families read the manuscript and gave it their blessing, but to any who haven't and wish that I had not exposed family history I apologise and hope you found it a respectful and affectionate record of our shared past.

I will just add that truth is often subjective. What one person believes happened is not necessarily the same for someone else. This applies particularly in personal relationships and within families. The response to this book from members of my families disclosed more information I could have pursued; but it made me realise above all how much other people's marriages are a mystery and that almost all families have and keep their secrets.

I have just returned from a walk to Swains Lane where I needed to buy some milk. My mother lived in Swains Lane in the 1930s and it was there, as an eighteen-year-old girl, that she fell pregnant by a neighbour's son. Mother must have been, for her generation, a remarkably free spirit. She was also much loved and someone I wish I had known better. If I inherited some of her waywardness – or according to my adoptive mother, degeneracy – I also hope I have inherited her good qualities.

This coda is about my two mothers who, though close in age and background, were very different women. My adoptive mother Jill has appeared so far as a cruel, unbalanced woman, who treated me badly. My natural mother, Joan, now appears as a kind and sympathetic woman much loved by her children, despite an erratic personal life.

But I do not compare them. Jill mothered me for fifteen years before throwing me out. Joan held on to me for my first nine months and then had no further contact until our one meeting three months before she died. Joan put me up for adoption and had nothing more to do with me. Jill carried the brunt of my adoption and its problems, and I think ended up being more hurt by it than me.

My adoptive mother, who gave me a childhood, was a troubled and difficult person. But her fallibility, paranoia and confusion taught me a great deal about the complexities of human nature and the hurt people can easily cause themselves. So I have been lucky having both of these mothers.

The missing link is my mysterious absentee father who, in the fallout from the war, made my mother pregnant and gave me life. That life, particularly with two mothers, has been too full to wonder much about him – but if by chance anyone knows who you are please get in touch.

Acknowledgements

My foremost thanks go to members of my family who appear in the book: to my sisters Priscilla, Janet and Caroline who read the draft manuscript and generously contributed their own memories of our shared childhood and corrected mine; and to my half sister Jill who guided me through the story of our mother and my natural family. I also give thanks to my cousin Tim Battle, to my Belmont schoolfriend Tony Aitken and to my oldest friend Shirley Tudor-Pole, all of whom played important roles in the story.

As a literary agent I have had the good fortune to have close contact with gifted writers and astute publishers, many of whom have been generous with their encouragement, criticism and support and I would like to thank the following: Carole and Richard Baron, Tim Binding, Peter Carson, Nicholas Evans, Eleo Gordon, Michael Holroyd, John Lanchester, Kate Saunders, Paul Sidey, Graham Swift and, particularly, Helen Dunmore and Philip Pullman.

Publishing a book by a literary agent may not an easy prospect for a publisher and I am very grateful to Simon & Schuster – and in particular to Suzanne Baboneau, Jane Pizzey, Lizzie Gardener and Hannah Corbett – for the care and enthusiasm which has made the process of publication so enjoyable.

Representing a fellow literary agent, friend and close colleague is also challenging so I give warm thanks to Derek Johns for his perceptive reading and astute agenting of this book.

I have dedicated *Problem Child* to my children and I also want to thank them deeply here; to Charlie and Flora, and to their mother Janey, for the happiness their childhoods gave me; and to my much younger daughter India for giving me still more.

Above all I thank Ingrid, without whose love and support this book would not have been written.